Expecting Moore

Moore Family Series

Frankie Page

Editing by Pagan Proofreading

This book was designed and created with the use of a licensed stock images and fonts from:

https://fonts.adobe.com/

https://www.stock.adobe.com

Asset ID: 248945741

Asset ID: 564388335

This story is for all those who had a bumpy journey on the way to their happily ever after. If you are still on that journey, keep holding on, you will make it there...

Contents

1

Robbie

February 1st

"Mack, get your ass in here!" Some days I really wonder why in the hell I put up with his shit. The slight pounding in my skull is warning me that a migraine is imminent.

"What's up boss?" Mack enters the back office, wiping his stained hands on a rag.

"What the hell is this?" I hold up a work order.

"Umm..." He leans in to inspect. "...looks like a work order for that Corolla I did last week."

"Yeah, I see that. What I want to know is what the fuck is this?" I point to the total at the bottom.

"Yeah, she got an oil change." Mack chuckles as he cocks his head and gives me a smirk.

I rub my temples in an attempt to ease the pressure building up. "You charged her for a conventional oil. But according to the parts list, you gave her a full synthetic."

"Sorry about that, boss. Must have mixed up the prices when I was ringing her up." Mack avoids direct eye contact, picking fake lint from his blue grease-covered jumpsuit.

"Hmm..." I stroke my chin, contemplating how stupid he reckons I am. "I can see that, but what about not chargin' for the wipers and install you did?"

Grabbing the back of his neck, Mack gives a suspicious laugh. "Ha, I must have calculated that wrong. You know math was never my best subject."

"Seriously, do you think I'm a fucking idiot? You didn't even include them in the total—" I shove the work order in his face, pointing at the line items.

Mack drops his arms and shrugs his shoulders, finally giving up the charade. "Come on, man. It was Mandy-frickin-Callaway. You can't charge a chick like that full price for anything." He attempts to reason with me.

Dammit, the sensation that a herd of elephants are stampeding in my skull is a sign that my migraine is about to be full-blown. I can be a charitable guy... I've cut deals and given breaks to people who couldn't pay the bill. But the damn Callaways are the last pricks in this county who need a fucking handout. *Why do I even keep Mack on staff?* Oh, yeah, that's right... When it comes to body work, his attention to detail is superior. Well, second to mine, that is. "It's coming out of your pay. Don't do it again," I scold.

"Sure thing, boss," Mack replies with a shit-eating grin. The little shit knows it will take a lot more for me to fire him—than giving discounts to get a piece of ass. This isn't the first time I've had to dock his pay. Honestly, the only reason I am pissed is that it just makes more work for me. Normally Tilly would handle this kind of bullshit, except, barely halfway through her pregnancy, she can hardly waddle into the bookshop, let alone my garage—I'm not going to force her to handle my crap too. "It was worth every penny," Mack singsongs, leaning back on his heels with his hands in his pocket.

I raise an inquisitive eyebrow at him; he holds his hands up in defense. "Seriously, a discount on an oil change and some free wipers gets you laid?"

"Well, it helps. What seals the deal is my charming personality." Mack gives me what I am assuming is his panty-melting smile—fortunately, I'm immune to that type of shit. No wonder he and Jake are best buddies. My baby brother is the biggest man-whore in this town; he could sell a woman in white gloves a red popsicle on a hot day. I'm assuming, with that grin, Mack isn't too far behind him. While I am sure some chicks find a grease monkey sexy (not that I've met one yet), there is no way he is pulling more tail than Jake. My brother milks that whole "hot hero" firefighter shtick.

I wave off Mack. "Get back to work. How about actually trying to make some fucking money this time?"

Mack laughs before he leaves my office. I'm fairly certain he mumbled some shit about me needing to get laid. *Fucker.*

I ignore him, start chewing on a few Excedrin and return to pulling my hair out as I go through the damn books. How the hell Tilly manages this shit, I will never understand. You need me to rebuild a Mazda rotary engine? Sure thing. No problem. I can't guarantee a wrench or two won't be tossed around along with a fountain of cuss words—but I will get it done. This, though, makes absolutely no fucking sense.

Whatever, I'll figure it out. My pops ran his junkyard and shop back in the day—practically by himself. If that old coot could figure this shit out, I know I can; we are both cut from the same cloth, after all.

"Robbie, what have I told you about messing with my system?" Tilly sighs, the annoyance in her tone clear as day. I was so caught up in trying to decipher this crap, I didn't notice my baby sister walk in. Glancing up from the books, I realize I probably appear as distraught as I feel. I'll most likely have a bald spot from struggling with this all day, trying to get everything together to file taxes for the last year. Fortunately, I have a guy who actually does them for me, but I can't go in there, toss a box full of papers at him and tell him to deal with it—I've tried, and he nearly kicked my ass for it.

"Well, I've got to figure out this shit, don't I?" I calm my features, realizing I am being a dick to Tilly for no damn reason. Glancing from her snow-covered hat down to her belly, which is pushing the seams of her winter coat, I know she trekked here in the snow to help me out. *How do I greet her? By being an ass, that's how.*

Tilly gives me a soft smile, replying in the new, calm, motherly voice she has developed. "I told you I would help you with this, Robbie. I'm sorry I couldn't make it in. The other day, the morning—well, all day—sickness wasn't letting me get far from my home."

Fuck, I just earned myself the "biggest asshole in the world" achievement. My extremely pregnant and exhausted sister took time out of what I know is her own busy workload to come and help me out. What does she get for her efforts? Her big brother being a complete and total jerk. "I understand. I told you not to worry about it."

Tilly levels her gaze. Her amber eyes, which match mine, look right through me. "I told you I would help you get your taxes together—and I keep my word. But seriously, I had everything organized and you've totally devastated my system." She motions to the stacks of work orders and invoices piled around the office. Picking up the work order I just reamed Mack out for, she sighs. "Seriously, again?"

I laugh as she shakes her head, Tilly has had to have the "talk" with Mack on more than one occasion. "Yeah, I already told him to cut the shit, and it is coming out of his pay."

She rolls her eyes at me. "God, he is almost as pathetic as Jake. I still don't understand how he thinks he will be able to handle a video store. That guy lacks any sense of business or responsibility. With his *extracurricular* activities, he will more than likely end up giving out free movies to every cute chick in town if they promise to..." She adds air quotes. "...watch it with him."

After our parents were killed by a dumb fuck drunk driver four months ago, we all received a chunk of inheritance. Not anything major, but enough to make some improvements in our lives. Jake used a portion of his to go in with Tilly and Scott on purchasing extra space and expanding Moore Books and Coffee. Jake is getting a section to set up a little video rental shop. Although Tilly isn't a fan of the idea, I'm excited. I can't stand the streaming selection, and Redbox doesn't carry the good old shit. I get little free time, but when I do, I want to go on a classic 80s action movie marathon.

"All right, get your butt outta my chair. I've got work to do," Tilly demands, gesturing for me to move.

I cringe as Tilly makes her way to my stool. She winces and grabs her lower back as she takes a seat. *Fuck*, I don't have an actual office chair. I fabricated a shop stool from an old tractor seat I had lying around at Pops' junkyard. Poor Tilly, whose belly seems larger than it should be, has zero cushion for her bottom and no lumbar support.

"Hey, why don't I take all the papers and shit to the house and you can work on it there?" I try to offer. It would make me feel less guilty if she could do this in some form of comfort.

"No, I'm fine... ugh." Her groan of discomfort gives away her lie. But that is my baby sister for you. She is selfless to a fault.

"Come on, that thing hurts my ass. I'm guessing it isn't pleasant in your..." I gesture to her growing stomach. "...current condition."

"Robbie, I'm fine. I'm pregnant, not an invalid. Now, the quicker you back off, the sooner I can finish." Tilly dismisses me with a wave.

I huff in frustration; she is about damn near as stubborn as I am. Arguing with her is no use. I concede and decide it's not a battle I'm going to win. "Is there anything I can get you?"

"Some hot cocoa and those sweetheart cookies Scott has been making would be perfect." Tilly looks up with giant eyes glimmering as she imagines eating one of those cookies.

"Sure thing, coming right up." I lean down, give Tilly a quick kiss on the forehead and let her get to work. As soon as I step outside, that anger inside me boils over. It is practically a blizzard out here, and she fucking risked her safety to come help my sorry ass. *Dammit*, I need to figure this shit out. I can't have Tilly hurting herself or those babies for my dumbass.

·♥ · ♥ · ♥ · ♥ · ♥ ·

"What the hell, man?" Scooting out from underneath the Jeep I'm working on, I look up to see Jax's red face and the tick in his jaw from his clenched teeth.

"Can I help you?" I raise a brow at my new brother-in-law. It's crazy to think this guy has unofficially been my little brother his entire life. He'd been best friends with Scott since they were in diapers and then moved in with us after his grandfather passed. Recently though, he officially became my brother when he and Tilly finally tied the knot the other week at the courthouse.

"Have you seen it outside? It is near whiteout conditions, and Tilly is here, sitting in your shitty little office when she should be home, curled up with blankets on the couch sipping tea. Not risking her and our babies lives because you are too stubborn to hire someone to manage your books." Jax crosses his arms over his chest, giving me his best "tough guy" impersonation. I am sure if the situation called for it, Jax could hold his own in a fight. But, at the end of the day, he's not as strong as he's making himself out to be.

I stand to my full height. Jax might be tall, but I'm taller and wider. Quickly he loses his composure a bit, knowing how thoroughly I can kick his ass if he tempts me. "Let me make something clear. I didn't ask her to come down here—she showed up on her own. I was trying to handle it, but this is Tilly, and she kicked me out of my office. Secondly, I offered to bring everything to the house, but Tilly refused. She didn't want me messing up her system any more than I already have."

Jax sighs in defeat. "I recognize Tilly can be headstrong. It's just... when I got home from the shop—we closed early because of the storm—she wasn't there, and I panicked. Thinking about her out in this shit... I worried that she might have slipped and fallen, or worse." I empathize with Jax. Tilly does what she wants. As her body becomes more debilitated from the stress of the pregnancy, her spirit counteracts—she's unyielding. Tilly refuses to back down. "Please, Robbie, you need to fix this."

I cross my arms over my chest and cock my head, looking slightly down at him. "How do you expect me to do that? I might be her brother, but you are her husband," I challenge back.

"Don't be stupid, Robbie. We both know the only reason Tilly is even here right now is because your stubborn ass refuses to hire help that you've desperately needed long before Tilly got pregnant." Jax attempts to stand tall again, finding a bit of the bravado he had lost.

"Look, I don't like strangers involved in my shit. I've told Tilly I will take care of it. But she seems to be a little selective on her hearing when it comes to that," I say, stepping into Jax's space. I'm surprised when he doesn't back down from the confrontation.

"Because Tilly loves you, and will never abandon you. It's your responsibility to man up and get over this ridiculous fear you have—let Tilly find a replacement for you. I know shit about business, but even I can tell you need the help, a lot more than she can offer."

I am so sick and tired of this fucking conversation. *You need help. Blah, blah, blah.* Tilly and I have been arguing about this shit for a couple of years now. When our dad started stepping down at the bookshop and she was taking it over, Tilly had indicated that I needed someone here full time. Though it hasn't always been smooth, we never changed our arrangement. I guess in all reality, this time, the issues with Tilly helping aren't temporary problems. If anything, it will get worse once the babies are born. *Fucking goddammit!*

I throw the wrench I was holding to the ground and the loud clunk makes him flinch. I storm off towards the back office with Jax on my heels. As I barge into the room, Tilly gasps, placing a hand over her chest—startled by my entrance. "Fine!"

"What?" Tilly asks, confused by my sudden outburst. She glances back at Jax for some sort of clarification.

"Hire someone to fucking help with this shit!" I declare, waving my hands around the office before rushing back to the bays. I purposely bump shoulders with Jax on my way out. I don't mean to be a dick, but dammit... I hate the idea of letting someone else in my shop, especially after what happened the last time. I'm aware I need the help. I might be stubborn, but I'm not stupid. I just really hope this doesn't come back to bite me in the ass.

2

Cassie

February 9th

"OUCH," I HISS, SUCKING the blood from my finger. The stupid
thorn got me, and not for the first time today. This is
flipping pathetic. Here I am—again—back living with my
parents, helping at their flower shop and stuck making
floral arrangements for a bridal shower. *White roses, how
cliché?* I don't mean to be catty; honestly, the arrangement
is beautiful. It's just... right now, the last thing I want to do
or look at is anything related to a wedding. Which is weird
coming from me—I love weddings. I've been planning my
own for as long as I can remember. But after recent events,
the last thing I'm thinking about is getting married.

"Níl ach braon beag fola ort." My father chuckles,
handing me a cloth to wrap around my finger. While the man
immigrated to the United States almost forty years ago, he
still enjoys teasing me in his native Irish tongue.

"Da, it is more than a little blood." I wave my finger at him.
Only a small droplet trickles down—I'm obviously being a
little overdramatic. But being the baby of our family and his
only daughter, I play it up as much as possible. Even though
I'm almost thirty, he still likes to view me as his little girl.

"*Próseche*. You are getting blood on the arrangements, Cassandra." Thanks to my unique heritage, I am fluent in English, Gaelic, and Greek. My mother's Greek heritage is the only reason I do not have a traditional Irish name like my brothers. While Da thinks my little antics are cute, they don't work as well on my mother.

"Sorry, Ma." I rush to clean and wrap my bleeding finger. When I turn back around, my mother is picking apart my arrangement and undoing all my work. I love her—she's my mother, after all—but she can be extremely nit-picky. Then again, when it comes to floral arrangements, she is a genuine artist. Numbers, math, have always been my thing. Burying myself in endless piles of data and spreadsheets calms and centers me. Flowers do that for her. Although she is proud of my education, I believe she still resents the fact I didn't inherit her gifts. None of us did. That didn't stop her from trying to make me the best florist she could. I think she assumed that, being her daughter, it would come naturally to me—*it didn't*. Sure, I am able to put together an arrangement or two, but I don't have the instinct that she does.

Ma sighs, pulling blood-stained roses from the arrangement and tossing them into the trash. "Cassandra, head home. Get cleaned up. I will finish up the order and we will meet you later tonight." She dismisses me, her brow scrunched in frustration as she figures out how to salvage the mess I've made.

Yup, my mother just politely kicked me out of the shop—again. Giving my parents each a brief kiss, I bundle up to face the freezing Minnesota winter. Although it's so cold my nostrils stick together when I take in a breath, I wouldn't want to live anywhere else. I was made for this weather.

· ❤ · ❤ · ❤ · ❤ · ❤ ·

Instead of going home, I stop at K.O. Murphy's, a pub my brother Killian owns. It is also conveniently within walking distance of my parents' house, which makes drinking here ideal. Not to mention, I mostly drink for free. I'm not a freeloader or anything; he just refuses to accept my money. I make sure to always tip everyone well to make up for the fact I don't have to pay. When he needs it, I volunteer to help wait tables. I might not be the best server, but it is a delightful distraction during times like these, where I'm not working and need something to do to keep myself from going mad.

Taking a seat at the bar, I flag down Sean, my brother's friend, who is also the lead bartender. "Hiya, Cassie, what can I get ya this evening?" Sean asks, his green eyes sparkling with the sort of mischief that matches his tone.

"Seriously, Sean? I am a little hurt you even need to ask." I feign insult, playing along with his game. Sean already knows what I want to drink. I've been drinking here almost exclusively for five years—ever since my brother opened the place after he retired from fighting.

Giving me his token flirty grin, he pours me a Murphy's Irish Stout. Yeah, given our family name and heritage, my brother has coined the Murphy's branding as much as possible. Even if the beer hadn't been created by a distant ancestor, it would still be my drink of choice. While Guinness is delicious, I feel this smooth drink doesn't get the attention it deserves. I take a sip of my beer and enjoy the mild coffee flavor. Glancing around, I notice that the place is packed, which isn't surprising for a Friday night. Thankfully, while busy, it doesn't feel overcrowded like other places. Maybe that is because I know almost everyone here?

"What kind of trouble are you planning tonight?" Sean teases while wiping down the bar.

"Just the usual," I toss back before giving him my most sinister smile. "World domination."

He lifts his chin, gesturing to someone behind me. "I am sure if anyone could do it, you two could."

Before I have a chance to turn around, I feel two thin arms wrap around me from behind, hugging my waist. "Hey, Cassie," Moira, my best friend, says. Squeezing me tight before sliding onto the bar stool next to me, she removes her jacket, revealing a cream blouse—her naturally vibrant red hair pulled back into a tight bun. She came here straight from the office. *Ugh, how I miss having an office to go to.* Moira lets out a deep sigh before offering me a soft smile. Ever since the breakup, she has been walking on eggshells around me. I really wish she would stop. "So how are you holding up?" Before taking off to help other patrons, Sean slides Moira a Guinness (because we haven't been able to convert her yet) and brings us some appetizers.

I roll my eyes at her question. "Fine, I guess. I am still looking for work. Hopefully I find something soon. I think Ma is going to kill me if I mess up another one of her arrangements."

Moira snort-laughs into her beer. Growing up alongside me, Moira knows my mother well and is aware of how particular she is about her flowers, and how she isn't afraid to show her disappointment in my lack of skillset. "I am sure someone will get back to you soon. You have only been looking for a few weeks."

"Yeah, it's just... I need to get back to work. I'm going crazy without my numbers. I need purpose." I pout and then toss a pretzel bite into my mouth, savoring the salt and warm cheese.

"Oh, speaking of jobs, guess who I talked to the other day?" Moira yells excitedly over the music, "Tilly!"

I smile, thinking of my old college roommate and friend. I feel bad for not keeping in touch with her. But that is life after college. You mean well, but eventually you all break off and go your separate ways. It doesn't help that Tilly refuses to use Facebook—or any social media for that matter—and lives almost two hours from me. "I haven't heard from her in forever. How's she doing?"

"Good, I guess." Moira's eyes tear up and her voice breaks a little as she speaks. "Her parents actually passed away a few months ago."

"Oh, wow, that is awful. I had no idea." I take a swig of my drink, trying to wash away the foul taste of guilt I feel. I can't believe she has been going through such a hardship and I knew nothing about it. Well, I guess Moira didn't either. Unfortunately, that doesn't stop me from being remorseful over not being there for my friend.

"Yeah, it sounds like she is doing better though. Tilly actually got married a couple of weeks ago," Moira says, then immediately retreats, knowing marriage has been a sore subject for me more recently.

"It's okay, Moira. I appreciate you looking out for me. But I need to move past this. I am happy that she got married." No lie, I am happy for her. It pains me a little, and I find myself a tad jealous. But I don't want to become one of those people who can't celebrate my friend's happiness, just because things are not so great for me right now.

"I know. I am sorry..." Moira clears her throat. "Also, she's pregnant."

"That's exciting. We should plan on visiting her soon. Or maybe invite her up here and take her out shopping for the baby," I offer, trying to heal some of the hurt and guilt in my heart. "I'm confused. What does this have to do with a job?"

"Actually, she called looking to see if I knew anyone in need of work."

"Oh yeah, she looking for someone to help at the bookshop?" That would make sense, needing some extra help with a baby on the way. Running a business isn't a simple forty hour a week gig. Knowing Tilly as well as I do, while she loves the shop, she wouldn't want to be gone from her child that much.

"I guess it is helping her brother out. He needs someone at his auto shop, to manage his books and stuff." Moira takes a quick drink. "I couldn't really think of anyone looking right now, well, except for you. Unfortunately, you'd have to relocate to Tral Lake—so I didn't think it would be something you'd be interested in. If you can think of anyone though, you should pass it along. Apparently, her brother is super nervous about letting a stranger come in and manage his books."

"Which one?" I try to recall her siblings. Who was it that was the mechanic?

"Her eldest brother." Moira pauses for a moment, tapping her chin. "Robbie."

I nod. "Ah, okay, I never met him. I really only ever met Jake, all those times he came to visit campus, and Scott at graduation."

Moira giggles, thinking of Jake. "If Jake needed an office manager, I would quit my job in a heartbeat." We both laugh. Jake was super hot. I'm sure he still is. The guy totally seeped sex pheromones from his pores. Tilly is drop-dead gorgeous, without even trying. She never needed makeup or anything else. She is just naturally stunning. Yeah, Jake, being her twin, inherited all those same qualities. I swear anytime he came to campus, I could hear the girls' panties drop as he walked by.

Goofing off, Moira and I continue to drink our beers and chat at the bar. Since the breakup, it's been nice getting to hang out with my best friend. It feels like forever since we have been able to do this—just the two of us. Eventually, we hit the drunk state of the evening, where we feel the need to pose for selfies at the bar and post them to Facebook. Scrolling through the newsfeed, we laugh at the comments our friends are leaving when something catches my eye. Moira notices and snatches the phone from me.

"Let it go, Cassie," she yells, turning her back to me and blocking the phone with her body.

"Moira, give me the darn phone," I chide. She looks down at the screen with a frown before huffing and passing it back to me. Studying the post, I can't help but feel the broken pieces of my heart shatter more.

"Come on, Cassie, you're better than him. He did you a favor, if you ask me," Moira pleads, trying to prevent the train wreck that is happening in my head.

"Sorry, Moira. I need to get going," I say, throwing a twenty down for Sean. Getting up, I run smack dab into a firm chest.

"Whoa, Cassie. Where ya heading off to?" Killian asks, his smile quickly turning to a frown as he notices the look of anguish on my face. "Hey, what happened?" Killian glances between Moira and me. "Did some drunk asshole try something?" He then cracks his knuckles, prepared to beat up one of his patrons if necessary.

"No, Kill, it's fine. I'm tired. I'll catch you both later," I say, walking away quickly and pulling my jacket snug around me. Off in the distance, I can hear Killian asking Moira details about what happened. I don't stick around to listen to the conversation because it doesn't matter. I need to get away from here. I love my family, and Moira, but right now everything reminds me of *him*. *I need to do something.* I don't even take a second to reconsider before grabbing my phone and calling my old friend. "Hey, Tilly, it's Cassie."

"Cassie? Oh, hi. How are you? I feel like we haven't spoken in ages." Tilly sounds excited and happy on the other end of the line. That is what I want to be again. I want to be happy, not constantly reminded of my heartbreak. How is it ever supposed to heal when the wound keeps getting picked at?

"I am doing good. I'm sorry for calling late, but I was actually just at the bar with Moira—she mentioned you were looking for someone to help at your brother's shop?"

3

Cassie

February 23rd

"OH MY GOD, CASSIE!" Tilly squeals as I enter her bookshop. Looking around, I take in the classic decor with a modern flair—it screams *Tilly*. In college, all she ever talked about was running her family's shop, and it is great to see her dream come true. As Tilly rounds the corner, I am shocked to see my petite friend's large, round belly. When I called her a couple of weeks ago, Tilly said she was twenty weeks pregnant—with twins, no less. But based on her size, I would assume she is almost ready to pop. Leaning in, she attempts to hug me as best she can with her enormous belly in the way.

"Wow, Tilly, look at you!" I yell excitedly. "You look absolutely stunning." Even if it seems as if she might tip over any second...

"I look like an elephant, but thank you." Tilly laughs, dismissing my compliment.

"Tilly," a deep voice scolds. I look behind the counter and see a tall, lean man with brown hair and the brightest blue eyes I have ever seen standing there.

"Oh, Cassie. This is Jax, my husband." Jax comes around the counter, putting his arm over Tilly's shoulder and extending his other hand to shake mine.

"Pleasure to meet you. I heard so much about you back during our college days." Tilly blushes at my comment. Jax winces briefly but quickly recovers, offering me a giant smile that is full of pure joy. Tilly and I didn't start rooming together until sophomore year. I quickly noticed that Tilly never dated and turned down many offers. I had asked her about it one night out of curiosity, and she had told me about Jax. How they had one amazing summer together, and he was her first love. But they broke up before she came to college because he was traveling for some dream job. Towards the end of the school year, Moira and I were able to convince her to start dating again—especially since she hadn't heard from him in two years.

I am all for genuine love and romance. I wouldn't blame her desire to wait for him, but he never called, and it seemed like it was time for her to move on. Although I haven't spoken with Tilly in a few years, last I knew, she still hadn't heard from him. Admittedly, I can't deny I am a little surprised to see them together after all this time. But, seeing how happy and in love she is, it seems they were able to move past whatever kept them apart.

Maybe there is still some hope for me.

"I'm excited that you agreed to help with Robbie's garage. He really needs it, and Tilly is in no shape to continue assisting him," Jax says, clearly relieved that I am here to take this task off Tilly's shoulders.

Tilly nudges his chest. "It wasn't that bad," she defends. Jax gives her a stare that says, "Don't argue with me; you are extremely pregnant and run your own business." "Anyway... I am excited you are here. We are actually about to close for the night, and then we can head back to the house. I am sorry we could not get your room fully ready. We just got back from our honeymoon in Greece and didn't have time to get it all situated. Scott went in and emptied all of his and Jax's old things. Then I put fresh bedding out for you. You'll have to suffer with a bunk bed, but they will deliver your new bed this week."

"I appreciate the place to stay, but you do not need to worry about a new bed for me. I'm sure your house is going to be crowded soon," I say, pointing at her stomach. "I'm happy to find an apartment." Tilly had generously offered me a room in her house rent free. But, honestly, the cost of living here is so low compared to the Cities. Unlike home, it wouldn't be that hard to afford my own place.

"Oh, actually, we are going to move next week. So, there will be plenty of space at the house. I already talked with Jake and he has no issues with you staying there." Tilly leans forward to whisper, "Between you and me, I think he's nervous about living there alone."

I chuckle. I already got Tilly's warning that if I decided to go down *that* path, I would need to be prepared for it to be nothing more than a casual fling. While Jake is hot as sin, fortunately for me, the last thing I am interested in right now is a relationship, casual or otherwise.

I'm taking a break, focusing on me. I repeat Moira's encouraging words in my mind.

I think Tilly was a little relieved when I told her as much, not that she really cared if I slept with Jake. She seemed more worried about me getting hurt when the relationship wouldn't go anywhere. I've never been one to just casually hook up, and Tilly knows that—I've always been a relationship girl. Unfortunately, those relationships never seem to go right.

"I hope you don't mind. Jake is a great guy and, honestly, hardly ever around. It will almost be like you have the entire house to yourself," Tilly says quickly, seeming a little panicked that I might back out on the arrangement now that she is moving out.

"I *was* looking forward to rooming together again, but I'm more than happy to help keep him company," I offer. I am not worried about living with the sex god. Nevertheless, I'll enjoy the eye candy and will take every opportunity to rub it in Moira's face. I practically had to tie her to a pole, so she wouldn't quit her job and follow me down here. When she found out I was going to be living in the same house as Jake, let's just say she got way more interested in the amenities Tral Lake has to offer.

·❤·❤·❤·❤·❤·

Bundling up Monday morning, I follow Tilly in my new-used Subaru Forester I bought before coming down here. I didn't have a car and relied on walking or public transportation. If truth be told, I've never been a huge fan of driving anywhere. Cian, my eldest brother, insisted that living out in rural Minnesota (versus the Twin Cities), I would appreciate the all-wheel drive. Pulling up to the garage, I can't help but chuckle at the sign: Moore Body and Lube. *Who would think to name their shop that?* I get calling the bookshop Moore Books and Coffee. It's cute and quirky. But this... this sounds like a bad porn flick. From what I have gleaned about Robbie so far, he seems to be a "no nonsense" sort of guy. The name doesn't really seem to fit him. Maybe he has more of a sense of humor than Tilly gives him credit for.

Tilly pulls out a key to unlock the shop and struggles to open the slightly frozen door. "Typically, Robbie would already be here, but he had an emergency call. There was an accident out on the county road this morning and someone needed a tow back to town. Robbie has the only tow truck in the area."

"Wow, I'm guessing he gets pretty good business then?" Thinking of the amount of auto incidents that could happen in this area and being the only local with a truck, I assume he must get nonstop business.

Entering the shop, I am surprised at how clean everything appears. The few shops I've been to before—well, I remember the floors being littered with various automotive fluids and tools scattered all around. Here, though, everything seems to be in its rightful place and freshly wiped down.

"Here's the office; it isn't much. I already spoke with Robbie. This will be your workspace. So, you can make whatever changes you need." Tilly sighs. "Look, I don't want to scare you..."

"Okay? Well, you are kind of making me worried now," I tease, although I get an uneasy feeling in my chest.

"Robbie, well, he can kind of be a stick in the mud as I mentioned. He isn't exactly thrilled about hiring someone he doesn't know to help manage his finances and stuff. It isn't my place to elaborate, so let's just say he had an unpleasant experience in the past. But, considering we know each other, he's been a little more accepting of the idea. Please, just don't let him scare you off."

I let out a relieved laugh. "Come on, Tilly, don't worry. I have two brothers myself. Have you met Cian? He is king of the grumpy-pants society. I'm sure Robbie and I will get along just fine."

"Yeah, I know. Just... please, if he gives you a hard time, let me know. I will kick his butt," Tilly offers with a wink, knowing that even though he may be a big tough guy, she has him wrapped around her tiny finger.

For the next couple of hours, Tilly and I go through the office and her organization systems, which I will admit are very impressive. I will eventually make some changes to fit more with my management style, but overall, everything is fairly straightforward. I couldn't stop laughing when Tilly showed me his ancient work order system. Most shops nowadays use an electronic system, but Robbie is still using an old school pad with copy ink. The stack of yellow copies spiked on a stand makes me cringe.

Afterwards, we walk out to the bays and I see two men working. The first is a younger guy, likely around my age.

He has long blonde hair, which is pulled back, and deep brown chocolate eyes. The muscle definition under his blue jumpsuit says he is in fantastic shape. Tilly introduces him as Mack, then whispers in my ear to be careful. He isn't much different from Jake (apparently they are best friends). The next man is older; I'd assume more than likely in his mid-50s. He is very handsome in his own right, with salt and pepper hair, and a short, well-groomed beard. While more mature, he seems to keep himself in good shape as well. He introduces himself as Chris.

"Darn it," Tilly says, glancing down at the time on her phone. "Hey, I need to get going. Will you be okay here? Robbie should be back soon."

I look over and see Mack winking at me. Ugh, he is going to be a headache—I can already tell. I turn to Tilly and give her a reassuring smile. "Of course. Get back to your shop. I will see you tonight."

"Okay." Tilly leans in and gives me a hug. "Thank you, Cassie, you have no idea how grateful I am."

Shortly after Tilly leaves, I let Mack and Chris know I am going back to the office to get situated. I'm not sure how much time has passed while I am getting familiar with the shop. I was apparently so caught up I didn't even notice the colossal beast of a man eclipsing the doorway to the office and scowling at me. Looking him up and down, I take note of the dark, disheveled hair and leather jacket. I can't help but gulp. Yup, I'm definitely in trouble.

4

Robbie

February 25th

THIS MORNING HAS BEEN an absolute shit show. First off, I get an early morning call about an accident out on the county road. Some idiot drove their new rear-wheel drive BMW on snowy country roads. *Dumbasses like him are what keep me in business*, I kept trying to remind myself as I had to listen to him whine about his poor car and "to be careful" as I pulled it out of the ditch. On our way back to the shop, I passed a minivan with a mom trying desperately to change a flat. I pulled over and could hear the screaming and crying of her two children in the back—ugh, the sound made me cringe. I hope Tilly's kids don't cry like that, at least not while I'm around. The woman was grateful that I was able to get her back on the road quickly. I took her flat tire with me and told her she could pick it up this afternoon and it would be as good as new.

The rest of the way, the BMW douche did nothing but piss and moan about my stopping to help the woman, and how I needed to get him into town. Apparently, he was late for work and it was *all my fault*. Getting back to the shop, I called Chris over to do a write-up for the BMW asswipe so I could get back to my office and catch up on paperwork.

When I opened my office door, it stunned me to see a slender woman with hair so dark it was almost black sitting at my desk and *working at my computer*. My instinct was to yell and figure out who the fuck this stranger is, but when she looked up at me with those steel, blue-gray eyes, it stopped me dead in my tracks.

The woman gasps, placing a hand on her chest, clearly startled by my presence. Taking a deep breath, she stands, shaking her nerves off.

I look her up and down. She's short—not as short as Tilly—but short nonetheless. Granted, when I stand at almost six feet, five inches, everyone seems tiny to me. Her silhouette is narrow with subtle curves; the dip in her shirt reveals that her chest is on the smaller side. However, it's more than adequate for her lithe frame.

Before my thoughts get too far from me, I quickly remember that this strange woman is in my office and going through my computer. As I'm about to ask what the hell she is doing, I hesitate at the sound of the slight throaty rasp of her sultry voice. "Hi, I'm Cassandra Murphy, Tilly's friend."

Oh yeah, with all the shit going on this morning, I forgot about my new employee. I'd assumed that Tilly would be here to handle introductions but, noticing the time, she probably had to go open the bookshop.

"I'm Robbie." I reach out and accept her extended hand, which is engulfed by my large one. "Did Tilly have a chance to go over everything with you?"

"Um, yeah. We went through her system for balancing the books, but thought it would be best to discuss my other responsibilities with you."

"Other responsibilities?" Cassandra looks back at me. She tilts her head and purses her bee-stung, plump pink lips.

"Yes, Tilly indicated you were looking for an office manager. While bookkeeping would be a function of my role, I'm assuming you have a lot more you'll need me to do around here." Cassandra glances around, taking a mental note of her surroundings.

An involuntary growl slips. I smirk as her eyes go wide with fear. Good, if she is afraid of me, maybe she will leave. I really didn't want to bring anyone on and only agreed to this to make Tilly happy. But if she quits, well then, I can easily get out of the deal. "For now, let's start out with the bookkeeping and see how it goes."

Cassandra seems a little insulted. "In addition to bookkeeping, I know I can help with—"

I raise my hand to stop her. "Look, I'm sure you are smart, probably overqualified to be working at some Podunk garage out in the middle of nowhere. But I like things done in a particular way. So, before you go and start messing with my business, and likely fucking shit up, I'd like to start with the books and work from there." I give her a pointed stare, letting her know this is non-negotiable.

Cassandra huffs, narrowing her eyes at me in a challenge. As she crosses her arms, they push up the bit of cleavage she has peeking from the top of her blouse. It takes all of my willpower to maintain direct eye contact and not sneak another glance. After thinking for a moment, Cassandra deflates and nods her head in agreement. With no additional conversation, I leave the office and head back to the bays. I need to distance myself from her. I'm not sure I can handle anymore alone time with her in my small office—well, now I guess *her* office. *Shit*, I knew that Tilly's friend was a female, but I wasn't prepared for... *that*. If I am going to keep my sanity, I need to keep my dick far, far away from her. Pretty girls and business don't work.

"What do ya think of the new girl, boss?" Mack asks, clearly already knowing she's a fucking knockout.

"I'm sure she will be gone in a week." I shrug at him with indifference, attempting to show as little interest as possible.

"Really?" Mack seems thrown off by my comment. If this were a cartoon, I'm pretty certain I would see hearts dancing in his eyes. *Great*, he already has a crush, not that I blame him. Fortunately, I can think with more than just my dick—can't say the same goes for my horndog employee.

"She's from the Cities; a girl like that won't stick around here long. I bet she is already bored and looking for a new job far away from here. Besides, did you see how she is dressed? Who the hell wears that kind of shit to a garage?" Cassandra looked fairly prim and pressed, ready to work at some sort of corporate office—not a shop that, despite my best efforts, has grease everywhere.

"I don't know." Mack shrugs. "I agree she is dressed a bit fancy, but I would chalk that up to nerves and first impressions. But, when she came out to the bay to meet Chris and me, she didn't seem uncomfortable or out of place here."

"Like I said—one week and she'll be gone." As soon as she realizes the nearest shopping center is an hour away, that there are no trendy restaurants or nightclubs, she will die of boredom.

"Care to put a wager on it?" Mack teases. To make work a little more interesting around here, we tend to make a lot of bets.

"Sure, pick your poison." I entertain his challenge.

"Hmm..." Mack ponders, tapping his fingertips together like an evil villain. "If she makes it through the week, all four of us go to Harper's and you're buying. *Dinner and drinks.*"

"Fine, if she leaves before the week is up, you have to shave those golden locks." Mack winces as though I stabbed him. He has always been proud of his long hair and refuses to cut it, saying that he will die before he allows someone to touch one strand of his golden mane.

After pondering my proposition for a moment, a Cheshire smile stretches across his face as he puts his hand out to shake on the deal. I grab it a little too firmly and shake on the arrangement. "Done. I look forward to a lavish evening at the bar." He pretends to flip his hair over his shoulder before walking off.

5

Cassie

February 26th

YESTERDAY WAS A TOTAL nightmare. Tilly warned me that Robbie might not be the most receptive to my working at his shop. I just wasn't prepared for the cold shoulder right off the bat. Except for our brief exchange in the morning, he avoided me like the plague. Unfortunately, I noticed the look in his eyes, the disdain—he doesn't think I belong here. I'll admit I had an error in judgement. I dressed up a little too professionally yesterday, but it is a force of habit. I am used to working in corporate offices, and it is customary to dress nice—especially on your first day.

Although day one didn't go as planned, I will not let that stop me. Robbie may think he has me all figured out and that I am some uptight, prissy girl from the Cities. But he's wrong—and I am going to prove it to him. I came to Tral Lake for a fresh start, and I will not allow him, or his sourpuss attitude, to ruin this opportunity for me. After the freak out my family had over me moving, there is no way I am crawling back home with my tail between my legs.

Sitting at the breakfast counter in the kitchen, I sip my coffee, scrolling through information on Tral Lake. I want to get familiar with what the town has to offer, which so far is fairly impressive. While there are no major shopping hubs, there are several small boutiques that stock local and handmade items in addition to the common brands I'd find at any major retailer. The stores have impressive advertising; I love that it's almost like a physical Etsy store around here.

"Hey, how was your first day?" I turn to see Jake, shirtless, standing behind me. I take a big gulp of my coffee, in an attempt to cover the little bit of drool he is eliciting from me.

"It was okay." I'm not interested in badmouthing his brother for being a jerk to me. Not to mention, shirtless Jake is slightly distracting.

"Just okay?" Jake gives me an inquisitive look. "Well then, I guess he likes you." Jake shrugs his shoulders before sauntering further into the kitchen. He leans back against the counter, taking a big bite of the apple he grabbed from the bowl. I don't know if he realizes he is doing it, but I swear he is actually attempting to seduce me—like it just comes naturally to him to do so.

At first, I'm drawn to the beautiful shoulder and partial sleeve tattoo he has. It's really breath-taking with deep black and colorful flowers. I'd never imagine something so feminine looking so appealing on a male. As my eyes continue to wander down, I clear my throat and look away, avoiding the well-defined V leading me to stare at the sizable bulge in his thin gray sweatpants. That's when I realize Jake is half naked, wearing the male equivalent of women's lingerie. "That is doubtful." I bite the inside of my cheek as I try to keep my eyes trained on his face. "But fortunately, I do not scare easily."

"That's good. You need thick skin to hang around Robbie," Jake says in a deep, husky voice—yup, he is definitely trying to seduce me.

"Jake!" Tilly yells from behind me. "Put your shirt on."

"What? Why?" Jake pouts, looking down at his delicious six-pack, rubbing it and trying to figure out what is offending about it.

"Cassie will not sleep with you—so you can stop now," Tilly says, causing me to choke on air.

Jake laughs at her comment. "I wasn't trying to—"

Tilly stops him. "You are totally giving her the *want to bang?* look right now."

"Well, if she is up for it." Jake gives me a sultry smile as he puts the suggestion out there.

I quickly dismiss his offer (this is not a journey I plan on taking). "While I appreciate the proposal, sadly no. Tilly's right, we are not going to sleep together."

Jake looks slightly insulted. "Why?"

"It's nothing personal," I reassure him. "You are definitely attractive, and I'm sure it would be enjoyable. But I recently had a bad breakup and I am temporarily on hiatus in that department." I see Jake is about to counter my reasoning, so I quickly add, "Also, you know I am a relationship type of girl. So, you see, we just aren't compatible."

"Oh, well, that makes sense. I am sorry to hear about the breakup by the way." Jake ponders for a moment. "If you ever change your mind, let me know. I'm sure I could help take your mind off your ex." He smirks.

I bite my lip, thinking over his offer one more time. As fun as I'm sure it would be, I quickly shake the visual from my head. "However, if you wouldn't mind, could I please take your picture to send to my best friend Moira? You might remember her—the spunky redhead. Anyway, she thinks you are super hot and would be completely jealous if she saw how you are standing in front of me right now." Tilly immediately bursts out laughing at my request as Jake's cocky smile grows.

"No problem." Jake shifts his position, making the bulge in his pants more prominent. "Is this good?"

I gulp and nod my head. I avoid responding, knowing I can't trust the words that might come out of my mouth. I snap a few pictures and quickly shoot them off to Moira.

Me: My new home has such an amazing view ::wink emoji::
Moira: [GIF of puppy dog begging with its tongue out]
Moira: Please tell me you are hitting that?
Me: You know I would never kiss and tell.
Moira: I HATE YOU!
Me: No, you don't. You know you love me.
Moira: I will be there bright and early Saturday morning. If you are really my best friend, you will make certain he looks like that when I arrive.

Jake saunters over (as I laugh out loud) and peeks at the text exchange. I shiver at his proximity. I will really need to work at getting my hormones under control if I am going to live here alone with him. Oh god, my brothers can never find out. Killian would beat him to death, and Cian would help bury the body.

"That can be arranged," Jake says in response to the text, taking the seat next to me and continuing to eat his apple.

"So, how was yesterday?" Tilly asks, changing the subject. Pouring herself a glass of apple juice, she sits at the end of the counter.

I shrug my shoulders. "It was okay. Robbie and I didn't talk much. But today is a new day. Hopefully, I can get him to add a little more to my workload."

"Yeah, Robbie can be a little reserved. But he really is a great guy. It's just..." Tilly looks off in the distance for a moment. "... he has some trust issues. I am sure, after you have been there for a bit, he will warm up to you."

"Robbie's a challenge," I declare. "But I never back down from a challenge."

·❤ · ❤ · ❤ · ❤ · ❤·

I arrive at the garage with a bag of pastries in one hand, and a tray of drinks in the other. On my way in today, I stopped by the café. Scott was kind enough to help me order all the guys' favorites. Although this might not be a typical office setting, bringing in treats is always a crowd pleaser and (bonus) a way to win over your new boss who hates you.

Walking in, I plaster on the biggest smile I can muster. "Good morning," I offer. "I stopped by the café this morning and got you guys a few things," I say in my most chipper tone, before setting the baked goods and drinks on the counter.

Mack rolls out from under the car he was working on. Quickly sniffing the air, he smiles before walking over. "Is that peppermint I smell?"

"Yes sir. Scott mentioned that the peppermint mocha was your favorite. I also grabbed you a chocolate croissant." I hand him his drink and pastry.

Mack drools slightly before taking a bite. "Oh. My. God. These are so good. Thank you."

Chris comes forward, looking at the options. "One dark roast with cream and two sugars." I hand Chris his coffee. "And one blueberry muffin."

"Thank you, Cassie, I didn't have time for breakfast this morning," he praises. Taking a sip, he groans as if savoring each drop.

Robbie continues working on the BMW he brought in yesterday, not offering a morning greeting or showing any gratitude. Whatever. I won't let him get under my skin. I leave his order on the counter before making my way back to the office. He can drink cold black coffee for all I care—*probably matches his heart.* It doesn't matter. I don't need him to like me. Just a little professional courtesy would be nice.

I look around and try to think of what to do. Honestly, there isn't much—at least not bookkeeping wise. It takes me no time to get all the current invoices and work orders organized. There is one heck of a project waiting for me in the filing cabinets, except I know that Robbie will flip his lid if I dare mess up his precious system. I'm still trying to figure out his sorting method. It isn't alphabetical, chronological by date, heck, not even by total cost. *Forget this,* I say to myself before grabbing my coffee and muffin.

Heading back upfront, I take a seat at the main lobby desk. I'm not interested in sitting here all day doing nothing. He might not want me messing with any of his management systems, but that doesn't mean I can't work on cleaning up and organizing the front area. I rearrange the space and ensure things are easy to find, labeled and color-coded. Once finished, I make my way out to the lobby area. I straighten up and scrub down the furniture. While Robbie seems to keep the bay area meticulous, his guest lounge could use some TLC. All the furniture is old and worn down; it looks as though it was salvaged and not maintained.

"What are you doing?" Robbie's deep voice booms from behind me.

Startled, I spin around and am surprised to see a scowling Robbie looming over me. My fear quickly turns into annoyance. "Working," I retort. "I would like to think that is rather obvious."

I take a step back when Robbie growls. Soon enough, I find myself trapped between him and the wall. "I didn't ask you to come up here and start changing things." Robbie crosses his arms. His blue jumpsuit is half hanging down and tied around his waist. His enormous arms, which are covered in thick black ink, and well-defined chest stretch the limits of his t-shirt. *Of course, he has tattoos.* I close my eyes and take a deep breath. I'd hoped it would stop my mind from traveling down a dangerous path. But as I get a whiff of diesel and cedar, involuntarily, I squeeze my thighs together.

It takes all my strength to keep my mind focused on the matter at hand. "No, Robbie, you didn't." I keep my voice level, stern. "Your books and invoices are all up to date. I thought you'd appreciate that, instead of messing around with your horrific filing system or allowing you to pay me to sit around and do nothing, I made myself useful. This front area seemed practically untouched, with stuff just strewn around."

"Yeah, but you moved shit. I can't find anything now." Robbie's eyes get dark as he takes a step closer to me—I can feel the body heat radiating off him.

"Well, I am happy to show you where everything is. I was thinking I could help cover the front desk. Greet customers, settle accounts—you know, administrative stuff. That way you guys can keep your focus on the cars."

Robbie scratches the scruff on his chin while considering my proposition for a minute. "Fine. But in the future, before you fuck with my shit, check with me," he huffs, before stomping back to the bays.

I let out the deep breath I hadn't realized I was holding and laugh to myself. I saw that look in his eyes. The one that said he liked my idea, and he is only angry he didn't think of it sooner. One day at a time, *I can do this.*

6

Robbie

March 1st

"WHAT IS SHE DOING?" I hiss at Mack.

"Looks like she's changing her oil," he replies matter-of-factly.

"Yeah, I see that. I am not blind." I rub a frustrated hand over my face. "Why is she changing her oil?" It's Friday afternoon. Cassie, much to my surprise, has made it through the work week—*fuck*. I've done my best to ignore her, shooing her off to Chris or Mack whenever she has a question or is looking for something to do. If they don't give her a task, she comes up with one of her own—some sort of project to irritate me with.

She's a persistent little thing. I hate how fucking hot that is.

After her first day, Cassie seemed to realize this was not a professional atmosphere and started dressing casually. *I wish she would go back to her fancy office clothes.* Despite the couple of fantasies I ended up having about biting buttons off her cream-colored blouse before bending her over the desk, the outfit at least served as a necessary reminder that she doesn't belong here—she'd only ever be a daydream. Her new wardrobe of skinny jeans that show

33

the curve to her perfect little ass—especially as she's bent over tinkering with her Forester—and her tight t-shirts that ride up when she stretches to grab something make her seem obtainable. Dirty thoughts that I know will never happen are one thing, this though—it's dangerous.

I just don't get it. What is her angle? Girls like her don't hang around a small town like this. None of them want to spend their day in the garage, working around a bunch of sweaty, filthy guys. Girls like her *especially* don't get their hands dirty.

Yet here she is, happily singing a song to herself as she inspects her air filter.

"Cassie mentioned she needed to schedule an oil change and check out a few things on the car. I guess she got it just before moving down here. I told her it was slow today, and I could look it over. She said she was bored, and you were being an ass not giving her anything to do." Mack shrugs his shoulders. "I mentioned that if she really wanted something to do, she could borrow my bay and tinker around to her heart's content. It's the best idea I've ever had." Mack cocks his head to get a better view of Cassie.

"Yeah, well, I'm not paying you to stand around and check out her ass," I growl, pushing Mack to the side.

He laughs it off. "So, when are we going out?"

"It hasn't been a week yet." I turn, going back to the BMW I have been killing myself with all week. I hate BMWs—it's not that I actually hate them. It's just working on them is a pain in the ass, especially getting parts. Not to mention, I have yet to meet an owner of a BMW who isn't an entitled douche. *I'll bet he is exactly the type of guy Cassie would date.*

Mack follows quickly behind me. "It has been a full work week."

"If she shows up Monday, you win," I say dismissively, before rolling back under the BMW.

Not two seconds later, I feel a hand grab my leg and pull me out from beneath the car. I am surprised as I look up to a seriously pissed off Mack. "I am not sure what your issue is, but you have been nothing but a dick to her since she started." He runs his greasy hands through his shaggy hair, dirtying it up. "If you actually took two minutes to talk to her, you would realize that she is a nice girl. Not some stuck-up, city bitch."

I laugh, trying to slide back, but Mack stops me. Furious, I stand up and lean into his face. "I get you want to fuck her, but understand this, girls like her will chew you up and spit you out like a piece of five-cent chewing gum."

"Hey, break it up." Chris comes over, separating us. "What the hell is the problem over here?"

"Ask the boss; he is the one being a dick," Mack hisses before storming off.

Chris gives me the stare down, silently asking me what the hell my issue is. "Mack is just upset I am not kissing his fancy new girlfriend's ass."

"Well, boss, you have been nothing but a jerk to her all week," Chris scolds me.

"Seriously, you too?" I huff, stomping back to my office—*her* office. Whatever, just the fucking office. Quickly, I take a seat on the shop stool and start rummaging around, looking for something to take my mind off her. Chris isn't far behind me. As he enters the office, he shuts the door.

"Robbie, you need to get over your shit. Cassie isn't Bee." I go to object, but Chris holds up his hand, halting my protest. "Bianca was a bitch, and you know I don't throw that term around lightly. But Cassie has been nothing but pleasant and hardworking. For Christ's sake, the girl was scraping out the paint booth the other day. I know you have trust issues, and that Bee did quite a number on you. But it isn't fair to punish Cassie when she's done nothing wrong."

Chris doesn't give me a chance to reply before walking back out of the office and slamming the door behind him. Running my fingers through my hair (practically pulling it out), I steam at the thought of Bianca. Chris is right, but after the shit *she* pulled, it is difficult to trust outsiders—especially someone from the Cities.

Dammit! I hate this. I know that rationally, I should give Cassie a real shot. Maybe if I didn't get hard thinking about her, it would be easier. The last time I let my dick do the thinking for me, it almost cost me everything. But I was young and stupid then. Now, I am older and have learned from the mistake known as Bianca. I can't keep punishing Cassie because my cock seems to have taken a liking to her.

Taking a deep breath, I run my grease-stained hands through my hair, messing it up even more than it probably was to begin with. *All right, Robbie, you can do this. Quit being a little bitch,* I repeat to myself several times in hopes of calming down, before getting up and going back out to the bays. Cassie is squatting in front of a shelf, organizing some parts. I need to get her a fucking uniform or something. Her pants are low enough that, in this position, I can see the line to her pink thong.

Clearing my throat, I watch as she startles. She stands quickly and knocks a few items over. "What are you doing?" I ask, crossing my arms over my chest. I know I told myself that I would try to be nice to her. But every time I look at her, I am reminded of how much Bee fucked me over. They look nothing alike, but it doesn't change the fact that Cassie is filling the role *she* once had, and it serves to do nothing but remind me of Bianca's betrayal.

"Sorry," Cassie says, glancing at the mess she made. "I was looking for a new air filter—don't worry, I'm going to pay for it. I'm not Mack. I noticed some gaps and was trying to get an idea if we needed to order any inventory."

Without thinking, I take a step forward, shortening the distance between us. "I handle the inventory," I say more aggressively than I intended.

I focus my eyes on Cassie's mouth as she sucks in her bottom lip. *A little taste wouldn't hurt, would it?* I take a deep breath, attempting to get my hormones under control. "I plan on doing inventory next week. If you are interested, I can show you."

Cassie gives me a giant, bright smile. It cracks the armor around my heart, which I had thought was impenetrable. "That would be great. Thank you. I will just put these away—"

I brace my arm against the shelf, further boxing her in and cutting her off. "No need." This close I can smell her perfume; it's like flowers and sunshine. "I'll take care of it." As Cassie's brow bunches, I realize she's about to object. "Finish up. When you're done, why don't you call the BMW douche and let him know his car won't be ready until next week? I'm waiting on parts. They should be delivered Monday."

"You mean Tristan?" Cassie says in a breathy tone. I'm not sure why but, as if my hand has a mind of its own, I reach up and tuck a loose strand of her black hair behind her ear. I don't miss the small gasp she makes. "Sure thing, boss." The reminder is like a bucket of cold water being poured over my head. Reluctantly, I take a step back to allow her to walk away.

"Wait!" I call after her quickly. This gets Mack's and Chris's attention, both of whom are now observing our exchange intently.

"Yes, boss?" Cassie looks back at me.

"Umm... well." She raises an eyebrow at my inability to form a sentence. *Fuck it!* "Look, we are going out to Harper's tonight. It is a bar in town we like to go to. It is nothing fancy, but they have cold beer and good burgers. Anyway, if you're interested, we are meeting there at about eight tonight. Drinks and food will be on me." I try to ignore Mack's stifled chuckle in the background over the awkward exchange.

Cassie gives me an enormous smile that sends a signal straight to my dick. "Sounds fun. I'll be there," she says before sauntering off. I groan as I watch the sway of her hips. I get this heavy feeling in the pit of my stomach. This is either about to be the best or the worst idea I've ever had. I pray it is the former.

7

Cassie

March 1st

THIS PAST WEEK HAS been grueling. Robbie has officially given me whiplash. One minute, he is all growly, making what I assume are his best attempts to get me to quit. The next, he looks like he wants to devour me whole. I hate that, despite it being a terrible idea, I want him too. If his gruff exterior and tattoos weren't enough of a turn-on, his brilliant mind for business would do me in for sure.

To say that I'm impressed is an understatement. He really has cornered the market in this area; he has an à la carte of services at an actually affordable rate. I found a few quick lube places, but they offer nothing more than that. Also, with Robbie having the only tow locally available, he gets a lot of extra business.

Sitting in my car in front of Harper's, I attempt to get myself under control. Except for Tilly, Jax, and Jake, I haven't really hung out with anyone. Even then, we have been mostly packing and getting everything ready for the big move tomorrow. I thought about declining his offer, given how hot and cold Robbie has been all week. But if he is warming up to me, I don't want to give him any reason to be grumpy with me again. Giving myself a once-over in the mirror, I gather my stuff and head into the bar.

Once inside, I am surprised by the atmosphere. I am so used to being at Killian's, other bars are usually off-putting. But this place seems to have that familiar feel, like everyone knows each other. Although it is busy, it doesn't seem crowded. There's music, but it isn't so loud that people can't hold a conversation. They decorated the walls with quirky farm equipment and old images of farms in the surrounding area.

"Yo, Cassie!" Mack waves me over to where he, Chris, and Robbie are sitting. Making my way to the table, I take a seat next to Chris, which unfortunately puts Robbie directly across from me. Glancing down at the table, I notice a few beers in front of the guys and a cocktail in front of me.

"Sorry, was someone else sitting here?" I ask.

"No, I figured that would be your kind of drink," Robbie bites. *I guess it's grumpy Robbie tonight.*

I raise my eyebrow and fight back my urge to snip at him. *You get more bees with honey.* "I appreciate the thought, but it is not my usual choice," I say, taking a sip of the martini. While not my preference, growing up with my brothers (especially Killian), I have a pretty strong stomach when it comes to alcohol. When he first opened K.O.'s, Moira and I had to suffer through months of weird concoctions that he and Sean came up with.

A woman with hot pink and black hair walks up to the table. Though her style has changed, I'd recognize her anywhere. "Cassie, is that you?" Letty squeals before leaning in and giving me a hug.

"Hi, Letty, long time no see," I say, returning the hug before sitting back down. Letty had hung out with us frequently while Tilly and I roomed in college. "I just got into town this week. Tilly called me looking for someone to help at Robbie's shop."

Letty smacks her forehead. "Wow, I feel stupid now. I can't believe I forgot that. Things have been hectic here. I just started taking over this place and I've been swamped."

"That is awesome. Congratulations!" I say before taking a quick sip of my drink.

"Oh fancy, when did you start drinking those?" she asks, inspecting the martini in my hand. We went out drinking enough back in the day. She knows I would never order this.

I chuckle. "The guys ordered it for me before I got here. It seems *someone* assumed that since I am from the city, I'd prefer some fancy drink. It's not bad though; it is pretty smooth."

Letty laughs. "Thank you. But don't worry, I'll get you something a little more to your taste. Would you be interested in a burger? I have been told we have the best in town."

"You have the only ones in town," Robbie grumbles under his breath.

"Robbie, you pain me." Letty fakes being stabbed in the chest. "The diner and the bowling alley both serve burgers."

"A burger sounds great, Letty, whatever you recommend. I am not a picky eater," I offer, laughing at her antics. It's been ages since I've seen Letty. I forgot how much fun she could be. I always enjoyed when she came to visit Tilly. It would end up being one wild weekend.

"Perfect, I'll hook you up, girl." Letty shakes her head before looking at the boys. "I am assuming y'all want the usual?" They nod their heads in unison. After Letty leaves to put in our order, the guys start talking shop, nothing overly exciting, but at least everything is going smoothly.

"How are you liking Tral Lake so far?" Chris asks casually.

"I really like what I've seen. I haven't had much time to explore this week, helping Tilly get ready to move and all. I plan on trying to visit a few shops after this weekend. I saw this one, Patty Cakes. They make homemade fudge. I am

41

going there for sure," I reply cheerfully, trying to avoid the glare from Robbie.

"Oh yeah, you will love it there. She makes the best sweets. All in-house too," Mack adds to the conversation. "What is it you used to do back in the Cities?"

"Before coming down here?" I think for a moment, debating over how much to share. I am not really interested in getting into the issues with my ex. I will keep it to the *Reader's Digest* version. "Well, before coming here, I was helping my parents. They run a floral shop. Then I would lend my brother a hand waiting tables at his bar."

"Oh, I thought you would have worked in an office or something?" Chris inquires.

"Yeah, I did. But I had been out of work for a little while," I reply dismissively. "So, when I heard Tilly had some work down here, I figured I could use the fresh start."

"Why did you leave?" Robbie asks, not conversationally. With his intense stare, it feels more like an interrogation.

"It just wasn't a good fit..." I try to think of a way to word it. "It was a toxic work environment. But hey, it all worked out, right?" I reply with a big smile on my face, which seems to catch Robbie off guard.

Letty approaches with a tall dark lager in her hands, and a small glass of amber liquid. "Here you go," Letty offers, placing my drinks on the table. Robbie raises an eyebrow at the beverages, and Letty seems to notice. "Got a problem, Robbie?" she asks, placing her hand on her cocked hip.

"No, just didn't figure you'd drink Guinness and whiskey," he replies, looking at me.

"Not Guinness," I say, taking a sip. "Murphy's is way better."

"Are you kidding, Robbie? This girl could probably drink all you boys under the table without breaking a sweat." Letty hollers, gaining some attention.

"Party girl... nice," Mack flirts. Robbie's deep growl takes me by surprise. I'm not sure what he is pissed about. I'm just thankful for the table hiding how I clenched my thighs. Clearly my body hasn't quite gotten the message that Robbie is a no-go zone.

"No, I am not a party girl. I can just hold my booze."

"Yeah, you can. Spring break senior year, this girl got us free drinks all week by winning little drinking competitions," Letty reminisces. That was a pretty fun spring break. When you are a fairly wispy looking girl, people underestimate you a lot. "While this chick can put shots down like a champ, she can usually be found with a Murphy's in her hand. She's why I convinced Ted to stock the bar with it."

"Aww," I coo, placing my hand over my chest. "I'm so happy I could convert yet another. Moira is still holding strong with Guinness, but she will come to the dark side soon enough."

"Let's see what you got," Robbie announces. I risk looking into those amber pools and see that twinkle in his eye. The one that says this guy loves a challenge as much as I do.

"I am already drinking and eating for free," I tease Robbie. "What motivation do I have to jeopardize having a hangover tomorrow?"

Robbie reaches and grabs his wallet. Opening it up, he pulls out cash and tosses it on the table. "How about two hundred bucks?"

"I'm game," Mack chimes in, reaching for his own wallet.

Robbie holds up his hand. "Mack, do I need to remind you about Super Bowl Sunday?"

"You underestimate me, man," Mack pouts. "I told you—I had a bad burrito that morning. You suckers are going down. I'm buying in."

Chris holds up his hands in surrender. "I am at a one beer limit. I am on call for the tow tonight."

"So, what do you say, sweetheart? You in?" Robbie taunts.

I've never been one to back down from a challenge, especially not from some arrogant jerk, who thinks because he probably has a good hundred pounds on me, it is a sure deal. And I am not about to start now. "Okay, your funeral."

"Yes." Letty claps excitedly before running off and coming back moments later with a large tray of shots, lime, and salt. Robbie and I remain in the stare down we've been in since she left, while Mack pumps himself up. Letty quickly divvies out the tequila. There's enough for ten each.

"Here, Chris." Letty offers him his burger. "I put a hold on yours, assuming you don't want to eat too much before drinking these." She gestures to the rest of us at the table.

"Rules are simple," Robbie says gravely, ignoring Letty. "Last one standing wins."

I don't respond and simply pick up my first shot and take it down—forgoing the lime and salt. Without hesitation, I throw back shot number two. Slamming the glass down, I look at Mack and Robbie, raising my eyebrow. "I thought this was going to be a challenge?"

Robbie smirks at me, and it's the first time I have seen even a hint of a smile from that man. Without responding, he does the same as I had done and takes two consecutive shots without lime or salt. Mack glances between the two of us and mumbles, "Fuck," under his breath as he attempts to repeat the challenge. If his gagging is any indication, the second shot was too much, and he rushes to the lime and salt.

I keep my eyes locked on Robbie as I go for drink number three, four, and five in rapid succession. Robbie, surprisingly, is able to match me shot for shot. Mack taps out after the third, calling us psychos.

As we both lift the sixth shot, I notice that Robbie is slowing down, but he pushes through and slams his glass on the table. I follow quickly behind him. I won't lie... I know I am pretty drunk—it has been a while since I've had this much. But I haven't reached my limit just yet. I grab my seventh one, as Robbie hesitates, looking from me to the drink. After a moment of consideration, Robbie sets down the shot. "How about we call it a tie?" he suggests diplomatically.

I take in his handsome features. The deep amber color of his eyes that makes me think of my favorite whiskey. The stubble that covers the sharp angles of his strong rectangular jaw. How his dark, disheveled hair, which is normally pushed back, is now slightly hanging over his eyes. I hate that this past week, while he has been nothing but a jerk, all I could think about was him wrapping his large, inked, corded arms around me. I smile at him before lifting the glass to my lips, taking it down and slamming it on the table. I am sure I will probably regret this in the morning. But, right now, the sweet victory (plus the look of shock and awe on Robbie's face) makes it totally worth it.

8

Cassie

March 2nd

THE BRIGHT SUN CRUELLY shining through the blinds wakes me. I'm not sure why they're open or who opened them. But it seems like a sick prank the universe has pulled on me. I'm also surprised by the amount of sunlight. I don't remember my room having so many windows. *I thought the walls were a light shade of blue?* These walls look greener. Yes, I definitely drank way too much last night if I can't tell the difference between blue and green.

I'm unquestionably not ready to be awake. Pulling the blankets over my head, I turn and face away from the offending light. I stiffen as I brush up against a firm, warm body. With my eyes still closed, I take a few deep breaths to calm my nerves. *Okay, Cassie, you need to be an adult and assess the situation. Maybe it isn't as bad as you think?* Opening my eyes under the blanket, I see an unbelievably delicious, naked, muscular, tattooed body. Risking a glance down at myself, I notice I am also very much naked.

Slowly, I lower the blanket from over my head. I cover my mouth, hoping to stifle my surprised gasp. *Why am I nude, in bed, with Robbie?* My shock quickly dissipates to awe as I study his handsome face, so relaxed compared to what seems

46

to be a permanent scowl he has most of the time. Lying on my back, I squeeze my eyes shut and try to recall what happened last night.

· ❤ · ❤ · ❤ · ❤ · ❤ ·

Eight hours earlier

"Well, I think it is about time I call it a night," Chris announces. We finished our shot challenge about an hour ago. Mack never really recuperated, even after eating his greasy burger (hoping to absorb some of the liquor). Not wanting to waste any alcohol, I continued drinking my beer and whiskey with my dinner. I know I'll pay the price tomorrow with a massive hangover. But the satisfaction of showing Robbie that he isn't as big and bad as he thinks is too delectable to pass up. "Do you guys need a ride home?"

Robbie and I continue to stare, each daring the other to break. Mack chimes in by slurring, "I do."

"I'm good," Robbie and I reply in unison, not breaking eye contact once.

"Are you both sure?" Chris verifies, his tone laced with concern.

"Yeah, I can walk home," Robbie confirms.

"So can I. Or I'll call a ride. I am not ready to go just yet. Think I might have another beer," I taunt Robbie, making sure to emphasize that I am not done drinking yet.

Chris mumbles something about us not killing each other before he gathers up a drunken Mack, leaving Robbie and me by ourselves for the first time since arriving at the bar. "What's your story?" Robbie asks abruptly.

"What do you mean?" I'm caught off guard by his question and aggressive tone.

"You don't make sense," he adds, though his inquiry is not any clearer to understand.

"Thank you?" I'm uncertain what else to say to a statement like that.

"You don't belong here." Robbie crosses his arms over his chest, leaning back in the chair.

"Well, geez, thanks. You sure know how to make a girl feel welcome." My retort is sharp and direct before I stand up to grab my coat. I sway a bit, but quickly gather my bearings.

"Where are you going?"

"Away... from you," I sneer. Tightening my jacket around my waist, I walk out of the bar before he says anything else. I step outside and let the chilled winter air sober me up a bit. While cold, it feels as though spring isn't too far around the corner. I make it about a block down Main Street before a strong arm grabs me and turns me around. I pivot with my fist raised, ready to defend myself as Killian taught me. But when I see Robbie's scowl, the fear quickly fades into anger. "What is your problem?" I yell at him, pushing at his chest.

"You," is all Robbie says before bending down and crashing his mouth hard against mine. At first, I am too stunned to reciprocate the kiss. But as his pillowy lips press firmly against my own, I can't help but sink into him. Growling, Robbie turns and slams me against the wall of a nearby shop. His mouth travels from mine, down to my neck. His hands work their way under my jacket, rubbing just underneath my bra.

This has never been me. Though some minor public displays of affection haven't bothered me in the past, I have never been known for getting hot and heavy on a sidewalk. I consider protesting, my mind telling me that he's a jerk, my boss, and he is drunk—I'm drunk. That I am not a one-night stand kind of woman. That I'm taking a break from guys and relationships. Ultimately, however, none of it matters. Because his fingers and hot mouth feel so good, I am not sure I ever want them to stop.

"Let's go back to my place," Robbie demands more than suggests. Releasing me from the wall, he takes my hand and leads me down the sidewalk and back to the garage. As we make our way, we frequently stop for him to push me back against a wall and devour me. We can't seem to go more than a couple of steps without touching each other. This is absolutely crazy!

Climbing the stairway to his apartment above the shop, everything is a bit of a blur as we remove our clothes during our make-out session, leaving them like breadcrumbs along the trail to his bed. I'm in nothing but my thong as Robbie picks me up and tosses me on the mattress. His eyes study me like a vicious predator. I have never felt so exposed in my life. I'm no stranger to sex. I've had a few hot tumbles in my time. But I'm not sure I've ever had anyone look at me the way Robbie is now.

I study him in return—it only seems fair, after all. As I imagined, his gigantic frame is packed with muscle from head to toe, his body covered with various tattoos. I had seen the black ink on his forearms, but I never imagined he would have so many tattoos painting his body as though he is a human canvas. My breath catches as my eyes travel down and notice the large member that stands proud between his legs. I really shouldn't be surprised, given how enormous the rest of him is.

Crawling over me, Robbie props himself up—kindly, he avoids crushing me. "I want you so much..." he says against my mouth as he consumes me. "I've tried so hard to ignore this—ignore you. But you and those fucking pouty lips and that tight ass... it's all I have been able to think about all week." The revelation (that he has been struggling with this crazy attraction as much as I have) sends a flood of lava to my core.

Robbie kisses his way down my body, stopping just above the waistband of my underwear. Looking up at me, his eyes glimmer with a spark of mischief. He wraps his fingers around my thong, and with a quick tight snap, he rips them from me. I am so shocked by the display of such a dominating man, I have no time to prepare for his fiery mouth pressing down below. Unable to focus on anything other than the sensation of him doing a mixture of sucking, kissing, and licking, I don't even bother trying to stifle my moans.

He first slips one, then two fingers inside of me. I feel the tension building in my gut. With a few more pumps of his digits, I quickly unravel around him. My limbs feel like jelly as my nerves are still buzzing with electricity from my orgasm.

His lips lightly brush against my skin as he makes his way back on top of me. When he kisses me deeply, I can taste myself on him. In my state of euphoria, I already feel my body gearing up for more of his attention. "You are so addicting, Cass," Robbie whispers against my mouth. I moan in reply, wrapping my arms around him and pulling him closer.

"I need to feel you inside me," I beg. If I was thinking clearly, I may have been ashamed of my desperate behavior. But he's caused this new ache, this emptiness, and I need him to fill the void he's created. He's awoken this hungry beast deep inside me, and the only sustenance she requires is him.

Smiling, Robbie gives me another deep kiss as I feel him press against my center—gently inching himself forward. The entire time, I am moaning into his mouth. I thought what he did before was unbelievable, but this... I don't think there are words to describe how exquisite this feels. "Fuck, Cass, you are so fucking tight," Robbie groans, stilling inside me and allowing my smaller frame time to adjust.

As soon as my inner muscles adapt to his large intruding member, Robbie thrusts himself firm and steady. As my body relaxes, I fall into rhythm with him and bask in the sensation of the areas he's stroking as though they have never been touched before. Instinctively, I wrap my legs around him, using my heels to dig into his rear—forcing him deeper. I claw at his back. I feel myself tense. "I-I'm going..." I pant, unable to form a full sentence as the buzz within my core vibrates through my entire nervous system.

This seems to spark something within Robbie. He quickens his pace. The sounds of our shadowed silhouettes colliding fill the room before he slams deep inside me. "Oh fuck, Cass..." is the only warning I get as his heavy frame goes taut, and he releases his hot load. His orgasm triggers the last of mine, pushing me into an ocean of ecstasy surrounded by warm white light. "That was..." he mumbles into my neck. He seems just as exhausted as I am.

Rolling off before tugging me against his side, Robbie is silent as we both stare at the ceiling. I know I should get out of bed. I should go home. But I don't think I could stand up if I wanted to. And that is part of the problem—I don't want to. Robbie's fingers gently tracing a pattern on my arm is the last thing I feel as I drift off into a deep slumber, realizing I am definitely in trouble.

· ♥ · ♥ · ♥ · ♥ · ♥ ·

Present

Robbie drapes his arm over me and pulls me closer, bringing me back to reality. Nuzzling into my neck, he whispers, "Good morning." The display of affection is in complete contrast to the wild animal who caused this pleasant ache between my thighs.

"Good morning," I reply tentatively, the realization of what happened last night settling in. This isn't me. I don't get drunk at a bar and sleep with some guy I barely know—some guy who has been nothing but a jerk to me from the moment we met. Not to mention, on top of it all, I slept with my boss—*again*. Slipping out from under his arm, I get out of bed and quickly attempt to gather my clothes.

Robbie's handsome, sleepy face turns and grimaces at me. "Where are you running off to?"

"I need to go home," I snip out a bit too harshly.

Dropping his shoulders, he shakes his head. "Is something wrong?" He sits up and pulls on a pair of shorts. I turn my gaze away, fearful of how my body may react if it gets any more of an eyeful.

"No..." I don't want to hurt his feelings more than I already have.

"If nothing is wrong, why do I get the sense that you are tucking your tail and about to flee my apartment?" Robbie asks, the stern demeanor I am all too familiar with firmly back in place.

"I'm sorry, but this was a mistake." I'm already half dressed in my jeans, boots and bra, and I no longer care about finding the rest of my clothes. I throw on a random hoodie of his and grab my purse. I'm about to leave the apartment when he grasps my arm, turning me towards him—similar to what he had done after I fled the bar—his eyes pleading with me not to run off.

Robbie tucks a loose strand of hair behind my ear. "Last night, I thought—" I cut him off before he can say anything more.

"You're my boss," I remind... *both of us*. Robbie drops his hand as he looks at me, hurt and confused. I force myself to continue, needing to do the right thing. "Look, I had a nasty breakup a few months ago. I was naïve enough to think that dating my boss was a good idea. Even though everyone warned me how bad it could turn out. I ignored them. I thought he was the one...." I pause, taking a deep breath to hold back my tears. The last thing I want is to appear weak in front of him. "Anyway, you don't need all the gory details. Let's just say... it didn't end well. I came here for a fresh start, and I think it is best if we just forget this ever happened."

Robbie backs up, as though I burned him. "Fine, it's forgotten," he says before sharply turning away to get dressed.

I don't waste another minute. I run out of his apartment, doing the ultimate walk of shame back to my car. *Great, one week in a new town and I'm already repeating the same mistakes.*

9

Cassie

March 2nd

Pulling into the driveway, I notice a familiar car sitting in my spot. I quickly park and rush into the house. I find Moira sitting at the breakfast counter drooling over Jake, who, as promised, is shirtless and wearing low hanging grey sweatpants. Moira is so fascinated that she doesn't even notice me.

However, Jake does and he smiles, taking in my disheveled exterior. "I thought you said you were taking a break in that department," he teases. I didn't think about appearances before coming home wearing a sweatshirt four times too large with my hair a mess and makeup smeared all over. Jake's comment breaks the spell he had over Moira and she turns and gasps.

"What happened to you?" she asks, tilting her head before raising her eyebrow at my ensemble.

"Just a long night," I answer dismissively. I really don't want to discuss *what* happened, and I especially don't want to discuss with *whom*. "Sorry... I am going to go upstairs and take a quick shower. I'll be down in just a few minutes."

"No worries. I am sure Jake will keep me company while I wait." Moira's attention goes back to Jake, who is proudly on display for her in the kitchen.

I chuckle under my breath as I make my way upstairs. Luckily, I avoid Jax and Tilly. The last thing I need is more questions about my state of dress, or my actions the previous night. Quickly disrobing and entering the shower, I scrub all the wonderful memories off me, every detail from the last few hours. While it was incredible, I need to forget it ever happened.

The sex may have been amazing—possibly the best I've ever had—but a relationship is more than that. It's about chemistry, and ours is explosive. And not in a good way.

I get dressed and trek back downstairs. I'm surprised to see not only Jax and Tilly in the kitchen, but also Scott. "Hey, take a seat. Do you like pancakes?" Scott asks as I enter the room.

"Who doesn't like pancakes?" I joke with him.

Scott whips up a delicious breakfast that helps absorb any of the remaining booze in my system. Fortunately, my hangovers never last too long. A hot shower and carbs usually cure me. I'm happy about that. I'd hate to be miserable while Moira is here visiting.

The sound of the front door opening and closing increases my heart rate. I know by the musky smell of his cologne mixed with an undertone of diesel exactly who just walked in. I don't need to turn around to know that Robbie is staring at me. I can feel his eyes boring into the back of my skull.

"Hey, Robbie, you hungry?" Scott asks, already getting a plate ready for his brother.

"Starving," Robbie replies. He takes the only seat near me. His enormous frame fills the space, causing his shoulder to brush against mine. I bite my lip, suppressing my gasp at the shock wave of electricity his touch sends through my body.

"Moira, this is my eldest brother—Robbie. I don't think you two ever met." Tilly makes introductions.

"No, we haven't," Moira confirms and, being her typical flirty self, she gives him a good once-over.

"Hi," Robbie grumbles as he shovels food in his mouth, paying her little attention.

"This is your new boss?" Moira asks me. I simply nod in reply, the air in the room suddenly feeling in short supply. Looking up and across the counter, I watch as she mouths, "Oh. My. God," and fans herself. I stifle my laughter by taking a sip of my orange juice.

The rest of breakfast goes smoothly with casual conversation. Robbie doesn't look at or talk to me. Fortunately, he doesn't seem as cold as he did earlier this morning. Jax goes over the moving plan for today, which honestly doesn't require much. They barely have a truck's worth of stuff, but they are excited to have everyone over today to check out the house. Tilly was telling me the other day how Jax inherited the house from his family; his great-great-grandfather built it originally. She really hasn't explored it yet, since the tenants who were renting it just recently moved out. But she said from the little she's seen, it is absolutely gorgeous.

I'm happy to see her excited and ready to move on to the next chapter of her life. She took likely the worst moment of her existence and somehow turned it around to come out on top. While Chad pulling the rug out from under me and shattering the illusion I thought was us—happy and in love—might be the worst moment of my life, Jax and Tilly are proof there is a rainbow after the storm. I glance over to Robbie, who's scowling as he drinks his black coffee and reads the paper. My happily ever after is out there—it's just not with *him*.

Prior to Chad, Robbie was exactly my type. Tall, dark, and brooding with a side of tattoos and a leather jacket. I wouldn't be shocked if he had a motorcycle. I wanted a bad boy with a chip on his shoulder and a heart of gold. A wild stallion only I could tame. After many heartbreaks, I learned *that* is just a fantasy. I thought Chad would be different, but he was just a bad boy in a more presentable costume. I need to stop chasing after guys I think I can fix, guys I hope will change for me. There is nothing *wrong* with Robbie; he just isn't *right* for me. The next time I give someone my heart, it will be because they want it. Not because I force it on them.

The sound of the front door once again opening and closing pulls me from my thoughts. I'm left wondering who else would be here this early, until I see the bouncing pink and black curls of Letty. *Darn it!* I feel a little nauseated, but quickly realize she hadn't seen me stumble in this morning. She has no reason to suspect anything. "Morning, bitches!" Letty yells, leaning in and giving Tilly a big hug before she notices Moira. "Oh. My. God. Moira, I haven't seen you in forever." She squeals, dishing out another embrace.

"Yeah, I figured since Tilly stole my best friend, it was time I visited," Moira teases.

"Yes, speaking of... Seriously, you should have seen Cassie last night. She was kicking ass and taking names. It was just like spring break," Letty offers and I cringe, hoping the pieces don't start falling together.

"Oh yeah, who was the poor sucker?" Moira asks, chuckling. Having witnessed me take down many patrons at K.O.'s, she is well aware that my iron stomach is still very much intact. People get so amazed at my ability to hold my liquor, it has kind of become a sideshow at the pub. Killian even made it into a game, saying if anyone could outdo me, their tab for the night would be free.

"This poor sap here." Letty pats Robbie on the back. "He tried, but dropped out after the sixth shot of tequila."

"I just value my liver," he retorts.

"Sure." Letty rolls her eyes. "What happened to you guys last night? You both stormed out of there?"

Oh no, what do I say? Moira and Jake obviously know I didn't come home last night. Besides Tilly and Letty, I have no friends around here that I can pretend I stayed with. Not to mention, I can't risk the drama right now.

"You know..." Robbie shrugs his shoulders and I hold my breath. "I was an ass; she stormed off. I chased after her, not wanting her out in the cold, drunk and angry. I twisted her arm and convinced her to come crash at my place to sleep it off." His voice is so cold, so detached that even I don't believe we had sex last night.

I side-eye Moira—she doesn't seem to suspect anything. "That explains why you looked so brutal. Tequila always leaves you looking sexed over." Letty laughs, and the other girls follow suit.

I let out the breath I didn't realize I was holding, before joining in. Fortunately, the topic is dropped as Letty catches up with Moira. But as I look at Jake, who's glancing between Robbie and me with a knowing smirk, a lump forms in my throat—*he knows.*

10

Robbie

March 4th

I'VE BEEN FUCKING DREADING today. Saturday, I barely made it out unscathed. Thanks to the move, I was able to avoid Cassie easily enough and without being too obvious. But at the shop, there will be no hiding it. Chris and Mack have already been on me about my attitude towards her.

But after Friday night, I don't know how to be around her. I am torn between wanting to throw her down on the nearest surface and fuck her, and keeping my dick as far away from her as possible. She's right though. Us hooking up, it's a terrible fucking idea. But damn if it wasn't incredible. All weekend I replayed each blissful moment I spent buried deep inside her. I hate that it felt so... *perfect*. Which is probably just more of a reason I need to keep my cock on lockdown. One week, one night, and she already has me thinking girly shit like how "perfect" we felt together.

Last night, I couldn't sleep, so I came down to the shop early this morning. I've been sitting here staring at the clock, waiting for her to come in like a sad puppy. *Dammit! Get your shit together, Robbie.* If my pops were around, he would kick my ass for being such a pussy. The sound of the front door opening has me sitting at attention, in a picture-perfect pose. I wait anxiously to see her stroll in. I'm disappointed when it is Mack who saunters over instead.

"What's going on?" he asks, raising a brow at my unusual behavior.

Getting myself back under control, I mask my features, returning to the tough exterior they are all too familiar with. "Nothing," I say before turning and heading into my office. I don't know what the hell I was thinking, sitting and waiting for Cassie to show up. What did I expect? She'd come in this morning through the fog with her blouse open and hair blowing in the wind like some bad 80s music video. Then I'd lay her out on the hood of one of the cars and get another taste.

In the office, I go through a few files, really just doing some busy work—anything to distract myself. It must have worked because I didn't even notice Cassie standing in the doorway, her dark hair piled on top of her head. I assume the baggy hoodie she's sporting and her face bare of makeup is her attempt at being unattractive. But unfortunately for her, if anything, her plain appearance makes her even hotter—it makes her look like she belongs.

When she clears her throat, I am pulled out of my daze. I realize I must have been sitting here staring at her like a lovesick idiot. "Were you still planning on showing me how you like to handle the inventory today?" she asks cautiously.

Fuck, I forgot I had told her that last week. "Yeah," I grunt. "Let me get a few things together and I will meet you up front."

Cassie nods in agreement, before turning and leaving. I watch how her hips sway underneath her hoodie. I stall in the office, thinking of any excuse to get out of doing this. But as I rack my brain, nothing comes to mind. If I am being honest with myself, despite how pissed I am that she stopped this as quickly as it started, I know she is right and pursuing anything together would likely be a colossal mistake. I've barely known her for a fucking week, and during that time,

I've done my best to avoid her, all while being torn about how much I want her. When I'm near her, all I want to do is pull her close, feel her warm skin against mine.

Friday, besides learning how sweet she tastes, I discovered there is a lot more to Cassandra Murphy than meets the eye. I had her pegged as some stuck-up suburban socialite. She is anything but.

Deciding to man up and face her, I grab my inventory checklist and make my way out to the bays. Cassie is sitting on a little rolling stool chatting with Mack and handing him various tools. Seeing her sit there, with a socket in her hand that is now slightly tinged with grease, is hot as sin. I get the sudden urge to throw her down on the creeper and convince her with my cock that there is no reason we can't fuck, like I know we are both desperate to do again.

Cassie's honey-smooth laughter echoes through the shop. At first, I bask in it. Then quickly, my jealousy takes over. She's laughing at something Mack said. I'm not close enough to know what she's laughing at. But Mack is just as much a man-whore as Jake. I am not sure the guy even knows how not to flirt with a girl. "We don't have all day, Cassie," I yell to her a lot rougher than needed. But thinking that Mack might try to put a move on her pisses me the hell off.

Cassie looks at me like a deer caught in the headlights—confused and wondering what she did wrong. Mack rolls out from under the car. His scowl confirms I am being too much of an asshole again for no damn reason. "Yeah, coming," Cassie replies sheepishly before sliding off the stool and setting down the socket she was holding. Mack gives her a sympathetic look before she cautiously approaches me, treating me as though I am some sort of rabid animal.

I take a deep breath, attempting to get my frustration under control. "Sorry," I say in a calm tone. "It's just... our cutoff time for ordering today is at two."

"Sure," she says tentatively. "Well, let's get started."

"So here is my inventory checklist." I show her my binder. "I have a list of all the parts and shit we keep in stock, and what the inventory level should be. I do a count of what we have on hand, then mark how many we need to order. It is pretty straightforward—even Mack could do it."

"Sounds like it." She is being careful, clearly holding something back.

I cross my arms over my chest and look down at her. "What?"

"It's nothing. Let's get started," she says dismissively. "How do you want to do this?"

"No, tell me." For the second time today, my demand is more aggressive than warranted. At first, she looks nervous, but then she shakes it off. She mimics my pose before frowning at me.

"Do you hate technology or something?" Her tone tells me I pissed her off.

"No," I growl. "This is how my pops did it for decades; it's how he trained me. I've never once had an issue. It works—there is no need to change it."

"How long does this take you to do?" she asks, tapping her foot.

"I don't know. It isn't like I time myself. But probably a few hours, depending on how many times I get interrupted."

"How often do you have to do this?" She gestures to the giant shelf of various parts.

"Every couple of weeks. Why? What's your point?" I'm fed up with her interrogation.

"Well," she says sarcastically. "If you stepped out of the Dark Ages and switched to an electronic POS system, your inventory count would be done automatically. All you would have to do is pull a report and order what you need. We would be able to more *efficiently* manage the inventory and customer records."

"Sure, but what's the point? I've been doing it this way, while you were still gossiping with your girlfriends over which boy band member was the cutest. It works. There's no need to change it," I say with finality. But the fire that is burning in her eyes tells me she doesn't give a rat's ass.

"You are being ridiculous. Just because something isn't broken doesn't mean it can't be better. I bet you could free up so much more of your time if you upgraded your system. Even offer online scheduling and estimates."

"Well..." I step closer to her, and I don't miss how her eyes turn dark and stormy. "I'm about to free up a bunch of my time, because this is now your job." I throw the words back at her since she has been dying for more stuff to do. My original plan was to ignore her and hope she goes away. Now, my new plan is to keep her busy as hell, so she doesn't have time to sit and laugh with Mack.

Cassie closes the distance between us, her slender frame pressed against mine. "Fine, so you are going to waste money paying me to do something a computer could do in a fraction of the time." Feisty Cassie is sexy as fucking hell. I want her pissed off at me all the time.

"Computers break down; the systems are unreliable. We are out in the fucking middle of nowhere. Five people sign into Netflix, and the entire system will shut down or move at a snail's pace." As we have a stare off, I struggle with the urge to lean down and capture her pouty bottom lip between my teeth. I shake the thoughts from my mind. "I will count, and you will write what we need." I shove the binder at her, effectively ending the discussion. With a huff, Cassie takes it from me and I immediately miss her warmth.

"Fine," she breathes out. I go to count the first item on the list before she adds, "If you upgraded your system, it would prevent Mack from giving away *accidental* discounts." Cassie does air quotes and we both laugh, the tension between us seemingly more palatable. Good. While she might not want to pursue anything further between us, now that she's here, I'm not sure I want her to go.

11

Cassie

March 8th

UGH, AND HERE I thought the first week sucked... This week was brutal.

Although most of the time Robbie was his surly self, that wasn't the issue. Actually, I'm pretty certain the surliness is just Robbie. This week he assigned me several new tasks. I'm basically glued to the front desk or the back office. The optimistic part of me wants to believe that this means Robbie has accepted me in my role and is giving me adequate responsibilities to justify my position. On the other hand, it terrifies the realist in me, who suspects that he is just altering his strategy. Last week, pretending I didn't exist and wasn't worth his time wasn't enough to push me away. So now, he is going to overwork me and hope I give up.

The worst part, I can't tell if this is still derived from his initial hope of having me quit because he didn't want someone new in his office, or punishment for sleeping with him. *Or*, worse yet, retribution for declaring I will not sleep with him again.

Why do you have to be so stupid, Cassie? Can't you ever learn your lesson?

Fed up, I grab my phone and call Moira. I still hadn't told her about us hooking up, mostly out of embarrassment. But I need her voice of reason before I drive myself mad with all the *what ifs*.

"Cassie," Moira shouts into the phone. Based on the loud music in the background and her giggling, she must be at K.O.'s. I should have known better. For years, we've spent almost every Friday night (Saturday nights also) at my brother's bar. It was silly of me to think that just because I moved away, she'd be sitting at home, alone, just like I was.

"Hi, Moira. Is this a bad time?"

"Nope, I'm just at K.O.'s." I hear some shuffling and talking in the background. "Sean says hi."

"Tell Sean I said hi back." Moira is talking in the distance again, presumably to Sean.

"How are things going down there? I miss you."

"I miss you too. Actually, I wanted—"

"Oh. My. God. Jake, he's so hot. You have some serious willpower, girl. There is no way I could live in that house with him and not already be banging his brains out daily. Unless—"

"NO! I'm not sleeping with Jake. But I need to—"

"I really should have slept with him when I was down there. But then, I figured that would be a kind of shitty thing to do to Tilly and all. I mean while I'm not as close to her as I am to you, it'd be like me sleeping with Kill or Cian. It's just wrong to sleep with your friends' siblings. But then again, maybe she wouldn't care. Isn't Jax like her brother's best friend?"

I slap my forehead. I'm such an idiot. I didn't just sleep with my boss; I slept with my friend's brother. While she warned me about Jake and didn't seem to care if I slept with him, for all I know, it was one of those scenarios where she was just being nice, knowing that I'd never hook up with him anyway.

"Moira, I really—"

"Cassie, are you still there? I can hardly hear you?"

"Moira," I shout again.

"Ugh... Cassie, this place is pretty crazy tonight. Kill's got this new local band playing, and it's packed. The lead singer is so yummy. I wish you were here. Look, can I call you tomorrow?"

"Yeah, that's fine."

"Awesome, love you. I'll call tomorrow."

As the line goes dead, I drop my phone on the bed. Feeling defeated, I lie back and do the only thing I can do—I let the tears fall.

What's wrong with me? I don't understand why I put myself in this position again. On more than one occasion, he made it clear he didn't think I belonged here. He's been going out of his way to make me quit. But the second I see him with his signature scowl, my panties get drenched. *Classic Cassie,* getting all hot and bothered by Mr. Unattainable.

A knock on the door pulls me from my pity party.

"Come in," I say quickly, sitting up and wiping away the tears.

"Hey, Cassie." Jake opens the door to my room. "I was just about to go out and..." He studies my appearance for a moment. "What's going on? Is everything okay?"

"Oh yeah, everything is fine." I put on my best smile. "Did you need something?"

Jake crosses his arms over his chest. "Come on, Cassie, clearly something is wrong. Your face is all red and puffy—*you've been crying.*"

"Seriously, it's nothing. I think I am just a little homesick."

"I can't imagine ever being away from home. I'm not sure how Tilly managed during college."

"It's tough. I mean, I'm glad to have gotten away. I needed a fresh start. It's just that, so far, this fresh start hasn't gone according to plan."

"Let me guess... *Robbie?*"

"Yeah, you could say that."

Jake frowns, and I immediately realize my mistake. I'm such an idiot, badmouthing his brother.

"Wait, I'm sorry. I didn't mean it like that—"

Jakes features turn from anger to confusion. "You have nothing to be sorry for. I just can't believe Robbie. I know what Bee did was fucked up, but that happened forever ago. He has no right taking it out on you. I mean, you uproot your entire life and come down here as a favor to Tilly and help his sorry ass. Which, from listening to Tilly bitch, he desperately needed."

"Who's Bee?" I'm not sure why, but out of everything he said, the only thing that stands out is the name. I have this sudden knot in my stomach; it aches with jealousy. I don't really understand why.

"Ugh, his ex." Jake rolls his eyes. "She's a total psycho. Don't worry—*she's long gone*. But she sure did a number on him. To be honest, I never liked her. She just reeked of crazy."

"Oh." Part of me is desperate to ask for more details. But I know I'm on thin ice already and would hate to push my luck.

Jake waves his hand in front of his face. "It doesn't matter. So, what has my dickhead brother been doing?"

"It's nothing, really—"

"Look, Cassie, I know we don't know each other all that well. And you probably think I'm just some colossal idiot who knows he's hot and uses it to sleep around."

"What? No, I don't—"

"It's okay. I'm not insulted. Honestly, for the most part, it *is* true. But can I let you in on a little secret?"

I nod my head in agreement.

"I'm fantastic at reading people. Scout's honor—it's why I get laid so easily. Being hot isn't enough. It helps. But being able to read someone, understanding her tells, is how I know if I'm treading in dangerous waters."

"I never really thought about it that way. It's a good point though. If you are a guy looking for casual sex, being able to read if the girl you are about to hook up with has commitment fever is probably a good thing. You must be great at poker?"

Jake gives me a gigantic smile. "Yeah, you'd think by now, my brothers would stop gambling with me. So come on, Cassie, spill it. What's going on with Mr. Stick-up-his-butt?"

"I slept with Robbie," I yell quickly as if ripping off a Band-Aid, then immediately cover my mouth, in shock that I finally admitted it out loud and not only that, but to his brother.

"Yeah, I know." I look at Jake, confused. I mean, I kind of assumed he knew that morning. But how certain he seems of the fact makes me wonder if Robbie already told him. *Oh. My. God. Did Robbie already tell him... tell everyone?*

"It was pretty obvious, well, at least to me. When you came home looking like you'd been sexed up good and proper while wearing my brother's sweatshirt. I may not be a rocket scientist, but it wasn't hard to put together. Then, when Robbie came over and had that dopey grin on his face, I knew he'd finally gotten some."

"He had a dopey grin?"

Jake laughs. "Yeah, when he first walked in and saw you. It was only for a second; Robbie is a pro at closing himself off. He's the only one who has ever been close to besting me on game night. So, now that we got your big secret out of the way, tell me what the problem is. Was it bad?"

"What? *No.*"

"While my brother isn't a monk, I'm guessing he is out of practice—"

"No, the sex was amazing. That isn't the issue. The problem is that I slept with him in the first place." I take a deep breath to build up my nerve. "My ex, he was my boss. Let's just say when that relationship ended, so did my career

68

and reputation. It's why I wanted to start again, somewhere new. I was in town one week, which was filled mostly by my new boss being a giant jerk. One moment, acting like I don't exist and the next, like I'm a tasty snack and he's starving. After all that, we have a few drinks and then—*boom*—we are all over each other. Now this week, after we hook up and I tell him it can't happen again, he's dumped a gazillion tasks on my plate. I'm just so confused. Why would I want to sleep with someone who has made it clear he didn't want me there? Why would he want to sleep with me if he hates me so much? Is all this added work a new ploy to push me away? Why do I want to sleep with him again?" I sit silently, realizing I just overshared. But it was like the dam burst, and there was nothing I could do to stop it.

"Robbie doesn't hate you. *Believe me*, if he did, you'd know. He isn't one to play nice."

"This is him being nice?"

Jake chuckles. "Not exactly. I'd say it's more that... he likes you and doesn't know how to handle it. As far as him giving you work, trust me when I say, he wouldn't let you near his precious business if he wanted you gone. If he's giving you more work, it means he wants you to stay. It's his way of opening up to you."

"Why do I do this to myself?"

"You did nothing wrong, Cassie."

"Didn't I? The last time I got mixed up with someone I worked with, it ended catastrophically. So bad that I had to leave the position I worked extremely hard to obtain. Not only that, but I couldn't find a new position that was even remotely equivalent, because of the rumors. Even after leaving my job, my ex is still rubbing everything in my face by galivanting around with his new *fiancée*. To make matters worse, last time everything imploded from an actual relationship. This thing with Robbie was some crazy one-night stand. Oh. My. God. My first one-night stand was with my boss, who is hoping I'll quit. He already had a low opinion of me... I can only imagine what he thinks of me now. Do you think he's told Chris and Mack? Do they all think I'm some slut who sleeps around the office?"

"Cassie, *breathe.*" I look to see Jake squatting in front of me and holding my shoulders. It is only then I realize my chest is tightening up and I can't catch my breath. *Oh no, this can't happen again.* "You can get through this," Jake says with confidence, his amber eyes locked with mine. As I sit and look into them, I notice the outer edges are a beautiful hint of green.

"Can you try taking some deep breaths with me?"

I nod my head in agreement and work to copy Jake's respirations. After a few moments, I can feel the panic settling, and my breathing regulate.

"You're doing a great job. Do you need something?"

I shake my head. "No, I think I'm fine now. I'm sorry... this is so embarrassing—"

"Cassie, you have nothing to be embarrassed about. It sounds like you have a lot on your mind. I'm not sure what happened with your ex. But if you want to talk about it, I'm all ears. It sounds like he deserves a good ass-kicking. As for Robbie, I can't tell you what he's thinking. Like I said, the guy can be Fort Knox. That being said, my brother might be an ass, but he's not a dick. He isn't the kind of guy who flaunts his sex life, or I'm fairly sure the lack thereof. I understand casual sex for someone who's used to a relationship might be shocking. I promise you, coming from a guy who basically has only casual sex, Robbie doesn't think any less of you. Only a hypocritical dickweed would think that way."

"Really?" I ask tentatively.

"Really." Jake reassures me with a smile. "Do you like pizza?"

"Yeah," I say, though I'm confused by the sudden change of subject. "But seriously, Jake, go out. I'm in no shape to be seen in public. I think I might just shower, then curl up and watch a movie or two."

Jake stands up and starts taking off his jacket. "What movie?"

"Umm... I was actually thinking of watching *The Conjuring* movies. I know it sounds ridiculous, but being in a new house, I thought it might be fun to watch creepy movies."

"Thank god," Jake says excitedly. "I love horror flicks. I mean *seriously*. Usually Tilly and I would watch them together, but Jax isn't the biggest fan. He's more into the romantic chick-flicks—*no offense.*"

"None taken. Funny enough, while I love romance, I actually can't stand the movies. If I want romance, I'd rather read a good book."

"Okay, now the important question. What kind of pizza?"

I wince, thinking of how many times I've fought with Kill and Cian. I'd always get outnumbered. "Pineapple, jalapeno, and bacon. But seriously, I'm not picky. I'll eat whatever you want to order."

Jake's grin grows wider. "You know, Cassie, I think you and I are going to be best friends."

12

Robbie

March 11th

"YOU DO NOT KNOW how long I've waited to get my hands on you." I gently caress the hood of my pops' pride and joy.

"Eleanor?" Cassie says from behind me.

"No, that was a reinterpretation of a 67' Mustang Shelby GT500. This, however..." I take another moment to bask in the beauty of her factory highland green paint (which is going to be a bitch to match perfectly) before giving my attention to the beauty standing behind me. "This is a 68' Mustang 390 GT Fastback."

"It was in a movie, right? It looks familiar." Cassie comes closer to study the car. Immediately, I can feel the stiffening in my pants as I catch the scent of her floral perfume. I've never once cared about flowers in my entire life. Mom loved them—always had beautiful gardens and arrangements on the table. I caught myself the other day at the market, sniffing the fresh flowers (trying to figure out which scent Cassie was wearing).

"*Bullitt*." I try to get my mind out of the gutter.

"Oh yeah, that's right. Sorry. It's a beautiful car. Did someone bring it in? It looks like it hasn't seen the light of day in some time."

"She hasn't hit the pavement in a while. This actually used to be my grandfather's car. When he passed, my dad inherited it. And, well, now..." I don't bother explaining further, as Cassie seems to get the point.

"Why hasn't she been driven in so long?"

"I don't think my dad had the heart to take her out after Pops died. God, did my dad love this car."

"Was your dad into cars too?"

I laugh at the notion. "Nah, my dad never got into cars. His passion had always been books. But *this*..." I glance at the Mustang. "...was the one exception. My pops ran a local junkyard just outside of town. One day this car got towed in—from what I was told, it was a salvage. Pops was actually going to scrap it for parts, but my dad saw it and flipped. My dad enjoyed reading, but he also watched a lot of action films—he loved Steve McQueen. Anyway, he begged Pops not to destroy it. Excited that for the first time his son was showing interest in cars, the old man couldn't refuse. Long story short, they rebuilt it together. The only car my dad ever restored... He learned to drive in this car, took my mom to prom... *Fuck*, I'm pretty sure I was conceived in the back seat of it." Cassie laughs at my comment, causing me to casually readjust myself. Fuck, I love the sound of her laughter. I also really love how easy it feels to talk to her. Like I could tell her anything and she wouldn't judge or put me down.

"Sounds like a really special vehicle."

"Growing up, I couldn't wait to drive this thing. But dad babied her, refused to let anyone but Pops drive it. He probably only agreed to that because *technically* it was in Pops' name. Then when he died, my dad put her in storage and he never drove her again. I remember we practically started World War III over it. I told him if he hated the damn car so much, he should give it to me. That a thing of beauty like this didn't deserve to be locked away. He was so pissed at me. It was one of the few times I ever saw him actually angry. That's when I learned he was keeping her safe. He and Pops didn't always see eye-to-eye. Pops was constantly hounding him to get his nose out of the damn books and put his hands to good use. This car was probably the one and only thing they ever agreed on."

"I'm guessing your grandpa must have loved having a grandson who inherited his passion for cars."

"You have no idea." Growing up, I spent a lot of time at the junkyard while my parents worked on getting their business off the ground. Realizing I'm taking a dangerous trip down memory lane, I quickly shake the thoughts from my head and bring myself back to the present. "Did you need something?"

"Oh," Cassie says, dejected—the warm smile she had now replaced with a mask of professionalism. *Shit*, why did I have to ruin this. The first time we've really talked about something not work related, and I end the conversation like an asshole. "I was actually hoping we could talk for a moment... in the office, please."

I nod and follow her lead, taking a seat at the desk out of habit. *I should really get her an office chair.*

"Look, I'm no good at this. But if we are going to work together, it is important we clear the air," she finally says, determined. Her chest puffed out, she looks me straight in the eyes.

"Okay." I cross my arms and lean back. I've been expecting this. Honestly, I'm surprised it has taken her so long.

Cassie takes a deep breath. "The night we..."

"Had sex," I finish for her.

"Yes, that." I smile; it's adorable how nervous she is right now. "I don't normally do things like that. I mean, I've never..."

"That was your first—" I sit up at full attention. If I would have known she was a virgin, I wouldn't have...

"What? *No.*" Cassie crinkles her nose and shakes her head. I'm momentarily relieved that her first time wasn't with me after one-too-many shots of tequila. But that is short-lived as a burn of unexplained jealousy washes over me.

It's ridiculous, but I want to kick the ass of any guy who's ever laid a finger on her. "I am trying to say... getting drunk and sleeping with someone. I don't do things like that. Not that I was too drunk, nor am I using alcohol as an excuse." Cassie speaks at a hundred words per minute. "Ugh, this was so much easier with Jake," she mumbles under her breath. That burn is now a raging fire as I stand and slam my hands on the desk. Cassie jumps.

"You slept with Jake!" I roar.

"What? No!" She scowls at me.

"Well, you just said this speech was a lot easier to give my brother—the king of that sort of thing."

"No, just stop. I'm not sleeping with Jake. Geez, why are you being so difficult? He helped me prepare to talk to you. To practice what I wanted to say. He really sucks at that by the way—he is not surly enough to play the role of you."

I calm down and rein in my anger, not wanting to scare her.

"Look, I know you don't like me. Since day one, you've been nothing but unkind, making it pretty clear that you don't want me here. I heard about your bet by the way—*thank you for having such little confidence in me.*" *Fucking Mack. I'm going to kill him.* "Now you have dumped a bunch of work on me. I want to know if this is your new tactic to make me quit. Do you have a new wager going? I came to Tral Lake to get away from an unpleasant situation, a toxic work life. I wanted a clean slate. But if you really don't want me here, I will leave. I'll even tell Tilly it's because I'm homesick. That way she won't be mad at you. I just need to know if this is you punishing me for sleeping with you."

In two seconds, I'm around the desk, holding Cassie's shoulders and tilting her chin up to look at me. "Cass, I'm sorry about that first week. I should have never treated you that way. You didn't deserve it. It had nothing to do with you. I promise you I'm not punishing you for that night. If we're being honest, I just wanted to keep you away from Mack."

"Mack? So, you think that I'll just—"

"No, I guess... I don't know. But I know Mack. The guy is ruthless. When I saw him flirting with you Monday, I got pissed. So, I made sure you were too busy to be bothered by him. Actually, I made the both of you too busy. Chris had a really light week." I give her a playful grin. "I'm sorry. If you want to quit, I understand. I promise I'm done with the games. If you stick around, maybe we can start over?"

"You were jealous of Mack?" she asks, almost baffled.

"Yeah," I growl. "I promise I won't take it out on you or him anymore. I need you, Cass, and that isn't easy for me to admit. While I was trying to keep you occupied, I honestly needed the work done. I've been looking into expanding for some time. You got more accomplished in one week, than I have in years. I'm good with fixing things, but I don't know the first thing about business."

"Hard to believe, considering you have such a successful business already."

"That was just luck. Simple supply and demand. This though, it's not that simple. I have a lot more to consider and think about. There is a lot more risk this time. Please," I plead one last time.

She silently ponders what I am saying. I've never felt so nervous or exposed. I've never begged anyone for anything until this moment. Cassie takes a step back from me. It feels like my entire world is shattering. And not just because I'm losing a brilliant employee, but because I'm losing *her*.

"Cassandra Murphy," she says, extending her hand out like she did on her first day. "My friends call me Cassie though. It's a pleasure to meet you."

I smile. For the first time in a long time, I genuinely smile at this raven-haired beauty before me. My large hand engulfs her tiny one. "Robbie Moore, welcome to the team."

13

Cassie

March 20th

THE SKY IS BLUE. The sun is warm and bright. And the days just started to get longer. It's the first official day of spring. Despite my love of fall and winter, the change in season is always welcome, although I never get too attached to the warmth; it isn't uncommon for a freak snowstorm or two to pop up between now and mid-May. But for how much heat that sun is putting off, I think winter and snow are officially over for the year.

What's more wonderful is work. Ever since our talk last week, things have been going smoothly. Sure, Robbie can still be a bit of a grumpy-pants, but it isn't mean or malicious. It's just him. I still have a fairly hefty workload, but I love being busy—especially since it helps keep me distracted from the not-suitable-for-work thoughts that I have about my boss. By the time I get home, I'm so wound up I feel like I might burst. As much as I love hanging out with Jake, having the house to myself for much needed *alone time* has been a lifesaver. Not that I think Jake would care if he overheard. He'd probably offer me pointers. In a truly educational way, not a "this is a lame attempt to fool around" way. That being said, I've definitely been pushing my B.O.B.'s batteries to the limit while getting pretty exploratory on my Kindle.

For the first time in what feels like forever, I am just... happy. Despite the lingering sexual tension between Robbie and me, working with the guys has been great. This job might not be the crazy executive type stuff I thought I'd be doing when I was in college. But I love how laid back everything is. No uncomfortable heels, constricting pencil skirts, worrying about staining my blouse right before a big presentation in front of a room of investors. Best of all, no water cooler gossip.

I've never lived outside of St. Paul before, but Tral Lake was made for me. The community is small enough that no one is really a stranger. A majority of the businesses are small and locally owned. And there's hardly any crime, nothing like the Cities. The only thing that's missing is my family, well, my brothers and Moira. If they came down here, then this place really would be perfect. I know it will never happen. They all have their own lives up there. For the first time, though, I feel like I have a life here—one that is all my own. *Not built around someone else.* Or influenced by my parents' opinions of what I should do.

In celebration of the pleasant weather, I walked to the shop today. This might be my favorite thing about Tral Lake. Unless you live on the outskirts of town, pretty much everything is within walking distance. The walk from the house to work is almost perfect. In the morning, on my way in, I stop into Moore Books and Coffee and grab breakfast. On my way home, I pass by Patty Cakes, which gives me the opportunity to stop in and grab delicious treats. Probably the only negative thing since moving here is my newly developed sweet tooth—good thing I enjoy walking so much. At the rate I have been devouring Patty's dark chocolate mint fudge, I'd be as large as a hippo in no time.

The bell dings over the door as I enter the shop. Patty looks up from her tablet, giving me a big toothy grin. "Why isn't it my best customer?"

"Stop," I say playfully. "I'm sure I am not your *best* customer."

"Well, this week you have been. Pretty sure you've been here almost daily."

"I can't help it," I whine. "I'm convinced you put some secret ingredient in your stuff to make it addictive."

Patty lets out a big laugh, before shaking her head at me. "If only. Another pound of the dark chocolate mint?"

"Make it two."

Patty eyes me suspiciously. I raise my hands up in defense. "It isn't all for me. Jake has been having sympathy cravings. He and Tilly have been going nuts for anything dark chocolate."

"Sympathy cravings? Doesn't that usually happen to the dad?"

"He says it is a twin thing." I shrug my shoulders, as though that explains everything (at least it does when Jake says it).

Patty shakes her head. "I want to know that boy's secret? I have seen what he eats, yet he doesn't have an ounce of fat on him. Good thing I gave up on my figure years ago, otherwise I would still need to run almost five miles daily to keep slim."

"Patty," I scold. "You are gorgeous." It is no lie either.

Patty laughs. "I never said I wasn't beautiful. Just that if I wanted to lose these love handles, I would need to start running again, or eat like a rabbit. There is no way I can manage my shop and not sample the merchandise."

"Seriously? You look great. If I worked here, I'd need a wheelbarrow to take me to and from home."

Patty and I both start laughing as she boxes up my fudge order. I pull my phone out of my purse when my special tone for Moira goes off. "Excuse me," I say to Patty. She just waves me off, letting me know she is not insulted by my accepting the call. Normally I'd never answer a call while at the counter. I've always thought those people in line at the store talking away, not paying attention to the clerk, were rude. But Moira and I haven't been able to connect this week except via text.

"Hey, chica," I greet Moira.

"Cassie, I miss you," she cries on the line. This is the frequent routine we have now. While we didn't hang out much while Chad and I were together, we still saw each other semi frequently, even if it was just to grab lunch. After the breakup, it was almost daily—especially since I was bored and unemployed. Now that I've moved to Tral Lake, I have only seen her the one time. "St. Paddy's Day wasn't the same without you. I can't believe you ditched me and stayed down there."

"I miss you too. I'm sorry. I was feeling rundown this weekend and not up for the celebration. I wish you were down here. Spring in Tral Lake is absolutely stunning. Not to mention, they have the best fudge I have ever tasted," I say, winking at Patty as she finishes ringing me up.

"Ugh, don't even mention fudge," Moira groans. "My bloating is finally going away. I figured you would be done attempting to keep your crimson tide at bay by now."

"What?" I ask Moira as I step outside the shop.

"I just figured your PMS cravings would be over already. Usually, you are a couple of days ahead of me. Stupid Aunt Flow. No wonder you didn't want to party this weekend. Granted, that's never stopped you before."

I pause and start doing the math in my head. "Darn it," I whisper.

"What was that?" Moira asks.

"Sorry... walking home right now. It is a little breezy. Can I call you back later?"

"Sure thing. I'm on my way to K.O.'s for Wednesday night bingo anyway. Wish me luck."

"Good luck," I say quickly, before hanging up the phone.

I back track a few blocks to the local pharmacy. Rushing inside, I beeline directly towards the family planning section, buying one of each brand. I get a sad look from the cashier as I check out. If I weren't so panicked right now, I'd worry about the potential gossip from me purchasing a large volume of pregnancy tests in a small-town pharmacy. But right now, all I care about is getting home as soon as possible and proving that there is nothing to worry about. It's not like this is the first time I've been late. Just like before, I've been super stressed with the move and everything that's happened with Robbie. That's it. Nothing to worry about. *Sure, keep telling yourself that.*

14

Robbie

March 21st

I GLANCE AT THE message for probably the hundredth time today.

Cass: I need to take a personal day

That's it. No other explanation. Simply, she needs a personal day. No mention of her being sick or a family emergency. A personal day. What the hell is a personal day? This must be some sort of fancy corporate thing that she is used to. Fortunately, it is slow, so it isn't like she couldn't have the day off if she wanted it. I just hate this vague text. *Something feels off.*

Since our talk, I thought things were going pretty well between us. Sure, we might have the occasional disagreement about her upgrading my system. Not to mention, the sight of her still gives me a semi for most of the day, making me tense until I can relieve myself. Otherwise, we've been getting along. I'm no longer steering clear of her. Hell, the other day she was even laughing at some crude joke I made to Mack about nuts and bolts. I was scared shitless for a moment, thinking she might get offended, but nope, she practically keeled over laughing.

"Something the matter?" Chris asks.

"Nah, everything is fine," I say, going over some proposals Cassie prepared for me. With her help, I am finally looking for another shop location. I almost put my plans of expanding on hold again. Tilly was right, it was too much for me to manage on my own. With Cassie here, I feel like I can confidently move forward with the idea. She has all the brains while I have the brawn. The match is almost perfect. *There's that damn word again.*

"Is everything okay with Cassie?" Chris asks, looking around to make sure we are alone. "You didn't do anything, did you? I thought you were both getting along."

"Are you fucking serious, Chris?"

He holds his hands up in defense. "Look, in the beginning, you were a pretty big jerk to her. After that night at Harper's, with the daggers you were shooting at each other, I thought she would walk out or murder you any moment. Things have seemed better recently, but it just feels odd that she wouldn't show up suddenly. I thought maybe you two had it out about something."

I rub my hand over my face, letting out an exhausted sigh. "No, we didn't have a fight about anything. I thought things were going well. But this morning she sent me some cryptic text telling me she needs a personal day. What the hell is a personal day?"

Chris shrugs his shoulders. "Not sure. I heard my niece mention something about a mental health day before. Maybe it is something like that?"

"I guess," I reply.

"Well, why don't you go check in on her," he suggests.

"What? Why?"

"Obviously, you are concerned. If something is wrong, her family is nowhere nearby. I'm sure she could use a friend."

"Yeah, I guess I could go make sure everything is okay. That's what a good boss would do, right?"

"There you go, big guy. Don't worry, we will close up everything here."

I give Chris my best evil death stare, which he shrugs off—not surprising, given the man has known me since I was a kid. Some might think I'm not the easiest to get along with, but they never had to work with my pops. Chris had the pleasure of working for him since he was a teen.

Quickly, I grab my leather jacket and keys. Since it is nice out, I decide to pull the Harley out of storage and clear the dust from her pipes. I'm dying to get the Mustang out on the open pavement, but she needs a bit more TLC before that happens.

I'm relieved when I get to the house and see her Forester parked in the driveway. For a moment, I was worried she might not even be here. That maybe she had to go up to the Cities or something.

In the past, I would typically just walk into my childhood home. But having her live here now, it doesn't feel like my home anymore. So instead, I ring the doorbell, not wanting to barge in. I end up tapping the button a couple of times. I almost give up, thinking she might be out for a walk, when the door finally opens. The sight of Cassie has me on high alert.

She is still wearing her pajamas at four in the afternoon. Her hair is a mess, her face red and puffy, and her cheeks are stained with tears. Right now, she reminds me of Tilly and how fragile and broken she looked after we lost our parents. *Fuck!* "Cass, what's wrong? Is everything okay?" I ask, pulling her into a big hug. She doesn't respond; she just sniffles into my jacket.

I gently scoop her up into my arms and carry her back into the house. Carefully, I set her down on the couch and retrieve a box of tissues before taking a seat next to her. "What happened? Did something happen to your parents?

84

Your brothers?" The unpleasant memories of how devastated we were at the news of the accident flashes through my mind. Honestly, most of it is a blur. While Tilly found solace in Jax and the shop, Jake in women and starting the video store, Scott in expanding to a large kitchen—a dream he and our mother both shared—my grieving wasn't as constructive or healthy. It mostly consisted of copious amounts of whiskey and burying myself into whatever engine I could get my hands on. It's why it has taken me nearly six months to open the storage units my dad left behind for me.

That night with Cassie, it was the first time I actually felt alive since they passed.

Cassie blows her nose before responding, "No, they are fine."

I breathe a sigh of relief, thankful that she isn't going through what we just had to go through.

"What are you doing here?"

"I was concerned; your message was a little vague. I wanted to make sure everything was okay."

"Everything is fine," Cassie replies dismissively.

"It doesn't look like everything is fine." I point out the obvious. "Remember, Cass, we're starting over. Forget for a moment that I'm your dickhead boss. Right now, I am just Robbie Moore, your slightly less dickheaded friend or at least acquaintance. You can talk to me. I've been known to give sage advice every now and again."

Cassie gives me a sad smile before nodding. "I guess I am going to have to tell you... eventually. I had to go to the doctor this morning."

I feel the blood drain from my face; she is sick. It must be bad if she is in tears. "Are you okay?"

"Yes." She takes a deep breath. "I mean... I'm not sick."

"Well, that is good, right?"

She takes another deep breath before huffing out, "I'm pregnant, Robbie."

"Pregnant?" I ask in reply, letting the words process in my mind. *Pregnant.*

"Yeah, I just found out."

"Does that mean you are moving back home?"

Her brows furrow at my question. "Do you want me to?"

"No, not exactly. I just assumed you'd want to move back and be closer to the father. But—"

"Well, if I moved back home, I would be moving *away* from the father."

I feel dumbstruck as realization hits me. "Oh."

"Yeah, *oh.*" Cassie sinks back into the couch, pulling her knees to her chest.

"Are you positive?"

She lets out a sad chuckle. "Believe me, after the ton of tests I took at home and the one at the doctor's office, I'm *positive.*"

I lean back against the couch next to Cassie. "How?"

"Really?" She gives me a pointed stare.

"I know *how.* I just mean, how? I am sure I wore a condom, and you're on birth control, right?" Cassie shakes her head. I don't know if that no was to birth control, or the condom, or all of the above. I've replayed that night several times over since, but I honestly can't remember wrapping up. It isn't like me to forget something like that. I am always responsible and careful. *Yeah, unless you have six shots of tequila and a week's worth of built-up sexual tension, apparently.*

"I'm sorry, Robbie. I was going to come talk to you later. I just needed some time to process."

"Stop apologizing, Cassie. It's not your fault."

"I know. It's just..." As we sit in silence, I try to think of what to say or do. *I'm going to be a dad.* There was a time when I'd thought that by now, I would have three or four kids, just like my parents. But after everything that happened with Bianca, well, let's just say plans changed.

"Well, what now?" Cassie asks, probably just as dumbfounded by the situation as I am.

I close my eyes and try to imagine my dad and Pops. What should the responsible man they raised do? That's when it hits me. "Simple, we get married."

15

Cassie

March 21st

Is he serious? Get married? Just like that. "You are joking, right?"

Robbie swallows hard. "No, you're pregnant. Getting married is the right thing to do." He sounds almost robotic, as though he's on autopilot.

"I hardly know you, Robbie." I rub a hand over my face in frustration.

He just shrugs his shoulders as though that's a minor detail. "I mean, we will get to know each other over time. I'll find us a place to live. My apartment is not big enough for all of us. Besides, kids should have a backyard. I can always talk to Jake about maybe us moving in here, taking over. See if he wants to live in—"

"Stop," I yell. "Just stop it already. Do you hear yourself?"

"Fine, I'll find us a new place," he replies as though that is the bigger issue.

"No, Robbie, I am not going to marry or move in with you." I get up and storm out of the living room and upstairs to my bedroom, slamming my door. Robbie is not far behind me as he comes barreling in.

"What then? Are you going back home?"

"No." I crinkle my nose at the thought. If Ma and Da were disappointed over Chad, I can't imagine how much of a letdown this will be for them. "I wasn't planning on going back home. But I am not marrying someone who's practically a stranger, because he feels obligated to *do the right thing*." I sneer at him, "This isn't the 1800s; a woman having a child out of wedlock isn't that big of a deal."

"*Stranger* seems like a bit of an exaggeration," he mumbles. "I'm not saying this is ideal. But let's be practical here. I'm single, you are single, and we are about to have a child together. Why wouldn't we get married?"

"Do you love me?"

"W-well—"

"Exactly, Robbie," I sigh, feeling emotionally drained. "People should get married because they love each other. Because they want to spend the rest of their lives together. Not because of one drunken night. And not because it's convenient." He rubs his chin, likely attempting to process the situation, just as I've been trying to do. "Look, can we just stop for a minute? Press pause on the situation? This is a lot. We don't need to decide anything right now. Actually, it is probably best we don't make any rash decisions right now."

Robbie nods his head in agreement. "Okay. Why don't you take tomorrow off?"

"Are you trying to get rid of me? Do you want me to quit?" I ask, insulted.

$\cdot \heartsuit \cdot \heartsuit \cdot \heartsuit \cdot \heartsuit \cdot \heartsuit \cdot$

"How could you?" I wipe the tears from my eyes. Since the breakup, I was careful to hide the pain while at work. Be the model of professionalism. But everyone has their breaking point.

"Don't you think you are being a tad melodramatic, Cassandra?" Chad says, disinterested. He doesn't even bother to look up from his computer.

"Melodramatic!" I shriek. "I haven't worked my butt off for the past six months doing countless hours of research and perfecting this proposal, just to have it handed off to Erik. He has only been with the firm for two months. He's never laid a finger on this project. This is my hard work, and I'll be damned if he's going to take credit for it."

"Cassandra, similar to the complaints we've received from other staff members recently, this display is completely unprofessional. Therefore, we are asking Erik to take the lead. There is concern that you are allowing personal problems to affect your work. This merger is too important to the firm to risk it on someone who, frankly, is emotionally unstable."

"Are you fucking kidding me?" Internally, I wince at the use of the profanity. Swearing isn't like me. But I'm just so angry right now.

"Cassandra," Chad scolds. "One more outburst and you will leave me no choice but to report you to HR. I have been lenient with you so far. But I can't keep making excuses for you."

I stand their stunned. Speechless.

He sighs, putting on a mask of concern. "Look, why don't you take the rest of the day and tomorrow off. A long weekend might do you some good. On Monday, we can discuss this after you've cooled off."

I nod, dropping my head in defeat. Chad accepts a call and shoos me quickly out of his office. I hurry to my desk to find some solace within my cubicle walls.

"Did you see her at the meeting today?" Veronica (who sits across from me) whispers, likely assuming I can't hear her. Or maybe she knows I can, and she doesn't care.

"I know." I presume she's talking to Amber; they seem to be the primary office gossips. "What did she expect? It's what happens when you sleep your way to the top. Eventually upper management realizes you just aren't qualified. Sucking dick will only get you so far."

"Oh. My. God. Did you hear about her begging him to take her back?"

"Seriously?"

"Swear to god. Apparently, she came into the office when he was working late, wearing nothing but a trench coat and heels."

"No way!" Amber says.

"Mike was on security that night. He saw her in his office begging on her hands and knees."

"What a slut! Isn't he with Katie?"

"Yeah, she is so sweet. What a bitch."

"Like Chad would ever cheat, especially on a sweetheart like Katie."

·♥·♥·♥·♥·♥·

"What? No!" Robbie says, squeezing his eyes shut. I notice the vein twitching in his thick neck. "I just thought you might want a few days off to process everything."

"Oh."

"You don't have to, just, dammit." He huffs, rubbing his hand over his face. "Look, you can come in if you want. But the offer's out there if you need the time off."

"Okay," I reply. We stand there silently looking at each other.

"Do you need anything? Crackers, soup, tea, or something?"

I smile at his kind gesture and shake my head. "No, I just need some time to let all of this settle in."

"I understand." He ponders for a moment. "Can I ask you something?"

I nod. Though I'm ready to curl up and hide from the world, Robbie being uncharacteristically affable makes it hard to say no.

"I know you said you wanted time to think. I respect that, but I have to ask..." He swallows hard, clearly uncomfortable. "Are you going to keep the baby?"

I hadn't really asked myself that yet. I'm not sure what has motivated his question, but when I search deep down the answer is clear as day. "Yes, I'm keeping the baby."

"Okay." He lets out a deep breath and seems relieved. Taking a step towards me, he reaches out. At first, I think he's about to hug or kiss me. Instead, he tucks a loose strand of my hair behind my ear. "If you need anything, call me. Day or night, all right?"

"Sure," I whisper. Robbie gives me one last longing look before walking back downstairs. As I hear the front door open and close, I breathe out a sigh of relief. When the first plus sign popped up on the plastic stick, the thought of having to tell Robbie terrified me. I momentarily considered not even telling him and returning home. But as uncomfortable as it was, I know it was the right thing to do. He has a right to know. If he made the choice to have nothing to do with us, that would be his decision, not mine.

I'd spent hours imagining how he would yell at me, blame me, accuse me of getting pregnant intentionally, and several other horrific scenarios. *He's not Chad.* I never once imagined his response would be to get married. If the situation weren't dire, I'd probably laugh.

Flopping back onto my bed, I stare at the ceiling. How is it that I (the self-proclaimed relationship girl) have my first drunken one-night stand and end up pregnant? What kind of karmic joke is this? Even though I had taken eight tests at home between last night and this morning, I had hoped that the doctor would tell me they were all wrong. Maybe I had done something to give myself multiple false positives—user error? But when she came back with the bloodwork, I almost fainted.

The doctor was exceedingly kind during my meltdown in her office. I assume I am not the first to find out she's *unexpectedly* expecting. After I regained my composure, we went through the "dos and don'ts" of pregnancy. When the topic of alcohol came up, I almost had another panic attack. I had mentioned to her that the night we got pregnant there was a lot of alcohol involved, and since then I've had a few beers. Fortunately, she assured me it shouldn't be an issue this early on.

The ding of my phone alerts me to a new message. I grab my cell off the nightstand and see there is a text from my brother.

> **Killian: Hey, sis, just checking in and making sure everything is good. Haven't heard from you in a while.**
> **Me: I'm fine, Kill. Thanks for checking in.**
> **Killian: Are you sure? We missed you this weekend. Ma and Da were pretty disappointed you skipped the parade.**

I sigh, for as long as I can remember, I have always marched with my family in the St. Paddy's Day parade. This was my first year missing it.

> **Me: I know, sorry. Had a lot going on this weekend.**
> **Killian: Okay, well, we miss you. If you get a chance, I know Ma would love it if you came home for a visit. I think she feels guilty, like she forced you to move away.**

Me: I will visit soon. Ma did nothing wrong.
Tell her to stop worrying. I moved away for
a fresh start. That's it.
Killian: How about you call and tell her that?

I toss my phone down on the bed, ignoring another message that comes in. More than likely, it's Killian still guilt-tripping me about being here.

Absentmindedly, I rub my hand over my stomach. "How am I going to tell them about you?" My parents are going to be so disappointed in me. Not only did I get involved with my new boss, but this time, I ended up pregnant. I should probably tell them and get it over with. They are going to be upset regardless, but maybe if I do it in person, it will lessen the blow? Robbie did just give me a long weekend. The longer I keep it from them, the more it will hurt them when I finally do. Especially Da—this will probably crush him.

With my mind made up, I pack a bag. Jake is on call at the station, so I shoot him a quick text letting him know that I am going home for the weekend. *Time to get this over with.* Who knows, maybe they will take it better than I'm expecting? Robbie didn't freak out like I planned. *You don't honestly believe that, do you?*

16

Robbie

March 23rd

Sitting at the bar, I stare down at my cell lying on the tabletop. I've been waiting, expecting Cassie to contact me. I wasn't all that surprised when I didn't hear from her yesterday. Part of me had hoped she would show up to work, even though I gave her the day off. Then I assumed she would have reached out to me last night, or at least this morning. We have a lot to discuss and I'm going fucking batshit crazy waiting for her. Here it is, ten at night, and still nothing.

Countless times I've picked up my phone, intending to message her. But I was at a loss for words. What the hell do you say to a girl you hardly know who you got pregnant after one night of hot, wild sex? The girl who turned down your marriage proposal? My dad and pops prepared me for a lot in my life, but never this.

"When did you start randomly coming to the bar on Saturday night?" Scott asks, sitting on the stool next to me.

"When did you?" I counter, evading his question.

"I don't know." He shrugs. "I guess since Jax moved back. Seeing how happy he and Tilly are, I was thinking it might be time for me to get out there."

"Yeah, Tilly has really messed everything up." I grunt, taking a swig of my beer.

"What the fuck, Robbie? I know Jax has a reputation for being flighty and you have your doubts. But seriously? Tilly hasn't messed shit up. This pregnancy is hard enough on her. The last fucking thing she needs to hear is you saying shit like that." Scott scolds me as he pushes my shoulder.

I grind my teeth. Logically, I know it isn't Tilly's fault. But right now, it feels that way. "If Tilly never got pregnant, Cassie would never have come here."

"What the hell, dude?" He pushes me off the bar stool and I stumble.

"Scott," Letty yells, "stop starting fights with your brothers in my bar. Take it outside." She tosses a dirty towel at Scott's head.

His cheeks burn red, muttering something to himself about how if only his brothers would pull their heads out of their asses, before he tosses the rag back to Letty. "Sorry, Letty. It won't happen again."

Scott and I both take our seats back at the bar. We sit in silence for several long moments before he speaks up again. "What happened with Cassie? I thought things were working out at the shop."

I sigh, rubbing my hand over my face. "I slept with her," I admit. There is no point in keeping it a secret. Soon enough everyone will know anyway.

"Dammit," Scott growls. I turn to study his expression. Was he jealous? I know Cassie stops in the café a lot. I feel my blood boil at the thought of Scott flirting with her every morning. Then I notice the smirk. "I owe Jake a hundred bucks."

"Seriously?" I shake my head.

Scott shrugs his shoulder before smirking at me. "Yeah, Jake called it when she moved here. Honestly, I didn't see her giving your grumpy-ass the time of day."

"Well, did you guys make a wager on me knocking her up?" I deadpan. Scott spits out the beer he was just sipping.

"*What?*" He asks loudly, gaining Letty's attention again. She gives us a pointed stare, gesturing with two fingers at her eyes and then back at us—letting us know she will not put up with our bullshit tonight. Scott coughs, trying to regain his composure, and waves her off. "This is just a hypothetical question, right? Are you and Jake fucking with me again? Like the time you convinced me that little shit totaled my truck?"

I laugh. It was probably one of the best pranks we ever pulled on Scott. I got a call for a tow. The truck was wrecked but happened to be the exact same make and model as Scott's; even the color was spot on. Anyway, I couldn't pass up the opportunity to fuck with him. He just bought that truck a few months prior and was proud as hell. Even dad jumped in on the action, coming up with some story about how he needed lumber and told Jake to use the pickup. I'm not sure if Scott was more pissed thinking Jake wrecked his truck, or realizing that we pulled one over on him.

"Nope," I say popping the P.

Scott takes a sip of his beer, successfully drinking it this time. "Shit, what are you going to do?"

"I'm not sure. She isn't exactly talking to me right now." I stare down at my own glass, finding little comfort in it.

"Why? Don't tell me you were an ass over this?" That urge to punch Scott comes back to the surface at his implication.

"You actually think I am that much of a dick?" I counter, crossing my arms over my chest.

"No." He contemplates for a moment. "I mean, not really. It's just... sometimes you are not the easiest person to talk to. You're not exactly known for being very empathetic."

I shrug off his comment, dropping my guard. Scott isn't wrong. I figure life is too short to sugarcoat things.

"Well, if she isn't talking to you, I assume something must have happened when you guys talked."

"I don't know. When she told me, at first, I didn't think she meant it was mine. I assumed that maybe it was her ex's or something. She said they had been engaged—not that long ago either. I assumed she would want to move near the father, maybe see if she could make things work. When she clarified that the baby was mine, I offered to marry her."

"You what?" Scott hollers at me. Realizing his mistake, he immediately turns to Letty, who is storming over to us. "We aren't fighting, I promise."

"You better not be," she admonishes, but has a small smile. Ever since she has taken over day-to-day operations, she has loved being *large and in charge* around here. Not that she hasn't practically been running the place for the past few years. But now that it is official, she has a new sense of confidence about her. Letty takes notice of our nearly empty beers, and hands us a couple more before moving on to other customers.

"No wonder she isn't talking to you," Scott murmurs, finishing the last of his drink. "I thought you were supposed to be the smart one. The practical, responsible, eldest brother. Right now, you are making Jake look like a fucking scholar."

I give him a pointed stare, reminding him I can easily kick his ass. Scott quickly regains some of his composure. "Sorry, Robbie, but you are being an idiot. You said you guys had a one-night stand, right? So, you haven't been dating or anything?"

"No." I shake my head. "We hooked up the night before Jax and Tilly moved. The next morning, she panicked. Told me it was a mistake and couldn't happen again. Work's been going well, though. It was tough at first, but we've found a rhythm."

"Bastard," Scott mumbles under his breath. I give him a questioning look. "Jake—he swindled me. He made the bet with me the day of the move. When you mentioned she crashed at your place, I thought nothing of it—given you are

98

well..." Scott gestures to me. "...*you*. Jake must have seen her come home, and mixed with the stories of the night before, the asshole already knew for a fact that you two slept together."

"Probably," I say, not really caring. Jake is honestly the last person you ever want to bet against; you'll lose every time. "She rushed out of my place half dressed in one of my sweatshirts."

"That sneaky bastard."

"Hey, at least *you* didn't gamble something as stupid as the name of your shop."

Scott bends over laughing, remembering that terrible mistake. "Yeah, a hundred bucks is a way less bitter pill to swallow. Anyway, she seems like a nice girl—probably too nice for the likes of you. She stops into the shop almost every morning, even picking up snacks for you sorry assholes. Jake's told me how much fun they have hanging out, watching movies and what not." Scott pauses a moment. "Robbie, she doesn't even know you. You guys hooked up once and then work together. No girl with common sense is going to just marry some guy she hardly knows, because he knocked her up."

"Well, what should I do then?" I ask, exhausted. I always know what to do. I always have a plan, a course of action. For the first time, I'm utterly at a loss with no compass to point me in the right direction. The last time I was lost, I had my pops to help set me straight. I love my brothers and sisters, but they've always looked to me for guidance, especially now with our parents gone. *Who am I supposed to look to when I'm lost?*

"I think the better question is: what do you want?"

I pause and think for a moment, Scott's question catching me off guard. "I honestly don't know. I mean, I know I want to help take care of the kid and be in its life." I can't imagine having a child and not being a part of its life.

"Is she planning on moving back home?"

"No, it seems like she wants to stick around. But who knows? Everything is fresh right now. I'm terrified that after she has had a few days to think it over, she's going to hightail it out of town."

Scott lets out a sigh. "I don't think Cassie's the sort of girl who just skips out. If she moves back to the Cities, she seems like the type of person who would make a calculated decision and would discuss it with you."

Probably, but then again, I never saw Bianca pulling half the shit she did. I shake my head, reminding myself to stop assuming what Cassie will do based on Bianca's actions. *She's not her.*

"What about Cassie? Baby aside, how do you feel about her?" Scott stares intently, attempting to get a read on me. His green eyes catch me off guard for a moment. Maybe it's because I've had one too many beers, but briefly, his expression looks just like mom's. Squeezing my eyes shut, I rub the bridge of my nose, willing the images of my mother out of my mind. When I think of my parents, the guilt seeps in. I lived in the same town as them. Literally just blocks away from their shop. Only a couple miles from their home. And I never took the time to see them as much as I could have. Sure, I was around whenever they needed me. Mom would frequently stop in, bringing me lunch or coffee. But I never just stopped by and visited for the hell of it. I missed out on so much. Tilly graduating from college, trips with Scott, going to the cabin with dad, weekly dinners, *fuck*, even just going out one night with Jake and being his wingman, or whatever other nonsense he spews.

I let out a deep breath—centering myself. I hate talking about feelings, especially my own. "I'm not sure. That night was... *intense*. It was the first time since... well, you know... I felt like I was actually living." I'm a little surprised at my admission. "It pissed me off when she said it couldn't happen again. I knew she was right though—it's a bad idea. Now with this baby though..."

"Your lives are entwined no matter what." Scott smiles at me when I nod in agreement. "I think you should ask her out, try to get to know her outside of work. No matter what, that simple boss and employee relationship is blown to shreds anyway."

Feeling like a total dumbass, I smile at Scott. He's right. There's really no need to ignore this intense connection anymore, no reason that we couldn't do it again. "Thanks, man," I tell him as I fish a couple of twenties out of my wallet and toss them on the bar top. Scott wishes me luck.

Grabbing my jacket, I rush out of the bar and practically run to the house. I am out of breath as I bang on the front door. After waiting for a few moments, and not getting any reply, I'm about to just use my key when the front door opens. All my excitement fades when my brother is standing there in his briefs.

"What's up?" Jake asks, rubbing the sleep from his eyes before they suddenly grow wide. "Is Tilly okay? Did something happen with the babies?"

"No." I shake my head. "I want to talk with Cassie."

"This late at night?" He frowns, rubbing his temple in confusion. "She's not here; she went home."

I clench my fists as I close my eyes, attempting to stop the room from spinning. *How could she just pick up and leave like that?*

I feel Jake place a hand on my shoulder. "What's wrong? Did something happen? Are you okay?" I open my eyes to see his brows drawn together as he looks me over. "Why don't you come inside? It's fucking cold out here."

I follow him past the door and plop myself down on the couch. Running my hands through my hair, I try to think of what to do. I could call Tilly, get her parents' address. No, Tilly's probably asleep. Letty? She might know.

Jake crosses his arms and studies me. "I'm not sure what's going on. But she should be back tomorrow."

"Tomorrow?"

"Yeah, she just went home to see her parents. I texted her a couple of hours ago to see how her visit was going." He frowns. "She didn't sound thrilled. Apparently, there is some family drama. Anyway, Cassie said she'd be home in the morning."

I breathe a sigh of relief. She didn't take off; she went home. Probably to tell her family. *Oh shit.* I shudder at the thought. "I'm going to crash here tonight," I tell Jake.

"Sure thing. I'm going to go back to bed. Unless you need something?"

"No, I'm good. I just need some sleep."

Jake nods before heading upstairs. Kicking back, I make myself comfortable on the couch while coming up with a plan for how to handle this situation with Cassie. How to break down the walls we both seem to have, so that we can hopefully get through this together. *Together,* I like the sound of that. It's the last thought I have before the sleep finally consumes me.

17

Cassie

March 24th

GENTLY OPENING AND CLOSING the front door, I tiptoe inside. I'd hate to disturb Jake this early in the morning if he is sleeping. Not that I think he would mind. Honestly, all I want to do is go upstairs and crawl under my covers and cry. Jake being the friend that he is, if he saw me, would want to discuss what's going on. I love that he cares, but right now, I just need some time to process.

Stepping into the living room, I stop dead in my tracks. Robbie is sprawled across the couch that he is much too large to sleep on. One leg is perched on the headrest, while the other hangs off onto the floor. He has an arm draped over his eyes with the other resting on his stomach. I stifle the chuckle threatening to slip from my lips as I listen to his soft snore. As funny as this is, *why is he here?* Shaking my head, I stop myself from jumping into the rabbit hole I was about to journey down. His being here probably has nothing to do with me. Even so, if I didn't think I could handle Jake, there is no way I can deal with Robbie right now.

Treading gently, I make it to my room, disturbing no one. I waste no time entering my en suite. After Tilly moved out, she insisted on me taking over her room. It was bigger and had its own bathroom. She assured me that from years of experience, I'd appreciate not having to share with Jake.

I finished my relaxing hot shower, before using a towel to dry off. As I'm about to put on my sleep shirt, I can't help but turn and stare at my profile. Running my hand over my belly, I look for any sign of pregnancy. But there is none. I simply look a little bloated—which isn't the flattering pregnancy glow everyone hopes for. The doctor said I was just about five weeks pregnant, which threw me off at first (since the timeline with Robbie and me didn't add up). After my mini meltdown, wondering who could have gotten me pregnant five weeks ago (and if it was some form of Immaculate Conception—because I hadn't been with anyone for months), she politely explained how they calculate gestational age based on the start of my last period. I still don't completely understand it, but she assured me that everything was fine.

At this stage, most women wouldn't even know unless they noticed their missed cycle (unlike me). While the whole situation is complicated, when I think about this baby, it feels like butterflies take up flight in my chest. Even if the events surrounding this pregnancy are less than ideal, I will not let that ruin this for me. I'd always assumed I'd fall in love, get married, and then have babies. Perhaps this is the best thing for me. I've always wanted to be a mother. Romantic love has never worked out right, and I am still recovering from the failure of my almost marriage. This baby though, I can love her (yes, *her*—I'm convinced she's a girl) unconditionally without fear of heartbreak. She will never cheat or deceive me—she'll never hurt me.

Tossing on my pajamas, I head back into the room and almost have a heart attack. "Jesus, what are you doing in here?" I hiss at Robbie, who has made himself comfortable on my bed.

"Sorry." Robbie holds his hands up in defense. "I didn't mean to scare you. I just wanted to talk."

"I really don't feel like talking." I sigh. "I need to be alone right now."

He frowns. "I'm guessing you told your family?" I just nod in agreement. "Didn't go well, did it?" Robbie assumes correctly. I wince at the notion. "Didn't go well" seems like a gross understatement.

·♥ · ♥ · ♥ · ♥ · ♥ ·

Last night

Moira was so excited when I told her I was coming home; she took Friday off and we spent the entire day together. I was grateful for the distraction, because as much as I wanted to be home and see my family, it's also the last place I want to be right now. I know I have to tell them. They will find out eventually and keeping it a secret will make it that much worse.

While eating lunch at our favorite deli, I told Moira everything. And I knew, being my best friend, she would help me come up with a way to tell everyone. As expected, at first, she panicked, frantically asking me how it happened. I felt like an idiot when I admitted I stopped taking birth control when Chad and I were engaged. We wanted to start a family right away. After the breakup, it never crossed my mind to start up again, especially since I had planned on taking a brief hiatus in pursuing romantic endeavors.

Moira felt terrible for not realizing I slept with Robbie. She thought something seemed off that morning. But she was too enthralled with Jake to focus. I know she means well, but I'm not sure the situation would be any different from how it is now.

After her freak out, we devised a plan for how to best break the news to my family. We agreed it would probably be best to tell them all together. To just get it done and over with in one shot. I'm so thankful she agreed to join us for dinner. I'm not sure if I'd be able to go through this without her here supporting me. At least, at the end of the night, I know one person in the room won't hate me.

As planned, after mentioning to Ma that we should have a nice family dinner, she successfully made certain that Cian and Killian would both be here tonight. Except now, as I look at their faces all gathered at the dinner table, I'm not sure I have the heart to see their disappointed expressions.

"Cassandra, I completely forgot. At the parade, Leroy mentioned he had an opening at his firm. I am sure he could get you a job there no problem," my ma mentions, bringing up the darn parade for the hundredth time since I have been home. I lied and told them I had to work Saturday, so coming home was just not practical. But apparently, having work ethic is an issue when you move away.

"I have a job, Ma," I reply with a mouthful of stew.

"I know, but wouldn't it be nice to come home? You will make so much more money. Not to mention, the benefits and retirement. I think you should at least apply," she presses.

"Cassie, you should come down to the pub tonight after dinner. Tommy is looking for a rematch. He is claiming that you forfeit your title since you didn't show up last weekend." Great, now even Killian is jumping on the guilt train.

"Not this time. I need to head out early tomorrow. I'd prefer to not have to drive with a hangover." I provide a partial truth. Moira nudges me under the table as a reminder to get this over with. But already feeling like they are ganging up on me, I am not sure I can. Maybe I should just call and tell them? Write a letter? Send them *a picture of the baby once she's born? Yeah, that sounds like the safest bet.*

"Come on, sis." Killian gently punches my arm. "Murphys don't quit. You can't give up your title like that. You need to defend it like the champ you are."

Moira kicks me this time, suggesting that I have stalled long enough. I sniffle and attempt to hold back my tears, but a few escape. "I can't, Kill. I'm sorry."

Killian's expression turns to one of concern, his playful tone now soft. "Is everything okay?"

"Cad atá mícheart, mo stoirín," Da asks.

As everyone stares at me, my heart feels as though it might burst from my chest. Closing my eyes, I take a deep breath. "Everything is fine. It's just..." I hesitate with a big gulp, swallowing down my fear. "I'm pregnant."

Everyone (except Moira) gasps around the table.

"I'm going to fucking murder Chad," Cian hollers, standing from the table and flinging his chair behind him.

"Cian, please, no," I plead, rushing after him and placing my hand on his arm.

"No, Cassie, you should have let us kick his ass when he cheated on you. I heard about the wedding with that skank. Now this?" Cian gestures to my stomach. "No, he's had one too many chances. The fucker needs to pay."

"Cassandra, is he really getting married to that woman? Is this why you moved away? Why didn't you tell us?" Ma asks, her lips pursed.

"I'm sorry, Ma. Yeah, the wedding is what sparked the move. But also, I needed a fresh start. A chance to get out on my own. You do not know how difficult it has been."

"Running from your problems doesn't fix them. Now..." She gestures to my stomach. "...there is no hiding from them either. You should come home. We will help you deal with this. I am sure Tilly will understand the change in your circumstances." I wince at her tone.

"It's not Chad's," I whisper so softly I think it's possible that no one has heard me. But glancing up and seeing Ma's frown, I realize I'm not that lucky.

"What was that?" she asks, her voice raised.

"The baby isn't Chad's," I say louder.

"What the fuck, Cassie! Whose is it?" Cian chimes in, though I can tell the question pains him. No doubt, he feels as though he somehow failed me. As though he didn't protect me like a big brother should.

"It doesn't matter, Cian. Can we please just drop it?"

"Like hell it doesn't matter, Cassie." Cian's expression softens. "I didn't even know you were dating anyone." Code for he hasn't had an opportunity to gain intel on whoever I'm seeing. "Now you come home after a month and tell us you are pregnant. Please, whose is it?"

"Robbie's," I mumble, looking down at my feet, ashamed at my admission.

"Robbie?" He repeats the name as more of a question, trying to place it. "As in Tilly's brother?"

I confirm with a nod.

Ma yells obscenities in Greek. "Cassandra." Her tone is laced with disappointment. "We raised you better than this."

I turn to look at Da, who's been silent during this entire exchange. "Da," I whisper. He is so ashamed he won't even look at me. The pained expression he holds reveals that whatever image he had of me as his precious little girl is now shattered—just like my heart. I think to myself, he is just one more man I thought would love me for better or worse, one more man who's just let me down.

I tune out the commotion of Ma and my brothers yelling. I didn't expect everyone to jump for joy. But then again, I wasn't prepared for... this. I look to Moira, who has been a silent observer. Growing up with my family, she knows better than to jump in. And that only adds fuel to the fire. When she notices me looking at her, she mouths, "I'm sorry."

I give her a sad smile. She has nothing to be sorry for. I knew my parents, because of their conservative and religious upbringings, would not take the news well. My overprotective brothers have always been a bit hot-headed. I'm sure if they had their way, I'd probably be fitted with a chastity belt. In their eyes, no man will ever be good enough for their baby sister.

Realizing there is nothing I can do to deescalate the situation (and not wanting to sit and listen to my brothers plot Robbie's murder), I wave everyone off and tell them I'm going to bed. Besides Moira, I doubt anyone heard me over their shouting. While they talk big, I know they wouldn't actually kill Robbie. Well, at least I hope not.

Once I'm in my old bedroom, I pull out my phone and see a message from Jake.

> Jake: How are things going in the Saint of the Paul?
>
> Me: I'll be home in the morning. Want me to grab breakfast on my way?
>
> Jake: Nah, thanks though. I am heading to the station early. Having fun seeing your family?
>
> Me: No, not exactly
>
> Jake: What's wrong? Are they still guilt-tripping you about missing St. Paddy's Day?
>
> Me: Sort of, we can talk about it later. I just want to get some rest before driving home.
>
> Jake: All right, I'll be at the station for the next few days. But if you need me, let me know. Or if you get bored, stop by. I'm sure the guys would love a visit ::wink emoji::.

I smile before tossing my phone onto the bed. Closing my eyes, I place my hand on my still flat stomach; I take deep, steady breaths. Whatever... it is over now. I'm sure they will come around, eventually. If not, at least I have you.

♥ · ♥ · ♥ · ♥ · ♥

Present

"Do you want to talk about it?" Robbie asks.

"No, not really. I'm exhausted and would just like to get some rest."

"Okay." Rising from my bed, he walks over to me. He pushes a loose strand of wet hair behind my ear. Studying my face, he pauses before stating, "When you're ready, we need to talk."

"I know," I say, barely above a whisper. Feeling his warmth while I am so emotionally drained is almost too much to handle. I hate the fact that all I want is for him to wrap his enormous arms around me and hold me close. I bite my bottom lip, which doesn't go unnoticed by his intense gaze. My self-control is dwindling, and I consider asking him to lie down with me. The words sit at the tip of my tongue, but I swallow them when Robbie presses a soft kiss to the top of my head.

"Get some rest," he says, his tone filled with genuine concern. As he opens the door, this distant voice in my mind yells at the top of her lungs to call him back. But I don't. She's officially silenced with the soft click that confirms he has walked out of the room.

18

Robbie

March 24th

"WHAT ARE YOU STILL doing here?" Jake asks, his hair dripping wet and towel hanging loosely around his hips. I swallow the jealous bile that rises in my gut. I fucking hate how, since the second I laid eyes on Cassie, I view every other guy as a threat. It's like this primal urge to mark her as mine in order to ward off other predators. And Jake is the biggest of them all. Okay, he is not a predator. Rationally, I know that my brother isn't the kind of guy to eye someone else's claim. But when it comes to Cass, the last thing I seem to be anymore is rational. Because seeing my charming brother prancing around half naked in the house he shares with my... well, I'm not really sure what to call Cassie other than "mine". That's a conversation we need to have. Regardless, though, seeing him like this and thinking about them living alone together has me two seconds away from going upstairs, throwing Cassie over my shoulder, and telling her she is moving in—end of discussion.

"I need to speak with Cassie," I grumble, before taking a sip of my coffee.

"Is there some sort of garage emergency," Jake teases as he rummages through the fridge. "National blinker fluid shortage?"

"No." I pause and consider telling Jake. He will find out eventually—especially since Scott knows. *Fuck*, now that I think about it, telling Scott was a shit idea. He sucks at keeping a secret. I'm sure he's already told Jax, who no doubt will tell Tilly. Then Tilly will tell Jake as soon as she hears. "We've got some unfinished business."

"I already know you guys hooked up. You don't have to put on some sort of show for me."

"I'm not putting on a show. It's personal."

"Personal, huh?" Jake muses, rubbing the short stubble he has on his chin. His grin turns into a frown as he crosses his arms over his chest. "What did you do to Cassie?"

His obvious defensiveness over Cassie brings my guard up. I quickly mimic his pose. "Nothing, asshole. Why does everyone think I did something to her?"

Jake shrugs his shoulders. "I don't know. It's just... Cassie suddenly takes a few days off and goes home. You show up drunk late at night, crying about needing to talk to her. Now, here you are in the morning, hanging around like a sad puppy. If I had to bet, I'd say you fucked up and are here to beg on your hands and knees for forgiveness."

Sometimes I hate how perceptive he is—the kid should have been a detective, not a firefighter.

"Yeah, she and I found ourselves in a situation the other day. We left some things unresolved."

"Good luck." Jake laughs and settles on the stool across from me.

"What do you mean by that?"

"Cassie happens to be my best friend, and as her best friend, I have a certain sway when it comes to her decision to forgive you. Dear big brother, I know you all too well. You've been out of the dating world a good long while, and the experience you do have doesn't count."

I go to protest, but Jake holds up his hand, halting my objection.

"This is long overdue." He eyes me carefully. "Bianca was a grade-A bitch. If I hadn't been so young and stupid at the time, I would have said something sooner. Especially before she..." Jake shakes his head. "It doesn't matter. Let me guess. That night with Cassie was amazing, life-altering. But the next morning, when the beer goggles were off and she saw what she'd done, she panicked. Especially because of the bullshit that happened with her ex—"

"What happened with her ex?" I roar, imagining the worst-case scenarios.

"Not my story to tell." Jake shrugs his shoulders. Jealousy rears its ugly head again, realizing that my brother knows more about Cassie than I do. "As I was saying, before I was so rudely interrupted, she hightailed it out of there so fast she left a silhouette of smoke. And, like the asshole you are, you let her. Didn't fight, didn't object. In true brooding fashion, you pouted. Finally, Cassie does the mature thing and addresses the issue. You can thank yours truly for that, by the way. Now that you guys have been getting along all peachy keen like, you realize that besides her being hot as sin, she is probably the most badass chick you've ever met—probably ever will. At that realization, your balls have finally manned up and decided to do something about the crazy sexual tension you both have been denying. How am I doing so far?"

Did I mention he was perceptive? Well, fortunately, I'm good at being evasive. "Who the fuck talks like that? Peachy keen," I scoff.

Jake rolls his eyes, not caring one bit that I didn't answer his question *and* insulted him in one shot. "Fine, don't tell me. Like I said, I'm only the lowly gatekeeper to our dear Cassie. I'm sure you can win her over with a big smile and your sunny disposition."

I study him carefully. "Do you have a thing for Cassie? Is this whole act some new play to get in her pants?" I ask, clenching my jaw.

"Who says I haven't already?" Jake levels me with his serious tone.

I'm not sure what happened, but suddenly I'm holding Jake by the throat against the wall. He eyes me for a quick second before a giant grin spreads across his face. "I knew it. You're a fucking goner, man," he rasps out.

I let him go and take a step back as he rubs his neck. Laughing, he shakes his head. "Seriously, dude, you should have seen your face. I wish Jax would have been here with his camera to capture that shit. Fucking priceless."

"So, you haven't?" I ask desperately.

Jake frowns. "Seriously? No wonder she's pissed at you. But to answer your insulting allegation: no, I haven't. Not that I didn't toss the offer out there." I growl, which makes Jake laugh. "Anywho, she turned be down. Granted, when I put the offer out there, I knew she wasn't my usual clientele. Can't blame a guy for trying though. All the other times I've seen her, she's been 'in love'," he says with air-quotes, "with some douchebag. You seriously can't get all butthurt because I made a pass at her. You'd have to be stupid not to. It's probably why she is never single or ready to mingle."

"Do you fucking hear yourself? You claim she's some great friend of yours. But then you go on to tell me how you've been dying to fuck her for almost a decade."

"Just because I think she is hot, like top five out of all the other chicks I've ever met. Doesn't mean that I'm actively trying to put my dick in her. I mean, come on, Tilly is drop-fucking-gorgeous—top five for sure. I might be biased... twin thing and all. But obviously, I have zero interest in banging my sister. Hell, I'm even willing to admit you aren't half bad—especially if you could ever move past your shit and find some happiness again."

Rubbing a hand over my face, I contemplate what to do. While he is a bit of a numbskull, he isn't all wrong. Cassie is definitely the most beautiful thing I've ever laid eyes on, and given some of the hoods I've had the privilege of working under... that's saying something. It isn't even just her looks; she is smart and not afraid to get her hands covered in grease. Jake is right. She is the most badass chick I will ever meet. "I'm fucked, aren't I?"

"Ha," Jake laughs. "That's why you are lucky to have me as a brother. Not only am I in with your girl and can root you on, I also happen to be an expert on women. Want to know a sure-fire way to give her the best orgasm she'll ever have in her life? So good, she will probably forget her name or at least that you are a grumpy asshole."

I think about his offer for a moment. It isn't the worst idea he's ever had. But I don't think orgasms are the solution here. Not that they would hurt, but I need something more. To pull out the big guns. "Nah, I think I'm good in that department. If that changes, I'll let you know." I stop and think of a different approach. "What does she like for breakfast?"

19

Cassie

March 24th

WAKING UP, I GROAN. As much as I would love to sleep all day, the few hours of shut eye I got will need to be enough. I have to work tomorrow, and if I hit the snooze button again, it will make going to bed tonight impossible. The smell of bacon cooking puts a smile on my face. *I thought Jake was at the station today? Maybe his plans changed?*

Quickly, I throw my messy hair up in a bun on my head, then pull on a pair of pajama pants before making my way downstairs. The sight before me halts me mid step. Robbie is in the kitchen, cooking. He has bacon going in one skillet and it appears scrambled eggs in another. Looking at the counter, I see a bag and to-go cups from the coffee shop.

Turning with the pan still in his hand, Robbie dishes up eggs on a couple of plates, before adding some bacon. "I thought you might be hungry," he offers with a disarming smile.

"I am. Thank you," I say cautiously before taking a seat at the counter.

Robbie pulls a triple chocolate muffin from the bag, placing it on my plate, which he then passes to me along with one of the cups.

"Scott mentioned you've been a fan of his white-chocolate-raspberry mocha recently. But I had him change it to a decaf, since caffeine isn't recommended during pregnancy."

I raise a brow, curious how he knows anything about pregnancy.

"I don't know much about having babies. I've learned some things from Tilly, mostly from watching her be so sick all the time and listening to her complain."

I take a bite of my eggs before smiling at Robbie. "These are good," I say, deflecting from the elephant in the room. I know we need to talk about the baby stuff. But I'm not awake or emotionally calm enough to deal with it.

"Thanks. It's the only thing I actually know how to prepare. I eat a lot of eggs and bacon." He offers me a smile.

I return it with one of my own, before continuing to dig into my food. We consume our breakfast in a heavy and suffocating silence. Even if I wanted to talk about the situation, I don't know where to start. Robbie startles me when his arm brushes mine, sending a jolt of electricity down my spine. Grabbing our plates, he walks them over and tosses them in the sink.

"I think we should go on a date," he then says abruptly.

"A date?"

He lets out a frustrated sigh, rubbing his hand over his face.

"Look, I know this situation isn't exactly ideal or what either of us had planned." I wince at his admission. His expression softens as he takes a seat next to me and continues. "Cass, let's be honest, this wasn't exactly planned. I don't mean it in a bad way—it is just a fact. Regardless though, I think we owe it to each other to give this, us..." He gestures between the two of us. "...a real shot."

"So, you want to date," I clarify.

"Yes, at least get to know each other better. I'm not sure where this is going to go. Maybe when it is all said and done, we discover we aren't compatible. I don't know." Robbie shrugs. "I understand why you initially wanted to stop things after that night. But let's face it, we will never have a standard boss and employee relationship. We can set boundaries if you'd like, keep things separate as best we can between our personal and professional life. I just..." He swallows hard. "I feel we owe it to this baby to at least give it a shot. If there is the slightest possibility of giving this child a home with two parents, we owe it to him."

"Him?" I tease, while mulling over Robbie's suggestion.

"Of course, *that* will most definitely be a boy," he declares with a playful grin, pointing at my stomach. I smile at this new carefree side of Robbie, one that I'm not sure I could have ever imagined before now.

He's right—we don't know much about each other. And spending time together isn't exactly the worst idea, even if the end result of this is simply that we are friends. It would make raising this baby together much easier. I'm not exactly sure Robbie is my happily ever after. But for better or worse, he will in some way be entwined with it. Unless he chooses to have nothing to do with this baby, he will always be a part of our lives.

When have you ever entered a relationship thinking about the practicality of it? Never. But maybe that's why all my other relationships failed. Maybe this time, I don't dive in heart first, and instead use my excellent reasoning skills to analyze the situation from a business perspective—*that* has never let me down before.

"Okay, I think *she* would like that," I reply with a smile, which he returns. Robbie opens his mouth to say something, but I halt him quickly. "*However*, we are taking this slow. I know that sounds ridiculous given our situation. Which is more of a reason to not rush anything. This isn't just about us, it's about her."

Robbie considers my condition for a moment before nodding in agreement. "Now that we got that out of the way, do you want to discuss what happened with your family?"

I wince at the memory. "There's not much to tell..."

"I'm assuming they didn't take the news well?"

"Ugh," I sigh, "that would be an understatement. My da remained silent, refusing to even look at me; he was so disgusted. Ma was probably praying for my soul. My brothers are plotting your murder." Robbie laughs, puffing his chest a little at the threat of a challenge. "Don't get too cocky there. While my brothers might not be as large as you, Killian is a retired undefeated MMA heavyweight champion. Cian, he is a well-trained and decorated Army Ranger. So basically, they both have the means and the knowledge to kill you."

Robbie's mouth makes an adorable O-shape as he puts the name and occupation together—my brother is a bit of a local legend. If you follow fighting, you'll know who he is as soon as you hear his name. "Your brother is K.O. Murphy?" I nod. He whistles then shrugs off the threat. "Fine, they are tough. But I'm not worried about it."

"Whatever, your funeral." I chuckle.

"I told Scott," Robbie says, quickly changing the subject.

My first instinct is to yell at him, but then I realize how silly that is. I just got done telling my family, why shouldn't he confide in his? "Okay. Was he mad?"

"No, surprised, but not mad. I haven't said anything to Jake or anyone else yet. I thought we could come up with a plan together. We should probably figure that out quickly though. Scott isn't exactly the greatest at keeping his trap shut."

"Okay..." I pause to think of the best way to handle this. "We could always tackle it like I did with my family. Get them all together... do it in one shot. I'm assuming Scott hasn't said anything yet, otherwise Tilly would probably be blowing up my phone. Except for our immediate family, I'd like to keep this between us for a little while longer."

"That sounds like a plan. I will warn you though, this is a small town and few people seem to understand boundaries. It won't take long for the news to spread."

My chest squeezes tightly at the thought of potentially being the focus of everyone's whispers... *again*.

20

Cassie

March 29th

"HOW HAVE THINGS BEEN going?" Moira asks.

"Okay, I guess," I reply unenthusiastically, while walking down the street and chatting with her on the phone. This has become a tradition of mine with the pleasant weather.

"Still no word from your family?"

"Nope," I say, popping the P.

"Have you tried reaching out to them?" Her tone is now laced with concern.

"No, and I don't intend to," I huff out. I know it is juvenile, but I'm still frustrated with how my family handled the whole situation. I didn't expect them to jump for joy, nevertheless, I didn't anticipate *that*.

"I know they hurt your feelings, Cassie, but it was a bit of a shock. Then you just disappeared, sneaking out before the crack of dawn. I'm willing to bet they are embarrassed and a little ashamed of how they reacted. They're probably too scared to reach out and are waiting to hear from you." Moira attempts to reason with me.

"Really, you think Kill and Cian are afraid to reach out? They have never been afraid to interject themselves into my life before. Remember when I was sixteen and was out on my first date with Finn?"

She sighs into the phone, no doubt shaking her head. "Yeah, I remember."

Of course, she does. Ever since the seventh grade, I had the biggest crush on Finn. It was sophomore year, and he had just gotten his driver's license and asked me out. I was so excited to go on my first actual date. You know, one where I get all dressed up, then the boy comes, picks me up, and takes me out. No being dropped off by Ma or having a chaperon. Unfortunately though, Killian and Cian heard about it (I'm guessing Ma mentioned something, because I sure didn't). When Finn knocked on the door, he was met by two large, muscular men—one of whom was openly carrying a Glock on his hip. They gave him the "we are watching you" and "if you hurt her, we will kill you" speech. While terrified, Finn still took me out. But then at the restaurant, we noticed they tailed us. Anytime Finn so much as looked in my direction, Kill would crack his knuckles or Cian would casually draw attention to his pistol.

After a very quick dinner, with little to no conversation, Finn drove me home, barely speaking two words to me the entire night. No goodbye kiss, hug, handshake, nothing. By Monday, the entire school heard about what happened and they labeled me "undateable" for risk of bodily harm by my brothers. I didn't get asked out again until college. Thankfully, I had learned my lesson and made sure not to mention anything to my parents. There was no way I was going to allow Kill or Cian to have me labeled "off limits" again.

"Then you know they're not sorry. The only reason they haven't reached out to me yet, is because they haven't devised a plan on how to get me to come home. So, no, I will not call them. I am not apologizing or going to plead my case. I am twenty-nine years old. Yes, I've made some questionable decisions when it comes to relationships, but I am a responsible adult. I will take care of this baby, on my own if necessary."

"Cassie, I know you're upset," Moira says cautiously. "You have all right to be. But I think you are reading too much into this. Your family loves you and they are just concerned. You are in an unfamiliar town, by yourself, pregnant."

"I'm not alone. I told you Robbie and I are working on getting to know each other. We are telling his family on Sunday."

"That's good. I'm glad you and Robbie are working things out. But Cassie..." She hesitates.

"What?"

"I love you. You are brilliant, self-sufficient, strong. But... when it comes to guys and relationships... well, it seems to be your kryptonite. I know you said that you and Robbie are going to take things slow, that you aren't going to rush into anything. Except, you kind of already rushed into something. You are about to have a baby with him. That's a big deal. I'm just worried that you are going to let having a baby with him influence your decisions."

"I told you, Moira, no more diving in headfirst with blinders on. I'm in no rush for anything. I only want to do what's best for me and the baby. Getting better acquainted with the father and remaining in a position that allows him to be in our lives is best for both of us. While he might not be happy-go-lucky, Robbie is a good man."

"I'm not saying he isn't." Moira lets out a frustrated breath. "I'll support you no matter what. I just don't want to see you hurt again. This was supposed to be your new beginning, time to focus on you. Now you are thrust into this situation with a guy you hardly know. I'm worried about you. I hate that I am not there."

"I promise, Moira, my guard is up. I've learned my lesson. My only mission is to provide the best life possible for my baby."

"Baby?" Jake asks from behind me. *Damn,* I hadn't realized I was home already.

"Hey, Moira, can I call you later?"

She chuckles. "Yeah, good luck."

I turn and smile at Jake, tucking my phone into my purse. "Hi," I say nervously.

"Hi, what's this about a baby?"

"Can we talk inside?"

Jake nods in agreement before following me into the house. As we both sit on the couch, I can't shake my apprehension. What if he reacts like my brothers had? Except this time, the fury is directed towards me? I swallow down my nerves. Though being able to tell him with everyone else would be easier, I can't lie to Jake.

"I'm pregnant," I let out with an exhausted breath.

"Seriously?" I can't quite tell if he is angry yet. Shooting up from the couch, he paces back and forth. "It's that asshole ex of yours? Chad, right? Do you need me to go kick his ass? Fuck, isn't he marrying that chick? Whatever, he doesn't matter. You don't need him. I can help you. We have more than enough room for a baby here. It is perfect actually; she can grow up with the twins."

"Jake!" I yell, finally getting his attention.

"Shit, sorry. Do you need something? Are you okay? Do you want some sprite and chicken tenders? That always makes Tilly feel better."

I give him a soft smile. "No, I'm good. Can you please just sit down? I'm not finished."

He takes a seat next to me, wrapping an arm around my shoulders and pulling me into his side. "Don't worry, Cassie, we got this. Whatever it is, we will figure it out."

"Jake, listen. There is more. Robbie—" I say, but Jake bolts up and panics.

"Fuck, I forgot about Robbie." He quickly shakes his head. "No, Robbie is a good guy. I know he likes you. If things work out between you, I'm certain he will help raise the baby as his own. If not, I will help."

"The baby is Robbie's," I yell in frustration.

As if frozen in time, he stops, looking at me with his eyes open wide and mouth gaping. I wait for the anger or rage, but am quickly shocked when he bursts out into a full-bellied laugh.

"What's so funny?" I ask, slightly offended.

He wipes away a tear. "I'm sorry, Cassie. But this is great."

"It is?" I'm both shocked and confused by his admission.

"Of course, I was worried that asshole ex of yours was the daddy and you were about to tell me you were going to go back home to him. Or even worse, try to get back together with him for the sake of the baby."

"You aren't mad?" I ask quietly.

Understanding dawns on Jake's features, as he gives me a sympathetic stare. "Your family, this is why you aren't getting along right now, isn't it?"

I sniffle and swipe at the wetness trailing over my cheeks. "Yeah, they didn't take it well. We were planning on telling everyone at the grill out on Sunday. But for a moment, I was worried that maybe you'd be mad and blame me or something."

"What?" Jake scrunches up his nose in disgust. "That's ridiculous—*shit happens*. I'm sorry your family is being an asshole about it. With us, you have nothing to worry about. Damn, Tilly is going to be so excited. Shit, I'm going to get to be a godfather to three babies now."

Laughing, I wipe away the remaining tears from my eyes. "Godfather?"

"You know it. So, I just gotta know... how did Robbie take it when you told him? Damn, I wish I could have been there to see his reaction."

"Yeah, he didn't take it the greatest at first. I mean, not bad. Just like you, he thought it was my ex's. Then after he figured out it was his, he said we should get married."

"Married," Jake roars, slapping his knee. "That sounds like something the big guy would say."

"So, you're really okay with this?" I ask tentatively, wringing my purse strap in my hands.

"Hell yeah. I think it's great."

A pang of sadness hits me in my chest. "I'm glad someone is excited about it."

Jake pulls me close again, resting his chin on the top of my head. "They'll come around, eventually. They're probably feeling like asshats from how they treated you."

"Maybe." I shrug. "My brothers, sure, they will calm down eventually. My parents though, I don't think you understand. They are very conservative. I remember when I was sixteen and my mom found my birth control. She flipped, even though I told her I was still a virgin... I just wanted to be safe. She called Father Flannagan over immediately for an emergency prayer session."

"Wow, that's tough."

"Don't get me wrong, they are good people. It's just how they were raised. As we've grown older, it's gotten better. While they still insist we attend mass on specific occasions, they no longer expect us to be as devoted as they are. I think they just ignore that we aren't exactly like them. But a baby, there is no way for them to pretend that their daughter didn't have a child out of wedlock. I'm terrified they will forever look at this baby like a stain on their family. What if they never love her?"

"I don't know your parents, but I'm sure that won't happen. Like you said, over time they have learned to accept that you guys are not like them. They just need time. I have no doubt that the moment they see their grandchild, it won't matter anymore how she came to be."

"You really think so?" I rest my head on Jake's chest and close my eyes.

"I do. My mom, when I told her I was joining the fire department, boy, did she freak out, screaming about how I was going to get myself killed. It actually took her a good long while to get over it. I remember the day I came home from my first big call. A barn on the outskirts of town caught fire. It was bad. The farmer got most of his livestock out, but he left a couple of goats behind. Before I knew it, I was running into the flames, frantically searching for a couple of baby goats. I rescued both of them, my first save. Damn, I was fucking proud. I was so excited I didn't even bother going back to the station to shower. I went straight home, sauntered into the kitchen chest out and covered in soot. Mom about damn near collapsed. I told her what had happened and how fucking amazing it felt. When she realized that I finally found my place and was happy, all her objections disappeared. So, the point is, if they love you, eventually they will come around."

"Thank you."

"Anytime. If you need me *for anything*. Let me know." He ponders for a moment before flashing me his mega-watt smile. "Look, I know Robbie is a little out of practice. He doesn't get around much. So, if it was bad the first time, don't hold it against him. I'll make sure to give him a few pointers."

I stop to think about Jake's words for a moment before it dawns on me. "Oh. My. God. Jake," I say playfully, hitting him in the arm. "Way to ruin a moment."

"What?" he asks innocently. "It's my duty as your best friend to ensure you have as many orgasms as possible. If you won't let *me* take care of it for you personally, I will make sure Robbie gets the job done."

Resting my head against his chest, I smile. This is what I needed. "Thank you," I whisper again.

Jake squeezes me tighter.

21

Robbie

March 30th

FUCK, I'M LATE. I hesitate before knocking on the door. *Why am I nervous?* It doesn't make sense. But here I am, heart ready to burst from my chest. I take a quick glance at my appearance in the window's reflection. I met up with Scott to buy a new shirt (he has his own date tonight and was looking for something to wear). Being a mechanic, pretty much everything I own has some sort of grease stain on it. It wouldn't surprise me if these black pants do—the spots are just hidden by the dark fabric. I'd considered wearing a black shirt, but I refuse to do black on black. Even if it is the same brand of clothing, the shade always seems off.

On my way home, I drove past some teens broken down on the side of the road. I stopped and looked at their car. Giving it a quick once-over, I surmised that their alternator was out. Easy fix (well, easy-ish) but not something I could do from the side of the road. We called Chris to tow them in and I gave the kid and his girlfriend a ride back into town. I knew I wouldn't have much time once I got home, but I had to shower and clean up. This is our first actual date, and I'd like to make it as nice as possible.

After verifying I am about as clean and presentable as I am going to get, I finally knock. Holding my breath, I wait for the door to open. When it does, it's like all the oxygen was sucked from my lungs. Cassie looks stunning standing before me in skinny jeans, combat boots, and a large sweater that hangs off her shoulder, revealing a thin tank top underneath. She piled her hair high on her head, with a few loose curls hanging down. The black liner is making her gray eyes more vibrant. Her lips are red and juicy, like an apple begging me to take a big bite. That smile though, it was the nail in the coffin.

"Hi," Cassie squeaks out, seeming just as nervous as I am.

Get it together, I chastise myself. Regaining some of my senses, I finally speak. "Sorry I'm late, had an unplanned roadside assist today. Are you ready to go?"

"Yeah, just let me grab my coat and purse," she says, waving me inside as she walks upstairs to get her stuff.

"Don't fuck this up," Jake states from the living room couch. He is sitting there, sprawled out in sweatpants and a t-shirt while drinking a beer. His hair is a mess, and he has bags under his eyes. Cassie mentioned she told him about the baby the other day after he overheard her talking on the phone. She said he took it well, but *this* doesn't look like my brother—he looks like shit. He should be out, or about to head out, if he isn't going to the station tonight.

I raise my eyebrow at him. "I wasn't planning on it."

He looks around the corner, verifying that Cassie isn't within earshot before he speaks up. "Cassie is a good girl, a lot better than you deserve. I know you both got baggage, but you need to forget about Bianca," he says her name with disdain, "and let go of whatever damage she did to you."

"Seriously? Look, Jake, I appreciate the concern. But I am trying to do the right thing here. You know, date, get to know each other. I'm not making any promises, but I am trying, okay?"

129

Jake lets out a sigh. His features soften a bit, showing his more empathetic side. "I know, Robbie. I'm just saying you have had this chip on your shoulder since Bianca. Just try to forget about her. Cassie is nothing like that bitch. You'll never be able to let her in if Bianca and what she did is always lingering and taunting you in the back of your mind. Cassie might be putting on a brave face, but I can tell this fight with her family is eating away at her. We are all she has right now. That means you need to step up. I am not just referring to taking care of the baby. I know you'd do that, regardless. I'm talking about with her. She's been through a lot. Fuck, she's *going through* a lot. If you aren't genuinely interested in pursuing something with her, more than just from a sense of obligation, let her be."

"I promise I only want what's best for everyone." Rubbing my hand over my face, I let out an exasperated breath. "Look, I will do my damnedest. I won't let the shit that happened with Bianca affect Cassie and me. I haven't even thought of her in years, to be honest." Cassie being here has triggered all the memories and feelings I've suppressed. In a good way, because Bianca doesn't hold a fucking candle to her. "You really are looking out for her."

Jake crosses his arms. "Yeah, I am. From the sounds of it, it's about damn time."

"Cassie isn't a damsel in distress that needs saving," I point out to my brother, who is always looking to rescue something.

"Just because she doesn't need saving, doesn't mean she doesn't need someone looking out for her. There is a lot Cassie doesn't show you, heck, a lot she doesn't show me. Unfortunately for her, I am pretty much a freaking mind reader. Trust me, she uses that sparkling smile as a distraction to make you go 'oh shiny' while she hides her pain away and tucks it deep down."

I am about to ask Jake what the hell he's talking about when I hear, "Are you ready?"

Turning, I see Cassie smiling in the entryway. I'm hoping it's a genuine one, not this mask Jake is convinced she wears like armor. Sneaking a glance back at Jake, he nods, giving me the signal. Everything is good. Thank god, that would be one heck of a way to start our first date.

"Yup," I say, heading towards her. With my back facing Jake, I throw my hand up in a wave. "See ya later." I make a mental note to finish our conversation another time.

"So where are we going?" Cassie asks as she takes a seat in my pickup.

"It's a surprise," I reply with a big smile.

As we drive out of town and into the countryside, we make general small talk. Cassie tells me some funny stories from when she and Tilly were in college. It makes me smile, knowing that they had a good time together. It took Tilly a while to get over Jax. Based on the stories Cassie is telling me, it sounds like I have her and Moira to thank for that.

Cassie glances around suspiciously when we slow down and stop in front of our destination. "Where are we?" she asks, as I get out of the truck and walk around to her side. Opening her door, I offer my hand to help her down.

"The junkyard," I reply with a grin.

"I can see that," she says, taking in her surroundings. "What are we doing here?"

"Come on, I'll show you." I take her hand in mine, leading her into the main building.

Entering, she lets out a small laugh. I cleaned the office up as best I could. There is a small table set in the center of the room, with two chairs, a candle, and a small vase of flowers. Jax helped me out by picking up a couple of burgers and fries from the diner and delivering them shortly before we arrived, so they would still be warm.

I glance over at Cassie, looking to get a read on her expression. I worry for a moment that I already fucked up this first date. "This is amazing," she says in awe. I let out a relieved breath as we stroll over to the table. "Why thank you, sir." Cassie nods and takes a seat in the chair I pulled out for her.

"Is this okay?" I ask, raising an eyebrow. I attempt to gauge if she is just being polite, or if I genuinely impressed her.

"Yes, this is perfect. This is the place your grandfather ran, right?"

"Yup, this place used to be his," I confirm, shrugging my shoulder. "He left it to me when he passed. Sometimes I get bored and rummage around the yard looking for parts."

"I've always thought places like this were beautiful."

"Really?" I agree there is a certain beauty to this place, but few can usually see it.

"Yeah, there is this U-Pull-It place south of the cities. It's a giant junkyard that you pay a small fee to enter and rummage around—pull any parts you need and pay them when you are finished. I actually went with Moira and her mom. Her mom is an artist and likes to repurpose items. We complained at first. Going to a junkyard didn't sound like fun to a couple of ten-year-old girls. When we got there though, I was left speechless. There was something so serene about seeing all those cars lying around in various stages of decay. I'm sure her mom would love this place."

"What kinds of things does she make?"

"All sorts. Furniture, garden art, murals—their entire house is filled with repurposed items."

"Like my shop stool?"

Cassie smiles. "Exactly."

"Well, she is more than welcome to come down here whenever she wants and look around, see if she is inspired by anything."

"Oh, wow, thank you. She'd love that." Cassie ponders for a moment. "I'm curious... It seems like you really respect your grandfather and share his love of cars. Why didn't you keep the junkyard open?"

"I love the place. Like I said, I come here a lot to dig around for parts. Also, I still take in salvaged vehicles. But fixing things has always been my passion. I don't think he intended for me to ever run the yard like he did. When he passed... the money he left behind, he specifically told me to open a shop in town if I wanted."

"That is really sweet of him. It must have been difficult for you when he passed. It sounds like you two were close."

I shrug. "It was tough at the time, but he lived a long, full life. I'm grateful for the time we got to spend together, which was a lot when I was growing up. He and grandma used to watch me during the day while my parents got the bookshop up and running. Then, after my accident, I struggled a bit. But he helped me forge a new path."

"Accident?" Cassie asks, confused.

"Yeah, I used to play football in high school, as a tight end. I was good at it too. Coach was certain that I'd get a full ride at some college to play ball and eventually get drafted. While I had hoped they'd win sooner, I dreamed I would go pro, join the Vikings, and be there when they won their first Super Bowl. But the summer before my senior year, I got hit hard in some pickup game with the neighborhood kids and broke my knee, along with tearing several ligaments."

"Oh, wow. I'm so sorry. That must have been devastating."

"It was, at first. I didn't really have any other plans. I mean, I am sure with PT and stuff I could have been back on the field, eventually. But since I had to sit out my senior year, scouts forgot about me. Honestly, unless it was to play ball, I wasn't interested in going to college. My dad supported whatever I wanted to do, but Pops was the one who had the hard talk with me. While I could have tried to play again, we both knew I would never be as good as I used to be. Most teams would consider me a liability. Also, with the injury, how long of a career would I even have? One good hit could take me right back out. So, I got into my second passion, mechanics. I'd been helping my pops tinker with cars in this yard since I was three."

"That's nice—you had something else to fall back on. While it might not be the NFL or anything, your shop is successful. I've noticed how people in the town talk about you and the garage. They think the world of you. I'm sure becoming a tight end for the Vikes and winning a Super Bowl would have been awesome. But it has to be nice, knowing how much your town loves and supports you."

"Yeah, my family has always been a keystone in Tral Lake. We are part of the first families who settled in this region. So, what about you? Did you always want to be an accountant?" I ask, trying to take a bit of the focus off me for a moment.

"I guess... I've always loved numbers and spreadsheets. It made the most sense. I figured it would be a way to do something I enjoyed and make decent money. Living in the Twin Cities can be expensive."

I grimace, thinking of the rent up there. We sit in silence for a moment, both just enjoying our dinner, before I start the hard conversation. "Look, Cassie, I know this situation is a little messed up. But I meant what I said before. I want us to get to know each other. So, I think we should get the hard part out of the way."

"What did you have in mind?"

"Tell me about your ex. I know you didn't give me the entire story before, which was fine. But given our current predicament, I think it is important we get everything out in the open."

Cassie stares at me for a moment, biting her red-painted lip and contemplating my request. After a few moments, she sighs before nodding in agreement.

22

Cassie

March 30th

I KNEW THIS CONVERSATION needed to happen, *eventually*.
This is definitely not something I really want to talk about on
a first date. But this isn't a normal first date after all. Don't
get me wrong, this private dinner here in the junkyard is
actually the most romantic thing anyone has ever done for
me. Even more memorable than Chad's proposal, which was
the conclusion to an argument we were having.

$$\cdot \heartsuit \cdot \heartsuit \cdot \heartsuit \cdot \heartsuit \cdot \heartsuit \cdot$$

*"Oh, Chad, look." I hold up the cream and lace invitation
in my hand. He just mentions that it's nice without even
looking up from his dinner. I roll my eyes, before
walking over and thrusting the letter in front of him.
"Melanie and Parker are getting married. Isn't that
exciting?"*

*Chad leans back, crossing his arms, and stares at the
invitation as though it's covered in doggie poo. "Sure,
when's the wedding?"*

"December 15th. A winter wedding sounds so elegant. Oh, Ma! I bet she'd make the most breathtaking bouquet. A mix of white and dusty blue flowers, cascading down, with eucalyptus. I know summer weddings are the traditional big-ticket events, but living in Minnesota, I think embracing our snow is just beautiful. Oh my god, wouldn't she just look gorgeous with a white fur cape. Melanie has the perfect complexion to pull off shades of pure white without looking washed out. I should call her, see if she needs any help planning. I'm sure Ma would offer her a discount on arrangements if she's interested."

"Do you hear yourself?" Chad sneers.

I stop, jaw hanging open. "What are you talking about? I'm just excited for Mel—"

"I know what you are doing, Cassandra."

"I'm not doing anything. Sorry... I get excited about this kind of stuff. Growing up, I spent most of my time at weddings helping Ma out. I think she's still disappointed I didn't inherit her creativity. I'm sure she'd be much happier if I had gone into wedding planning or something. Could you imagine a family business that can provide you a bundle deal for your wedding?"

"Fine," Chad groans before digging into his dinner.

"Fine?" I restate the singular word, confused by its context.

"We'll get married," he states plainly, before grumbling something under his breath.

"Are you serious? Chad, I wasn't—"

"Do you want to get married or not?"

"Well, of course I do. But I know how you feel—"

"I think it's time. I was speaking with my father. He was dropping hints about retiring soon and wanting to keep this a family firm. I think us getting married and having a few children is a wise decision."

"I can't believe it," I say excitedly, bouncing up and down. "I'm going to call Ma—she is going to be so happy."

·❤·❤·❤·❤·❤·

I shiver at the memory. *How stupid was I?* No matter, I'm not going to make the same mistake again. Robbie is a good guy. I don't doubt that at all. It's the reason I want to stick around, so he has easy access to our baby's life. But I won't forget for a moment that this is all just a formality. Although it's a nice gesture—to suggest we are dating. I know this is Robbie doing what he feels obligated to do.

"As I mentioned, I was engaged to my boss. I discovered he was cheating on me with another girl in the office. There isn't much else to it."

"I feel like you aren't telling me the whole story." Robbie leans back, crossing his arms. "I thought we were getting things out in the open?"

I roll my eyes. "Fine, you want the nitty-gritty details?" He nods. "I came home early from Thanksgiving with my family. I was bummed, our first holiday being engaged, and we were spending it apart. When I walked through the door to our apartment, he was balls deep in Katie, the office assistant. It felt like someone tore my heart from my chest and shredded it to pieces."

"He sounds like a fucking douche," Robbie growls.

"Yeah, same thing my brother said."

"Then what happened?" He asks, clearly not yet satisfied with my level of sharing. "Don't look so shocked. I skimmed over the resume Tilly provided me. It said you were employed there until the beginning of January. Then at Harper's, you mentioned the toxic workplace. I'm curious what happened next."

"Yeah, I wanted to quit immediately. I was heartbroken and embarrassed. After Cian was finished plotting Chad's dismemberment, he convinced me I should stay. I had worked so hard to get into the firm, even harder to get promoted to the executive team at such a young age. My brother insisted that if I quit, Chad would have really won. Cian was right. The next day, my brothers helped me clean out my stuff from his apartment. It was fairly easy, as I had only recently moved in. Most of my belongings were still in boxes. Not that I was allowed to bring much over, since Chad already had the place well furnished. Monday morning, I showed up to work, giving everyone my most professional smile."

"I take it he didn't make it easy on you?"

That's an understatement. "You could say that. As I mentioned before, the workplace became hostile and toxic. I wanted to be strong, but there was only so much I could take."

Robbie comes around the table, crouching before me and wiping a tear from my cheek that I wasn't aware I was shedding. My body shivers at his touch. "Cass, speaking from personal experience, there is a fine line between strength and stupidity. It was brave of you to go back to work and show him that getting rid of you would not be that easy. But if being there was killing you, it would have been stupid to stay. There is only so much abuse one person can take."

You have no idea.

"I was being serious when I said I wanted to get to know you. But I get the feeling you are at your limit for sharing this evening?" I give him a sad smile before swiping away the remaining tears. "Okay, I am not going to pry or force you to share beyond what you are comfortable with." I quickly notice a pained expression flash in his eyes. "When you are ready, I will listen."

"Thank you," I whisper. Robbie places a soft kiss on my hand, before getting up and taking his seat.

"I guess it's my turn?" I wait patiently for him to continue. I know I just shared some of my past, but that was pretty heavy for a date, no matter the conditions of how the date came to be. Robbie rubs his hand over his face before launching into his tale. "Her name was Bianca. I'd known her since we were kids, but we officially started dating our sophomore year. We were the classic story of high school sweethearts. I was the football player, and she was the cheerleader. My injury started sparking little fights. She was adamant that I get back into football. When I refused, she began pressuring me about going to college. She wanted me to get some big fancy degree in engineering or something. While I enjoy working on stuff, I had no interest in becoming an engineer. I thought we would get past whatever problems we were having... eventually. But the fighting just got worse. It pissed her off when I stuck around to help my pops at the junkyard. Then when he died, and I got the money, she wanted me to sell the yard and use the inheritance to move us away from Tral Lake.

"Instead, I kept the yard and opened the garage. Honestly, at that point, I should have seen the warning signs. But I was blind to it all. I figured all couples go through a rough patch, and this was ours. Once the garage was doing well, she actually started helping me in the back office. The fighting eased up after we got married." My jaw drops at his admission. "Though it wasn't perfect, I thought things were finally getting back on track. We were even talking about starting our own family. Then life threw us a curveball, some guy came into the shop. He got a flat while in town; I guess he was a location scout or some shit. He flashed his Hollywood smile at her, and then it all went downhill from there. One day, she stayed home from the garage, which wasn't uncommon. That night when I went upstairs, I found her closet and our bank account empty. Not just our joint, but the business account as well. She left me some letter explaining she just couldn't stick around here anymore, that she needed to pursue her dreams of becoming an actress. Some shit about if I loved her, I wouldn't keep holding her back. Apparently, that guy had some connections and said he could help make her a star. About six months after she left, I was finally served with divorce papers. Fortunately, the divorce went smoothly. She tried to get more money from me. But my dad made sure I kept the letter along with a bunch of other stuff. Once the judge saw how things went down, and that my own inheritance funded the garage, he denied her request. Said the accounts she cleaned out were sufficient payment."

"Wow," is all I could say. I guess that explains a lot. I had assumed there was a reason he was hesitant about hiring someone to help manage his finances. I just didn't imagine his own wife betrayed him.

"Yeah," Robbie admits sheepishly.

"How long ago did this all happen?"

He ponders a moment, rubbing his chin. "It will be nine years, this August."

My heart breaks for Robbie, now that I have a better understanding of him. Just like me, he thought he had his happily ever after, except fate cruelly tore it away from him.

We finish our dinner in a silence thick with pain from our personal wounds. As much as it hurts, it feels good to share this with Robbie. While I have disclosed little details with Moira, my brothers, and even recently, some with Jake, I've never told them everything. I've never wanted to. I had been ashamed by all that had happened. I couldn't bring myself to admit it out loud. For the first time since the incident, I genuinely want to share all the ugliness with someone else. Even what put me in Chad's path in the first place.

But I can't. Not yet. Not because I fear that Robbie will think less of me, which is a surprising revelation all of its own. No, it's because I feel that familiar tingle in my chest. The one I felt with Chad, with my other exes, even the day I met Robbie—except this time the tingle isn't a light flutter of butterflies. It is more like the pounding hoofs of wild stallions stampeding throughout my chest—the strength of which terrifies me. In the past, I've always let that feeling lead me, but I swore to myself I wouldn't do that anymore. It is one thing to ignore butterflies... How do you ignore a stampede of horses barreling at you?

Once finished with my meal, I carefully push my plate forward and stand. Robbie watches my movements with intensity. It only fuels this spark inside me. He pushes out his chair as I get closer, allowing me access to sit in his lap. Once seated, his hand carefully comes around and grabs my butt.

"What are you doing?" he asks in a deep, husky voice.

I respond by leaning forward and licking the side of his neck, before nibbling on his lobe. "Getting to know you."

"I..." He gulps. "I thought we were taking this slow?"

"We are." I breathe into his ear.

"This doesn't feel slow." Robbie thrusts up, allowing me to feel how hard he is.

At the sensation, my underwear soaks with my arousal. I consider for a moment, thinking this might be a bad idea. I want to take things slow. But just because I want to take things slow with my heart, doesn't mean I need to take things slow with the rest of my body. A body that has been buzzing in anticipation of his touch.

"I need you," is all I say before Robbie growls and moves his mouth to capture mine. The kiss is searing, even better than the last one. Our first interaction (while hot) was drunk and sloppy. This one is intense, passionate, purposeful. It is conveying a lot more feeling than I think either of us are willing to admit at this point. That's fine by me—we've done enough sharing for now.

Robbie stands, lifting me with him. I wrap my legs and arms around him. "You've got me." His statement holds more meaning than I can accept at the moment. Instead, I focus on his fiery mouth devouring mine. Initially, I was nervous that the intensity and passion we felt that night was all fueled by tequila and frustration. As my body hums, desperate to feel him everywhere, I realize it wasn't the alcohol that made me so wanton; it was all Robbie Moore.

Not once does he break our locked lips, as he walks us into an office off the main lobby area. It is dark and I can hardly see anything. Fortunately, Robbie knows this place like the back of his hand and has no issue leading us to what I presume is a desk. Setting me down, Robbie reluctantly breaks our kiss. He pulls up the hem of my sweater, ripping it over my head before tossing it over his shoulder. His mouth is back on me as quickly as it left. He travels down my neck, giving me small pecks and nibbles.

I reach between us and fumble with his pants as he tears off his shirt. Sliding my hand beneath the waistband of his briefs, I wrap my fingers around his stiff member. Even contained, it seems bigger than I remember. Robbie moans at my touch.

"Too many clothes," I breathe as I sit in a puddle of need.

He growls against my mouth before his movements become more frantic. Forcing me prone, he finishes stripping me down. I lean back on my hands, chest heaving, naked, and watch the outline of his silhouette as he removes his clothing. Once he is bare, we both stand, each studying the other. The only light in the room is peeking through the doorway. I reach up and begin tracing my fingers across his left pec. From the little I can make out, it appears this is the one bare area on his torso. The rest is covered with designs in black ink. As my thumb rubs over the tip of his bulbous head, I feel the moisture from his pre-cum. I bring my thumb to my mouth and suck off the sticky liquid, moaning at the salty, musky taste.

"Fuck," Robbie groans. I reach back down and squeeze him tightly as he thrusts into my hand. Reaching up, he takes my nipples between his fingertips. Gently he tweaks them, turning them into stiff peaks. I throw my head back and let out a moan of my own. I'm not sure if it is Robbie or the pregnancy, but my nipples have never felt so sensitive before. This alone has me on the verge of climax.

He continues stimulating one of my breasts as his other hand reaches lower and rubs between the apex of my thighs. I am so wound up; I cry out in ecstasy as his thumb traces small circles over my clit. Letting out a deep throaty chuckle, he sends another shock to my core. "So sensitive." As soon as one of his calloused digits enters me, that impending climax lets loose. I feel myself shake as my muscles contract around him.

"Wow," I sigh as I come down. Removing his finger, still slick with my juices, he raises it to his lips. I snatch his wrist, pulling the appendage into my mouth before releasing it with a pop. Robbie cups my cheeks, crashing his lips to mine in order to get a hint of the taste I greedily stole from him.

Stepping further between my legs, he rubs against my dripping center. I gasp into his mouth as he presses slowly inside me. Digging my heels into his butt, I pull him deeper, impatient to feel the entirety of him again. Once fully sheathed, Robbie rocks his pelvis against my nub. Still oversensitive from my climax, I tense at the sensation, squeezing him tightly inside me.

Robbie deepens the kiss as his hands travel down and dig into my cheeks. His hold is firm and bruising, but I love it. I've never been handled so passionately before and it is intoxicating. As I am about to beg him to have his way with me, he pulls out carefully before slamming back in. He sets a steady, punishing pace as he almost fully unsheathes himself before burying himself deeper with each thrust.

That inferno raging within my core has me built up with so much pressure I think I might explode. As if sensing my impending orgasm, he moves one of his hands between us, pressing his thumb to my clit like a magic button. I immediately unravel around him. Robbie continues pushing through my tensed muscles that are throbbing and squeezing him tightly.

"Fuck, Cass." His hot breath tickles my ear. "Give me one more."

I go to protest, feeling completely exhausted. But his lips crash down while his tongue lunges into my mouth. The hand he had between my legs makes its way up to my nipples. And just like that, I am off again, completely baffled at my body's continued response to his stimulation. All my nerve endings are on fire, coercing one more mind-blowing orgasm from me. I let out a loud cry of pleasure, which he swallows down. Robbie stiffens and I feel his rhythmic pulsations, followed by the warmth of him spilling inside me as he lets out a cry of his own.

Spent, he presses his forehead to mine. Our bodies are both soaked with droplets of sweat. Now that we have stopped moving, the cold air causes goosebumps along my skin.

"That was..." He takes a deep breath and exhales. "That was fucking incredible. Here, let me help you up."

Robbie reaches out to assist me off the desk, but my legs are like jelly and I almost collapse. Chuckling, he scoops me up into his enormous arms, before walking over to a couch on the other side of the room. Holding me close, he lays us down, acting as my big spoon. He reaches back and pulls a thick blanket over us. I shiver as he rests his hand against my belly. I struggle to ignore that pounding in my chest again. It's funny to think... we just had amazing sex on a desk a few feet from here, and before that, exposed our emotional wounds to each other. Yet, somehow, this feels like the most intimate thing I've ever done. My body easily relaxes into his as I drift off to sleep, safely nuzzled in his arms.

23

Robbie

March 31st

"STOP FIDGETING." CASSIE LOOKS at me like a deer caught in headlights, her steel eyes wide and vibrant against her black liner. Biting on her red-painted, plump bottom lip, she furrows her brows. "Everything is going to be fine," I remind her for what feels like the hundredth time this morning.

"I know," she groans. "Just... what if—"

"We've been over this," I say exhaustedly. I pull her into my lap, her sundress riding up as she straddles me. If I weren't certain that my nosey siblings are spying on us in the driveway, I'd consider calming her down with one more orgasm. It's how I was able to settle her nerves enough earlier, so she would finally get dressed and ready to go. *Not that I'm complaining.*

Since last night, things feel different. While bringing up the past wasn't exactly something I wanted to do, Jake was right—I needed to let *her* go. I hadn't realized how much shit I've been holding on to until after spilling my guts. It's been nine damn years, and this is the first time I've let anyone in. *How fucking pathetic is that?* I thought that night with Cassie was my first time actually living since my parent's accident. No, I stopped long before that.

Last night, as I watched Cassie sleep in my arms, I continued to really think about my marriage. The more I recalled, the more I realized that relationship had been over prior to us even graduating high school.

· ❤ · ❤ · ❤ · ❤ · ❤ ·

"I can't take this anymore," Bianca screams, throwing our framed wedding picture against the wall. As I watch the glass shatter and fall to the floor, I wonder... Am I more upset that we are arguing again? Or over the fact I need to go out and replace the frame. "Are you even listening to me?"

"Of course, you were saying you can't take this anymore," I repeat her words back to her.

Bianca whines while pulling at her hair. "God, it's like you don't even fucking care about me. Do you even love me?"

"Of course, I do." As I say the words, they leave a bitter aftertaste. I love her, right? This is what you are supposed to do. You meet a pretty girl, fall in love, get married, raise a family. It's what my parents did; it's how it worked for Pops and grandma. I treat her well. I never yell, even though she is always hollering at me. I'm thankful we don't have actual neighbors who can hear us. I've never raised a hand to her. I remember all the important dates, making sure she gets flowers and gifts. I tell her I love her every time I walk out the door (like Pops taught me), since you never know what might happen. We have started a business together. Okay, mostly I started it. But she's stepped up recently—ever since I got featured in the Tral Lake Times as the newest up-and-coming business owner. They made a big deal about me continuing the Moore tradition of establishing successful shops. For a bit, I was almost like a local

celebrity, everyone stopping me on the street or at the market and talking to me about their car problems. It thrilled farmers when I offered house calls for their tractors.

It felt good, and Bee finally seemed happy and proud of me. But now, here we are, having the same fucking fight again. I know people in love fight. I've heard mom and dad get into a few big ones. But is it supposed to be this often? It's like no matter what I do, it's never enough. I'm not good enough.

"Then let's go." Bee gets down on her knees before me, undoing my belt buckle. "We were never supposed to stay here. We were meant for something bigger and better than this dump."

I frown, going limp in her icy hand.

"What's the matter, baby?" she croons. "Don't worry, mama will make it all better." We've known each other since we were kids, but right now, I don't even recognize her. I take a step back and she lets me go before looking up at me. If this were a cartoon, I think steam would blow from her ears. I don't bother fixing my pants before walking out the door. At the realization I didn't tell her I love her, I turn to go back inside. But once I hear her scream and something shatter against the door, I walk away. It's fine. She just needs some time to cool off. Tonight, we'll talk, have make-up sex, and everything will be okay again. It has to be.

· ♥ · ♥ · ♥ · ♥ · ♥ ·

"Hey, are you okay?" Cassie frowns at me, her head tilted to the side with those juicy lips pursed. *Fuck, I really wish we didn't have an audience right now.*

"Yeah, I'm fine."

"Okay, you just zoned out for a moment."

"Someone kept me up late last night," I tease, pinching her ass. *Fuck, is she wearing a thong under this dress?*

"Hey." She playfully hits my chest. "You are the one who initiated round three. There I was, sleeping peacefully, not harming anyone. Then I woke up with you hard and rubbing against me, ready to go."

I look at her sternly. "Sleeping peacefully?" I scoff. "I woke up with you purposely rubbing your ass against me."

"Me?" She feigns innocence. "I must have been having a dream."

"It better have been about me," I growl, squeezing her ass tighter.

"Maybe," she teases. No longer caring about who's watching, I capture her bottom lip with my teeth. I work my hand between us and pull her thong to the side. My finger slides in with ease; as I thought, she's drenched. Cassie gasps as I add a second finger and my thumb rubs a circle on her button. Wasting no time, she rides my hand seeking release. I'm fucking jealous of how my fingers get to enjoy her wet, hot, velvety center. Only one of us is going to leave this car satisfied, and it won't be me. That's fine. I'll survive. I've spent weeks hard for her. I can get through one afternoon. Cassie though, I know she needs this.

Jake was right. Cassie is holding a lot back from me. I could tell that last night we didn't even skim the surface. If this is what she needs right now to help her get through this lunch, I'm happy to give it to her.

After I finish swallowing the cries of her orgasm, she goes limp against me. I carefully pull my hand from her center and reposition her thong. I suck my fingers clean, the taste leaving me painfully hard. Noticing my predicament, Cassie reaches between us, but I stop her before she makes contact.

"But you're—"

I give her one more kiss. "It's fine. We better get inside before Jake comes out here and gives us pointers."

Cassie's face goes pale. "Do you think they saw us?" She closes her sweater tightly around her.

"I'm sure most of them had the decency to walk away. Probably not Jake though."

"Oh my god." She buries herself in my shoulder. "There is no way I can go in there now."

"It'll be fine. But we better get going."

She hesitates for a moment before sliding off my lap and quickly fixing her hair and makeup in the mirror. Glancing down, I notice a wet spot on my pants. I untuck my shirt to cover it.

The relief from the orgasm was short-lived. As we walk up the porch, I can see Cassie trembling. I haven't met her family, but right now, I want nothing more than to kick all their asses. I've disagreed with my parents before. Fuck knows I've gotten into full-on fistfights with my brothers on more than one occasion. But right now, she is practically shaking from terror. Does this have something to do with more than just her family? It has to...

24

Cassie

March 31st

I CAN DO THIS. I can do this. I chant the affirmation to myself repeatedly. My pep talk is interrupted as I feel Robbie's giant hand engulf mine. "You can do this," he says with confidence.

I give him my best reassuring smile and nod. *I can DO this.* He's right—half of them already know. If Scott is as loose-lipped as everyone claims, there's a chance all of them have already heard, and this is nothing more than a formality.

We forgo knocking and enter the house. The last time I was here, the place was mostly empty with boxes piled all around. It's almost shocking to see it fully furnished, pictures now proudly displayed on the walls. With Jax being a professional photographer, I guess that shouldn't surprise me. I'm drawn to a giant floor-to-ceiling bookcase.

"It's new." Tilly startles me, confirming my suspicion.

"It's beautiful," I say in awe as I continue to admire it.

"Thank you. Jax built it for me as an early birthday present. I guess I have too many books and he wasn't satisfied with my stacking them in the corner idea. He mentioned something about babies and toppling books." She laughs. "Come on, let me show you the rest of the house."

Tilly walks me around, showing me the changes they have made since moving in barely a month ago. It seems impending babies are an excellent motivator for getting your house unpacked.

"This will be the babies' nursery." She absentmindedly rubs her belly. It's the only unfinished room in the house. "I was saving it for last. That way, I can take my time."

"You've done such an amazing job."

"I honestly didn't have to do much. At its core, the house is beautiful. My parents did an outstanding job keeping everything up-to-date while it was rented out. My mom always had an eye for detail when it came to decorating. I can't wait to see the gardens in full bloom. Truthfully, all we had to do was unpack a few boxes and hang up some artwork. This is the only room we are actually doing anything with."

"How've you been feeling?"

Tilly groans. "Good. I mean, except for feeling like I might topple over some mornings. Sometimes I worry about how big they will get. I'm not even in my third trimester yet, and I do not know how they can get any larger. Oh, I'm also convinced they are street fighting in there some days."

I laugh at the visual.

"Tilly." I hear Jax yell from downstairs. "Burgers are done."

At that, both of our stomachs grumble. We make our way downstairs and see that Jax has the kitchen counter set up buffet-style with assorted toppings. Everything smells delicious. Looking around, I notice two stacks of patties that appear almost identical.

"Okay, here is how it's going to go," Jake explains, holding color-coded flags in his hands. "Everyone is going to craft two burgers, one seasoned by the blue team and one by the red team, and add the corresponding flag. You will then use these cards." Jake holds them up. "To write down which burger you thought was the best. Once finished, we will add up the votes and determine who the official burger champion is. Only Scott and Jax know who prepared what. So, there will be no cheating."

"What's going on?" I lean up and murmur to Robbie.

Robbie whispers in my ear, the heat of his breath sending a shiver down my spine. "I guess they got into an argument about who makes the better burger. They decided to use today's cookout to declare a champion."

"What will the winner get?"

"Why, Cassie, thank you for asking. Isn't she as smart as she is beautiful, folks?" Jake says, acting like a game show host. "The winner will get their burger featured on Harper's menu and named after them."

"It won't be Harper's for much longer." That's when I notice Letty. I'm shocked to see her giving me the stink eye. *Why is she mad at me?* The nerves that I hoped were gone are now back. I thought this was going to be easy. But I haven't even said anything yet and I'm getting nasty glares.

After dishing up and flagging our burgers, we all sit down to eat. Taking a bite of the red burger, I moan. It is so delicious and flavorful. I love the unique mixture of spices. I take a few forkfuls of my salad before biting into the blue burger, which is equally delicious. *Damn, they are both good.* This one has a more classic and smokey flavor.

Looking next to me, I notice both of Robbie's burgers are already practically devoured. "Which one are you voting for?"

"Scott's," he says confidently.

"They are anonymous. How do you know?"

"Scott has been cooking meals in our house for decades. I know how he seasons his food."

"Well, don't spoil it for the rest of us," Jake remarks as he inspects each burger before making notes. Amusingly, he is taking this competition very seriously. After the brief time of living with Jake though, I know how much he loves these little games. We've even played a few when we've hung out. I never thought a simple game of Cribbage could be so cutthroat, until we played together. And don't even get me started on Battleship... It makes me miss my brothers. They were always so competitive growing up. I'm sure they'd love this.

"Has everyone cast their votes?" Jake inquires. We all nod, passing our votes over to Jake. He quickly goes through them and makes a note as to who the winner is. "This is a close one, folks... Winning three to two is... drumroll, please." Letty excitedly taps on the table to build anticipation. "The blue burger!"

"Yes," Scott cheers, jumping from his seat. Jax drops his head in defeat as Tilly rubs comforting circles on his back. "In your face!"

"Now that's just unsportsmanlike," Jax protests.

Scott crosses his arms. "Yeah, like you loosening the lid on the saltshaker wasn't attempted sabotage?"

"I thought they tasted saltier than normal," Robbie adds to the commentary.

As the boys argue over the winner, I use the opportunity to try to make small talk with Letty. "Have you picked out a name yet?"

"No," she says flatly, stabbing at her plate. What did I do? I saw her the other night when I picked up dinner on my way home. Everything seemed fine then. Did she already find out about the baby? *Does she have a thing for Robbie?*

"I have some news." Robbie gathers everyone's attention, causing my heart rate to speed up. Tilly and Letty are best friends. If Letty hates me, Tilly will for sure. If Tilly hates me, Jax and Jake will. Then Scott. *I can't do this.*

"What's going on?" Tilly asks excitedly. "Are you finally moving forward with the expansion?"

"Yes, well, we are working on it. But that isn't the news."

Tilly looks between the two of us, studying us carefully. "Well, out with it already!" she whines.

"We are having a baby."

"Robbie!" Tilly jumps up (as much as that's physically possible) and launches herself at Robbie, hitting him with a pillow she was sitting on. "What the hell is wrong with you? Out of everyone, I never expected you'd be the one to go and knock-up my friend."

I sit there stunned; I told him everyone wouldn't be as accepting of this. Great, now Letty *and* Tilly hate me.

Unfazed by Tilly's attack, Robbie holds up his arm, defending himself. "Tilly," he says sternly. "Do I really need to bring up the irony of what you are saying right now?"

At that, Tilly stops her assault before looking back at Jax and Scott, who are both laughing hysterically. "Pot meet kettle," Scott spits out.

Tilly scrunches up her nose. "Can you blame me? Yes, I get it. These babies weren't exactly planned. But at least Jax and I had history. When Cassie came here, I had *the talk* with Jake. I even talked with Scott. I just never imagined I'd need to have the talk with *you*." Tilly taps her chin. "Now that I think about it though, you are both perfect for each other."

"Wait!" Robbie seems insulted. "You never considered the possibility of Cassie and me hooking up?"

"No, I bet on Scott. He seemed more like her type." She motions to Jax, who pulls out his wallet and tosses two hundred-dollar bills at Jake.

"My money was on Jake." Jax shrugs. Jake takes the money, kissing each bill before folding and placing them in his own wallet.

It's my turn to give Tilly a look. "Oh, don't give me that look, Cassie. If I go through the list of your exes from college, Scott fits the bill. Tall, dark hair, tattoos, intellectual, can keep you supplied in coffee and baked goods, not to mention a total romantic. The only thing he's missing is a Harley. Besides, I thought it would be kind of cool. You know, Scott and Jax being best friends, us being friends. We could double date. I guess we still could. Hmm... maybe Letty?" Tilly looks at Letty, who is now shaking her head at the mere suggestion she should date Scott.

"It's nothing personal, Scott. But that combination will not work, Tilly."

Tilly shrugs. "Yeah, you're right. It's why I never tried before. He needs a nice, girl-next-door type—*no offense*. But you know what I mean, right?"

"Yup, I agree," Letty replies.

"Oh well, we will find someone for you, Scott." Tilly silently counts names on her fingers.

"Hey," Scott interjects, seemingly insulted. "I don't need my little sister's help finding a girlfriend. I'm getting out there and doing just fine on my own."

"Didn't your last date try to pull a Jedi mind trick on you?" Jax bursts out laughing, and everyone else follows suit. I'd laugh too if I wasn't so thrown off by the exchange right now. "Take me home, you will." Jax reenacts what I assume was the girl's pickup line.

"Don't worry, Scott, your brother will help you out," Jake offers proudly.

"Clean out your ears, Jakey-poo. He's looking for a girlfriend, not a hookup." Letty crosses her arms.

"So, you aren't mad?" I ask so quietly I'm not sure anyone hears me. But as everyone stops making fun of Scott and turns their attention back to me, it's like time has frozen for a moment. I prepare myself for the worst. But as everything comes back into motion, I'm surprised to see a very pregnant, crying Tilly rushing at me with her arms wide open.

"Of course not. I'm so excited. We are going to have babies." She bounces enthusiastically. "Oh my god, are you having twins also? How awesome would that be?"

Tears begin to fall at the realization that she doesn't hate me. Then what she just asked registers. "What?" I hadn't even thought of that. "I don't know... I'm not that far along. We haven't even had an ultrasound yet."

"Take that, Letty. I get to be godfather to three now," Jake taunts Letty, who is now smiling.

Crossing her arms, she snips back, "It's not about quantity; it's quality."

That's when it finally dawns on me. Letty wasn't mad about Robbie. She thought I was hooking up with Jake. *Oh my god, Letty was jealous.* That makes so much more sense now. I remember back in the day, all she would ever do is complain about Jake. I feel like such a dork.

But like Robbie said, everyone seems okay with this turn of events. Scott and Jake rubbed the fact that they knew first (and kept it a secret) into Jax's and Tilly's faces. Apparently, there is some story there... Then there was an argument over who was going to be the godparents to whose children. And somewhere in the mix, Tilly began telling me WAY too much about pregnancy. I'm a little overwhelmed, but I can't seem to wipe the smile off my face. This is how it is supposed to be. Everyone celebrating.

25

Robbie

April 12th

I DON'T WANT TO jinx it, but I think everything is going well. After we told my family, Cassie seemed to relax. As promised, while working together we've remained professional (well, *mostly*). There might have been a few stolen kisses when we were alone. I objected a bit when she said she didn't want to tell the guys yet. I respect her need for boundaries, but I don't enjoy pretending that we aren't together. Given what I know of her last relationship, I get wanting to ease into it. This is a small town—it's actually pretty fucking surprising that most don't know about us already. That will change soon enough, especially when she starts to show.

With the hours I keep at the shop—between actually being on the clock, project time, and on-call duty for the tow—it is super convenient working together. The only thing that would make it better is if we lived together. Then, even if I did get home late, I could see her before bed or first thing in the morning. This is how it was supposed to be. A partnership, something Bianca never understood. Cassie and I work together like a well-oiled machine. Then, outside of the shop, well, everything works amazingly well there too. She is so laid back. Like Saturday night, she stayed with me.

I was covering the on-call for Chris because he had some shit going on. As expected, I got a call during the middle of our movie. Cassie gave me a kiss and told me to be safe. Bianca would have flipped out.

"Boss, we got a situation," Mack calls to me from the back.

I rush over to see what is going on. He is leaning outside the bathroom door. "Shitter clogged again?"

"No, I think Cassie is sick," Mack states, frowning as he glances at the door.

I walk to the bathroom door and knock softly. "Hey, Cassie, are you feeling all right?"

"I'm fine," she says in a pained tone that is muffled by the door.

Mack wrinkles his brow before shaking his head. "No, she is not fine. We were talking up front. Then all of a sudden, she looked green and ran off to the bathroom. I'm guessing with some of the sound effects I've heard, she is throwing up."

I breathe a sigh of relief—it is probably just morning sickness. I pat him on the shoulder. "I'm sure she will be fine, Mack. I'll take care of it," I say, giving him a reassuring smile.

"Thanks, man. I'd go in there and check on her. But you know how I am a sympathetic vomiter. Just listening to her out here, I've almost thrown up twice."

"No worries. I'll get her situated, okay?" Mack nods before walking back to the bays. I test the doorknob and thankfully it isn't locked. I slip into the bathroom, and poor Cassie is sitting on the floor with her head leaning on the side of the toilet. We keep the shop clean, especially the bathroom. Even so, something about seeing her head on a public toilet makes me want to puke. "Morning sickness?" I ask quietly, in case any of the guys walk by. Squatting down beside her, I rub her back.

"Yeah, I don't understand. Until now, I've felt great."

"Tilly told me it is different for everyone. She didn't really start getting sick until the second trimester. So far, it hasn't let up."

Cassie groans. "I really hope that isn't the case."

I chuckle empathetically. For her sake, and well, I guess mine, I hope not either. "Cass, clearly today isn't a good day for you. Why don't you go upstairs and lie down? After I close up, I will stop by the diner and get you some soup."

"I should be fine now," she says, stumbling as she tries to get up.

"No, babe, you aren't. I'd feel better if you went upstairs and rested."

"Fine." She rolls her eyes at me.

I help her up off the bathroom floor and to the sink. I quickly wash off some of the vomit from her chin. Once she's ready, we walk down the hall towards the back exit. Fortunately, my apartment has two entry points: one from the sidewalk, and one from the back of the shop. Cassie seems a little weak right now. I scoop her up into my arms before she can protest.

"Hey, I can walk, you know."

"Sure you can, sweetheart. But I'd prefer carrying you over taking the risk of you falling down the stairs," I say, giving her a half grin.

"What's with the *sweetheart* and *babe*?"

I think for a moment. I realize I've never called her by a pet name before. I shrug my shoulders. "I guess I'm trying out some names, seeing what sticks."

Cassie scrunches up her nose. "I've never been a big fan of pet names."

"No?" I ask. Walking us through the door, I gently set her down on my bed. "Well, what do you like to be called?"

I look down at Cassie as she blushes slightly. "Umm," she stalls.

"You better tell me, honey, otherwise I am going to keep trying all these silly names until I find the one that fits."

She gives me an exhausted laugh. "Fine, I guess I really like it when you call me Cass."

"Cass, really?"

She nods her head at me. "Yeah, I mean mostly everyone has called me Cassie growing up. But I like Cass. It makes me think of my favorite show, *Supernatural*."

I think back for a moment. "Is that the show you were telling me about. The one with the two brothers hunting demons?"

"Yeah, that's the one. He is one of my favorite characters on the show."

I kiss her on the forehead. "Well then, Cass it is. Maybe we can watch it together some time."

She shakes her head at me. "No, I won't make you do that. It is a good show, but we have already talked about you not liking horror. I don't want to make you watch my show during your downtime."

I shrug, getting up from the bed and walking over to the kitchen to get her a glass of water and a bowl. "Hey, I will give it a shot. Tilly and Jake have had me watch a few good horror movies before. I don't hate them. I'm just not a fan of those campy slasher films with too much fake blood and bad special effects. Besides, it would be something fun to do with you."

"Okay, that would be nice."

"Here," I say, handing her the glass of water and setting the bowl beside my bed. "Try to stay hydrated but take small sips. Here is a bowl if you feel like you might be sick and can't make it to the bathroom. I don't want you rushing off and falling or hurting yourself."

Cassie rolls her eyes at me. "You are going to be one of those guys, aren't you?" I give her a quizzical glance, so she elaborates. "Ugh, one of those guys who treats a pregnant woman like she's made of glass."

I smile. "I ordered a bubble wrap suit for you the other day online."

"No, you didn't." She laughs and pushes at my chest playfully.

"Maybe not." I shrug noncommittally. "But of course, I am going to look after you and my baby. What kind of asshole would I be if I didn't take care of my girlfriend?"

"Girlfriend, huh? I didn't realize we were to the point of labeling our relationship." Cassie's tone is uncertain. I can't tell if she is happy or not, by how I reference our relationship.

"What would you call it?" I ask flatly.

"I don't know. We haven't been seeing each other that long. You told me that since your divorce, you've hardly even dated, let alone had a girlfriend. I get we are kind of in a unique situation right now. But I don't want us rushing into anything, just because you feel obligated to try to be with me."

Cassie's words are like a punch in the gut. I agree; we haven't been dating that long, but I didn't think this was that far of a stretch, especially considering we've spent almost every minute together. Not wanting to argue with her about this right now, I give her a small smile before getting up and walking to the door. "You should get some rest; I'll bring you some soup after we close up."

"Robbie, wait. I didn't mean—"

I hold my hand up, cutting her off. "Don't worry about it," I say as I walk out of the apartment. I take a few deep breaths, attempting to calm my nerves before heading back to the shop. I get that saying we should get married might have been a bit extreme, even though I still think it is the right thing to do. I can accept her hesitation at that. But we are dating, we seem to get along, the sex is amazing, and we are about to have a fucking child together. If not married, the least we could do is be in some sort of committed relationship.

Not wanting to get myself worked up, I shake the thoughts from my head. We have time, thirty-two more weeks to be exact. Granted, we have a lot to figure out in that timeframe.

Like a place to live. My family home makes the most sense, but I don't really want to kick Jake out. I guess we wouldn't have to. I make a mental note to talk with Jake about it later.

After an hour of wrenching on this Suburban I've been toying with since this morning, the door chimes in the lobby. Realizing Mack and Chris are elbow-deep in their own work right now, I stand. "I'll get it," I yell to them before they stop what they are doing. I'm the one who sent Cassie upstairs after all—the least I can do is cover for her.

Once I'm up front, I see two big guys in the lobby. The dude with tattoos (who seems strangely familiar) looks me up and down, before giving me an evil grin. "You Robbie?" he asks.

I stand with my arms crossed, not letting either of these asshats intimidate me in my own shop. They are both clearly fit, and based on the scarring on the tattooed one's knuckles, it seems he has been in a fight more than once. The second male, he has those cold, calculating eyes that let you know he has seen some shit and has possibly killed a man at least once in his lifetime. "Yeah, that's me," I reply with a sigh when realization dawns on me. As their glances turn murderous, I know what's about to happen. Before I have a chance to block it, a fist collides with my jaw.

26

Cassie

April 12th

"*DARN IT!*" I HUFF out, rubbing my eyes. Everything has been going so well. I didn't mean to upset him. I get that saying we are a couple isn't that big of a deal. It just feels too soon. I promised myself I wouldn't rush in. *It's what you always do*, that nagging voice reminds me, and she is right. I always close my eyes and freefall into a relationship. As soon as the spark or the connection is there, I just go for it. But not this time—*it's about more than just me now.*

No longer feeling nauseated, but still gross, I get off the bed and make my way to the bathroom to take a shower. Glancing around, I notice I don't have a single thing here, further proof of how new this relationship is. I don't even have a scrunchie lying around yet. The hot water from the shower helps loosen some of the tension in my body. The smell of Robbie's mint and eucalyptus bodywash mixed with the hot steam of the shower makes it feel like a spa in here.

Once finished, I wrap up in one of Robbie's giant soft towels. The thing is so huge I could probably use it as a throw blanket. Although this place has the bare minimum—what you'd expect from any other bachelor pad—Robbie definitely enjoys a few luxuries. The thought makes me smile. Such a masculine guy has the coziest towels I've ever used, and spa-quality soaps. I glance at the label and see it's made by a local goat farmer. I smile. Robbie loves his town. I notice most of what he owns or purchases is homegrown. If not from the town, within the state at least.

Picking up my clothes to get dressed, I immediately gag. They reek of vomit. There is no way I can put these back on. I quickly toss them in the tiny stacked washer he has in his kitchen. Looking around in his dresser, I grab a black t-shirt and throw my underwear back on—*at least I didn't get vomit on them*. He is far too big for me to wear a pair of his pants. Whatever, it is just temporary until my clothes are cleaned—it isn't like he hasn't seen me naked before. I snuggle up in his bed, loving the slight sent of motor oil and gasoline everything has. That, mixed with the scent of his soap on my skin, makes me smile.

Grabbing the remote, I turn on the little TV he has. It still shocks me that he doesn't have some sort of streaming service, just a Blu-ray player and cable. Not wanting to get up and grab a movie from the shelf, which there aren't many to choose from anyway, I flip through the channels, finally settling on watching some random movie on Syfy.

I must have dozed off; it is crazy how many little naps I take now, since becoming pregnant. I'm startled awake by some commotion downstairs. Not thinking, I get up and quickly rush down to the shop. The sight before me stops me dead in my tracks. Robbie's face is bloody and swollen, and Killian is about to throw another punch. "Stop it!" I yell. My brothers turn to stare at me.

This gives Robbie a brief opening, which he takes in order to deck Killian in the jaw. They are about to go at it again when I rush forward, working my way between the two. "Seriously, stop this. What are you even doing here?" I turn and ask Killian.

"We haven't heard from you in almost a month. I was worried that this asshole had you locked away or some shit," Killian hollers, attempting to throw a jab at Robbie again.

"Taobh amuigh, anois," I order my brothers to go outside. Robbie gives me a confused look.

"Dáiríre?" Killian whines, gesturing to Robbie.

"Yes, now!" I yell. Both of my siblings look a little sheepish. But thankfully they back off and head out the door. "Are you okay?" I ask Robbie, inspecting his face.

I go to touch his cheek; he hisses at my caress. "Peachy," he groans out sarcastically. "So, I finally got to meet your brothers."

"Yeah, I'm sorry, Robbie. While they can be a little hotheaded, I never imagined in a million years they would actually come here, let alone hurt you."

"Do I need to call the sheriff?" Mack asks from the doorway, carefully studying my appearance and my proximity to my boss.

I don't reply. Instead, I look to Robbie. Even though I don't want them getting in trouble, they did just enter his place of business and assault him. He has every right to press charges. Robbie's features soften, likely noticing the worried expression on my face. "Nah, Mack, it is fine. No need to get either of the Laffertys involved in this."

"Thank you, Robbie," I say relieved. "I'll go out there and talk to them. You won't have to see them again, I promise."

"There is no way I am letting you go out there!" he replies sternly.

"Excuse me?" I cross my arms over my chest. "They are my brothers; I will handle it. They may be jerks, but they would never hurt me."

He runs his hand exhaustedly over his face, wincing when he comes in contact with his bruising flesh. "You are not going outside like that, Cass." He points down to my legs, which I now realize are as bare as my feet.

In all the panic, I completely forgot I was wearing nothing but his shirt and my underwear. Glancing over to Mack, I notice him checking me out and giving me an approving nod. Robbie seems to see this as well and shoots him a terrifying look. "Stop staring at her and get back to work, you pervert."

Mack laughs. Walking away, he mumbles, "I fucking knew it."

"Here," Robbie says, walking around the corner and coming back with blue coveralls. "They are going to be way too big, but it's better than you standing around half naked." I slip the jumpsuit on before thanking him.

I turn towards the window and notice Cian looking in, his arms crossed as he studies us intently. I know that expression—if I don't come out there soon, they will barge back in. The last thing I want is for another fight to breakout.

"I'm going to go talk to them," I say, then give Robbie a soft kiss on his cheek, not wanting to hurt him.

He nods in agreement, and I turn to walk outside. Killian is pacing, likely pumped with adrenaline. He always gets this way when he fights. Cian is still glaring at Robbie through the window, probably not missing the kiss I just gave him.

As soon as Killian notices me, he rushes over and swoops me up into a hug. "I've missed you so much, Cassie."

I push him away, though I see his pained expression. "Whose fault is that?"

"No fair. You drop a major fucking bomb on us and then snuck out of town."

"Yeah, there was no way I was going to stick around listening to the both of you lecture me on what a screw up I am. *There's Cassie, screwing her boss... again*," I mock with a masculine voice.

"Don't be so overdramatic, Cassie. Even you have to admit this whole situation is fucked up," Cian states, getting straight to the point.

"I will admit it isn't ideal. But it isn't as terrible as you're making it out to be," I reply, crossing my arms defensively over my chest.

"Yes, it is," Cian states coldly. "You just got out of that shit show of a relationship with that manipulative asshole. Not to mention, the string of douchebag exes you had before him. Then you run off to some shit town, hook up with the first asshole you can find and get knocked up. It's fucked up. Cassie, your life is ruined. When this thing with him fails..." *Like they all do,* I chastise myself internally. "...you are going to be stuck with that baby—there is no moving on from that."

"It's not ruined, Cian," I yell. "I made a bad judgement call with Chad. But stop treating me like some sort of screw up. One time, ever, I went out drinking and had a one-night stand. This isn't some sort of common routine of mine. Sometimes these things happen."

"You were drunk?" Cian growls, I can see the fury boiling inside of him.

"He took advantage of you!" Killian booms, his calm demeanor gone.

"No! Now stop it. Yes, we were drinking, but I knew exactly what we were doing. It's just..." I let out a sigh. "You are going to make me say it, aren't you?" One look at my brothers tells me I am not going to be able to walk away without getting everything out there. "I can't believe I am about to say this to my brothers. Look, there had been this crazy intense sexual tension there all week. I dismissed it, not interested in pursuing anything. Especially because of the whole Chad debacle. I meant what I said when I told you guys that I was moving here. I wanted a fresh start. The last thing I intended was to kick it off by making the same mistakes again. I fully planned to take a break from dating and just focus on me for a while. Then we were at the bar, and I kicked his ass doing shots. One thing led to another, and well, I'm not giving you a play-by-play of the rest. Now seriously, you both look me in the eye and tell me that neither of you have ever had some drunken, lust-filled one-night stand."

My brothers look sheepishly between each other. "Fine, but still. You need to come home, Cassie. Ma is worried sick about you."

"Clearly she is *really* worried, since she hasn't bothered to call me once," I sneer back at Cian sarcastically. The flash of sadness tells me all I need to know. She might be worried, but it is more about her reputation than about me.

Cian's features soften. "Being a single mother is going to be difficult. Come back with me. I'll get us a place and help you both out. Eventually, Ma and Da will realize how stupid and hypocritical they're being. You should be with your family; we'll take care of you."

I'm about to ask what they are being hypocritical about when a loud voice booms behind me, sending a shiver down my spine. "What makes you think she will be a single mom?"

"Robbie, please go back inside. Let me handle this," I say, still keeping my eyes on Killian. I notice his fists clenching, and I am not about to let him hit Robbie again.

"No, Cass." I feel my lips turn up at the name. "Look, I've listened to enough of this bullshit. I get that you guys just want to protect your sister. Obviously, if Tilly were in a fucked-up situation, I'd want to kick the guy's ass too. But I am trying to do the right thing here. I fully intend on taking care of your sister and the baby. When she told me, I offered to marry her right then and there—"

"You're engaged," Killian states, seeming almost relieved by the unintended announcement.

I don't get a chance to correct them before Robbie comes up, draping his arm over my shoulder. "Yes, we are."

Shit, what the heck is Robbie thinking? Seeing the smile on Kill's face, I understand. *Robbie's just doing what he thinks is right—telling them what any big brother would want to hear, that their baby sister is being taken care of.*

168

"Is that true?" Cian asks, eyeing me suspiciously (not nearly as convinced as Kill).

"Yes," I admit, though reluctantly.

"This is great!" Killian yells before scooping me up in a big hug. "Ma is going to be so happy. She's been crying since you left... going on about her unmarried daughter getting knocked up."

"Yeah, well, she also needs to learn this isn't the Stone Age anymore," I grunt. "Are you going to apologize to my fiancé?"

"Shit, I'm sorry, man. You get it, right?" Killian shrugs his shoulders as though coming into someone's place of business and decking him in the face is normal man-speak.

"Yeah, I get it," Robbie replies with a similar lack of concern.

"Let's get a bite to eat. I'm starving," Kill smiles, rubbing his belly—and that's just like my brother. Sometimes I think the only things he cares about in this world are booze, food, and fighting.

"Sure, I know the place with the best burgers in town," Robbie says with a grin.

27

Robbie

April 12th

"OH. MY. GOD," THE fourth girl this evening says excitedly. "I can't believe K.O. Murphy is here, in Tral Lake." The girl squeals, "Can I please take a selfie with you?"

Killian gives her a gigantic smile, his split lip making him look like a madman. "Aye, sure thing, lass." He gets up and poses with his most recent admirer, listening to her talk about how jealous her dad is going to be, before he offers her an autograph. I suppress my laughter. I've noticed that whenever a fan comes near, he plays up the Irish thing, just like he did in his fighting days. I guess that is all part of his persona. Because when he is back to being just Killian, Cassie's big brother, he sounds like any other Minnesota-grown boy.

"I think I should start visiting small towns more often," he leans in and whispers after the girl scurries off. "I don't get this kind of attention at home."

Cassie has been nervously fidgeting next to me. When her brothers asked to go out to dinner, I knew she wasn't exactly thrilled. I won't lie—part of me wanted to send them on their way. But I have a feeling as soon as we are alone, Cassie is going to lay into me. *We're engaged.* What the hell was

I thinking? That's right... I wasn't. My dumbass just put Cassie between a rock and a hard place. I just really hope when this night is over, I haven't lost her. Because as it stands now, she hasn't even glanced at me since the whole exchange.

"Tell me about the garage. What kind of work do you do?" Cian interrogates. He's tough. I can't get a read on him. Fuck, I'm not sure even Jake could. I considered inviting him down to stop in and say hi. But the jackass is working tonight. While Killian seems to be accepting of Cassie and me now that we are getting married, Cian has seemed unfazed. I'm not sure if that is because he doesn't believe us, or because he doesn't care. I feel as though he couldn't care less if Cass had a baby with, or without the father in the picture. He'd drop everything and make sure they were both provided for. I know it's what I'd do for Tilly.

"Not much to tell really. We do basic maintenance and bodywork."

"That's an understatement," Cassie offers. "The place is practically bursting at the seams with business; he does everything. In addition, he also performs house calls for farm equipment maintenance and has the only tow truck in the area." The pride in her tone has me holding on to the tiniest thread of hope; she doesn't seem to hate me *at the moment*.

"Impressive." Cian takes a sip of his beer. "The shop seems small for that much work."

"Yeah, but Robbie is actually looking into expanding to a second location."

"Opening another shop, that is going to be a lot of work," Killian interjects; thankfully he seems more conversational than his brother. "I remember when I first opened the bar. Sean and I practically lived there for the first couple of years. It seems like only recently I feel comfortable enough to take a night off—especially on a weekend."

"Yeah, it's why I moved into the apartment above the shop originally. Additionally, my house was full, and they needed the extra bedroom."

"It won't be easy with planning a wedding. I assume it will be soon, before she starts showing. Plus, with a new baby," Cian states, "you'll be gone a lot. Not to mention, shorthanded while Cassie is on leave. Have you decided where you are going to live? I'm guessing in town won't be practical, depending on where you end up opening a second location."

"Cian," Cassie scolds. "We haven't discussed any of that yet."

Cian holds up his hands defensively. "I'm just making conversation. Stating facts. These are things you should be thinking about, Cassie."

"I know that, but we have time. This is a discussion I'd much rather have with Robbie—*alone*." Cian opens his mouth to say something, but Cassie cuts him off, scolding him in a language I don't understand. Once she's finished though, Cian seems to relax a bit—well, as much as someone like him *can* relax.

"So, Moore Body and Lube..." Killian chuckles, attempting to break the tense stare down between his siblings.

"Yeah, I lost a bet to my brother." I groan into my beer.

Killian and Cian both laugh. It seems we might have found a safe topic of discussion for the moment. As much as I hate reliving this embarrassment, I decide to tell them about it.

"I had the shop open for about five years at that point. Things were taking off. I'd been thinking of changing the name. It was originally Tral Lake Auto Services. Like an idiot, I made a bet with my brother at the start of the playoffs, siding with the Vikings to win the Superbowl." The Murphy brothers laugh. "Yeah, well, we lost to the Saints in the NFC Championship and Jake got the honor of naming my shop. Definitely not the sort of power you want to give a nineteen-year-old kid."

"What would have happened if you won?" Cassie asks.

"I would get to pick his next tattoo," I say with a big smile.

"You guys like high stakes; that is awesome." Killian laughs again.

"I was wondering what all the commotion was about... Now I see," Letty interjects, eyeing up the local celebrity in our midst.

"Hey, Letty. Sorry about that. My brothers are visiting and asked where they could get the best burgers in town," Cassie explains.

"No need to apologize. This is the most packed I've seen it in here since St. Paddy's Day."

"Aye, got a lot of Irish around here?" Killian puts on his charm. Letty rolls her eyes. Growing up with Jake (plus working at the bar), she's immune to these sorts of antics.

"Everyone thinks they're Irish that night. You can drop the act, Killian; I know you aren't as green as you're pretending."

"Act?" He feigns insult.

It's Cassie's turn to roll her eyes. "Kill, this is Letty. You've met her several times. She's Tilly's best friend."

As recognition dawns on him, his demeanor completely changes. "Letitia, wow, I didn't even recognize you. I love the pink and the ink. How've you been?"

"Good, I actually own this place—well, mostly."

"Seriously, it's impressive. If you ever need any tips or connections, let me know. I have an in with most distributors in the area."

"Thanks, I appreciate that. In the meantime, what can I get for everyone?"

"Surprise me with the house special. Also, can we get a few glasses of champagne and something sparkling for Cassie here—we need something to toast with."

"Oh yeah, you guys celebrating the baby?" Letty looks panicked at Cassie for a moment, not sure if she just unintentionally opened a can of worms.

"That and the engagement." Nope, it seems Killian is the one who tossed out, opened, and obliterated *that can* all at once.

"You guys are engaged? Oh my god!" Letty shouts excitedly, gaining the attention of the surrounding townsfolk. *Fuck*, by tomorrow morning, everyone is going to hear.

"You didn't know," Cian states skeptically.

"It just happened," Cassie clarifies with a forced smile and clenched teeth.

"We haven't told anyone yet. Figured one surprise at a time," I add to the story.

"Shit, man, sorry... I didn't think. I just assumed," Killian apologizes.

"Oh my god, Tilly is going to freak." I eye Letty, silently urging her to keep her mouth shut. "Don't worry, my lips are sealed."

Letty takes our order and the rest of dinner goes smoother. Killian did most of the talking, sharing some stories about his fighting days. He also ended up doing several more autographs and photo ops. The bar was packed with people who wanted to catch a glimpse of K.O. Murphy.

Once we were finished eating, I could tell Cassie was eager to get out of there. I'm sure part of her enjoyed seeing her brothers today, even with the fight and lying about the engagement. But it's drained a lot out of her. That, or she is gearing up to rip me a new one.

"Well, I think we should start heading home." Cian seems to notice that Cassie's ready to call it a night too.

Killian glances at his watch. "Yeah, if we get going now, I'll make it to the pub as it gets busy. Not that Sean can't handle it, but I like to at least make an appearance." Killian pulls his sister into a hug before turning and shaking my hand. "I'm sorry about earlier."

"No hard feelings."

Cian leans in and gives Cassie a hug, whispering something in her ear. When they part, I can tell that whatever he just said is upsetting her, which pisses me off. But she says nothing, and I don't feel like starting another fight when they are about to leave.

After they're gone, Cassie remains silent. I'm not sure if she is still troubled by whatever Cian said, or just eager to tear my head from my body. Once inside my apartment, I prepare for the yelling and screaming to begin. For her to pick up the nearest object and throw it at my head. I'm surprised when she kicks off her shoes and crawls on the bed before grabbing the remote and getting comfortable to watch a movie.

Not able to handle the suspense any longer, I make the first move. "Okay, Cassie. Let me have it."

"Have what?" She sounds genuinely unaware of what I'm talking about.

"Well, I kind of made us engaged tonight. You've made it pretty damn clear you don't want to get married. Now your family, and probably by now mine, think we're about to get hitched—*soon*."

"Yeah." She shrugs. "You were just doing what you thought was right. It obviously seemed to satisfy my brothers."

"Okay, so what do you want to do?"

"Do you not want to get married?" She arches her brow at me.

"No, I just know—"

"Well then, it's settled... we are getting married." With that, Cassie turns on a movie and snuggles under the blanket. I should feel happy now. I'm getting exactly what I wanted. Then why does it feel like she just dropkicked me?

28

Cassie

April 17th

"You made it." Tilly waddles over to me as I enter Moore Books and Coffee. Jax tries to get her to sit back down, but she just waves him off. "I sit all damn day, Jax. The doctor said it's healthy for me to get up and walk around." He grumbles something about wanting a second opinion. Tilly rolls her eyes before attempting to hug me. "How's my soon to be sister-in-law feeling?"

I thought Tilly was excited when we told her about the baby... No joke, after the barbeque, she has texted me daily with nonstop baby talk. It's a little overwhelming, but it's nice to have someone to discuss this stuff with. That being said, now that we've told everyone about the engagement, the texts have doubled. We are supposed to go to my parents' house this weekend and tell them we are getting married. I wanted to just call and inform them, but Kill was pretty adamant that I needed to do it in person. Oh, I also have to bring Robbie. Killian is positive that once we announce our pending nuptials, everything will be good. But I'm not holding my breath—and neither is Cian.

"I'm not sure what the hell you are doing, Cassie. But WHEN you change your mind, I don't care what time it is, call me. I'll come get you."

You know how Jake is good at getting a read on someone? Well, my eldest brother isn't just good; he's a master. There is no getting anything past him. I'd say it has something to do with his military training, but he has always been this way. The Army just helped him perfect the skill and put it to good use. Initially, I was mad at Robbie. But then, seeing how relieved Kill was—he's convinced it will fix everything with our parents—and how thrilled Letty was, I started thinking maybe this *is* the right thing to do.

It's not like I don't have feelings for Robbie. I do. If I let my heart take the lead for a bit, I'm sure she'd be head over heels with him by now. But she doesn't get to come out and play just yet. Not until Robbie is ready. While this isn't the magical fairytale I'd imagined growing up, looking at the situation logically and rationally, this seems like the best course of action. I'm just going to do things a little out of order. *Robbie and Cassie sitting in a tree, K-I-S-S-I-N-G, first comes the baby, then comes marriage, then hopefully comes the love.* If not, two out of three isn't bad.

"How are you feeling?" Tilly leans in and whispers as she gives me the best hug she can.

"Good." Mostly anyway. I am definitely dreading our checkup in a couple of weeks. It will be my first ultrasound, and to be honest, I am terrified. Not that I don't want to see the baby, it's just... what if there are two of them? My brief internet search eased my fear a bit, saying that the family history of twins is more relevant in the mother than the father. But given my luck recently, I will not breathe easy until I see only one happy peanut.

"I am so excited," she squeals. "Now with the wedding. I just can't wait. Have you started planning yet? Oh, who am I kidding? I'm sure you already have everything lined up."

"Oh, not yet..."

"You need help, let me know. Patty makes the best wedding cakes, well, any kind of cake. I never really liked sweets before, but with these two, I can't stop stuffing them down. Oh, Scarlett, she runs the Inn; it's absolutely stunning. It's where we are hosting the baby shower. That would be a perfect venue for the reception. Oh, or the apple orchard. Jax has been working with Eli to showcase it as the new hot wedding destination in this area. I'm sure Jax would be happy to take the pictures. We can get everything planned, don't worry."

Funny enough, I haven't been worrying about it... I'd always imagined some giant wedding with all the frills. It's what I was planning with Chad—the wedding of the year. Now, though, something small and intimate sounds more appropriate. I'm not sure if it is because I know this wedding is nothing more than a formality—checking off a box on the to-do list Robbie has. Or if it's because after Chad, I suddenly realize how ridiculous those wedding plans were? Like we were overcompensating for something—I guess we were.

Grabbing a muffin and some tea, I take a seat next to Patty as Tilly goes and greets Scarlett.

After everyone gets settled for the book club meeting, we discuss the novel we read last week, *Torment: Part One* by Dylan Page.

"Okay, who wants to start?" Tilly claps her hands excitedly. She loves nothing more than discussing our latest reads, but she usually lets others initiate the conversation. She tries to facilitate the group more than anything.

"I'm not even sure where to begin," Michelle states. I've only been a part of the club for a couple of weeks. I've learned that Michelle is the local Sunday school teacher. Tilly has told me about some of the books Scarlett has recommended to the group, and to say I was shocked is a grave understatement (though it has little to do with the fact that Scarlett actually reads these books). From the brief interactions we've had, her reading preferences are not surprising. No, it astonished me that some of these seemingly clean-cut and uptight women could read a book like this with an open mind.

"Let's start with Shay." Patty fans herself. "If I were young again, I'd definitely be jumping on his hog, *if you know what I mean.*" She then elbows a shocked Sally. How anyone is surprised by her antics, I don't understand? Patty is the cool grandma every girl wishes she had. Not that my Nana isn't awesome. But there is no way she would ever dye her hair teal or read any of these books. She is a good Catholic farm girl through and through (I should visit her and Papa soon... before I get too pregnant to fly to Ireland).

"Really, Patty? I figured you'd be more interested in James."

"It's not that I have any issues with Daddy James, but there's something about a lip ring that gets this old gal's furnace a-burning."

"Wow." Tilly laughs. She looks over her shoulder before leaning in and saying quietly, "Personally, I might have a little crush on Keenan. It is just so classic, him putting his life in danger to maintain some sort of contact with Mina. I'm getting some serious Romeo and Juliet vibes."

"Well, let's hope they have a *happier* ever after then those two," Sally comments.

"I'm team Shay all the way."

"Really, Scar?" Michelle says in disbelief. "He is her significantly older step-brother and has had a fairly inappropriate relationship with Mina since she was a young child."

"Keenan isn't any more age appropriate," Scarlett retorts. "Also, they are not biologically related. While maybe unconventional, I'd say his affection towards Mina is no worse than Keenan's."

"Yes, I agree. But unlike other step-sibling romances I've read, Mina doesn't seem to think of Shay as anything more than her older brother."

"What other step romances have you been reading?" Scarlett teases Michelle.

"What?" Michelle shrugs. "I've been exploring Kindle Unlimited."

"How dare you!" Tilly feigns offense—clearly playing up the fact that Michelle is reading e-books over visiting the bookshop. We all laugh, knowing that Tilly has a subscription as well.

I'm having a blast, debating the fictional relationship dynamics with everyone (it's so much easier than focusing on my own real-life drama). Who was behind Mina's attack? Who will come out ahead in this love-triangle? Or will they all somehow put aside their differences and turn this into a *why-choose* romance? Yup, book boyfriends are far less complicated than tangible ones.

"I'm hoping Big Daddy gets his own book. The entire time I was reading it, I kept picturing him as Jeffrey Dean Morgan," Mandy, the youngest in our group, adds to a conversation that seems to have gotten a bit out of hand.

"Hey, Robbie," Patty greets in a teasing tone. "Come to join our book club? Normally we have a *no boys allowed* policy, but we could make an exception."

All the ladies in the room turn to the large man standing in the entryway. I hear some murmurs (likely, everyone is wondering what he is doing here). I don't know who, but someone whispers about how she wouldn't mind him giving her a tune-up. I've never been *that* girl before, the one who feels the need to mark her territory. Perhaps it is because of Chad's betrayal, or the fact that Robbie is the father of my baby, or maybe it's just because he is about to be my husband. But my body reacts before my brain has time to catch up, and I saunter over to Robbie and give him a quick kiss. "What are you doing here?" I ask. As my consciousness reacquaints itself, I worry that the open display might have been a mistake.

Since the engagement, things between us have felt strained. When we went and told his family about the upcoming nuptials at Sunday lunch (which has become a new tradition since most of us don't have to work), he seemed like the normal Robbie. Except, afterwards, instead of going back to his place or doing something together, he told me he needed to go work on the Mustang. It was the same reason he cancelled our plans the night before.

I've tried not reading into it. Because with the way he lights up when he talks about what he's doing, I can tell that is his genuine passion. Even if football would have been successful for him, I think he would still do this in his spare time. I just hope this change in our short-lived routine is because he needed a moment to process everything. Despite getting married initially being his idea, and taking into account that he's the one who got us into this predicament, it is selfish of me to assume he wouldn't have any jitters about getting married—*again*.

I feel like such a jerk. Here I've been focusing on coming to terms with getting married for the sake of the baby and making my family happy, and I haven't stopped to think about how Robbie must feel getting married for a second time, especially after what his ex-wife did. Even if he wanted to get engaged because he thought it was the right thing to do, it doesn't mean he's excited about it.

"Sorry, I wasn't sure what time this was over tonight. I wanted to catch you before you left and see if you wanted to have dinner." Robbie and I ignore the numerous whispers about us in the room, especially the gasps after Tilly mentions we are engaged. We had assumed that the entire town would know about our engagement after Kill's big mouth. But it seems everyone was more focused on K.O. Murphy's presence, rather than what came out of his mouth. Because until this moment, outside of his family and Mack witnessing us kiss, no one in this town has said a thing about us—*at least not to our faces.*

"We're almost finished," Tilly says with a big smile. "How about you go sit with Jax in the back and we will come get you when we are done."

"Sure." Robbie tilts my face up to his and gives me one more quick kiss before turning around.

"Okay, so, where were we?" I immediately get back into our discussion and can't seem to wipe the smile off my face. Not wanting this meeting to become an interview about my newly discovered relationship, I keep the conversation limited to the book. Inside though, I am jumping for joy. Robbie and I just kissed, twice, in a room full of people. No doubt, we are about to be the talk of the town. I ignore that voice in the back of my mind, the one that reminds me about the last time I was *the talk* of anything. *This* isn't the same.

29

Robbie

April 21st

CASSIE'S ASLEEP NEXT TO me, her thin white tank top sheer enough that I can see the pink of her pebbled nipples. I thought after the forced engagement, she'd be mad, yell, leave. I was so stunned when she just seemed to accept it. I didn't know how to handle *that* type of reaction. Anger I could do; anger was the norm (at least it had been with Bee). So, instead of taking the initiative, I did what I always do—I buried myself in an engine and thought of how to address the situation. The other night, I intended to talk to her about how to get out of this and do the least amount of damage possible. But then she kissed me. It's not that she hadn't kissed me before. But this time, without hesitation, she laid one on me in front of a room of some of our town's biggest gossips.

The panicked expression on her face afterwards was fucking adorable. What made it better was the realization that she wasn't worried about everyone else in the room. She was concerned over how I'd react. Because, like the asshole I am, I'd been avoiding her as best I could while I processed everything. Since then, I've remained buried, but this time it's in *her* and not an engine.

Reaching up, I gently trace one of her stiff peaks. The soft hitch of her breath sends a signal straight to my cock. "Good morning," Cassie hums as I continue to play with her breast.

"Good morning." I lean down and kiss her deeply as my hand travels to the waistband of her underwear. She gasps as I rub her clit.

"Can we wake up like this every morning?" I smile at her request, because soon we will.

"Like this?" I tease as I plunge two digits inside her.

"Yes," she moans, "exactly like that."

Pulling down her top with my teeth, I suck her nipple into my mouth as I thrust my fingers deep inside and rub her nub with my thumb. Her cries become louder, her breathing labored. As her body convulses beneath me, I pick up my pace. Watching her cum has become my new favorite pastime. With the pregnancy, she is so much more sensitive, and the climaxes have been increasingly intense.

"Please, I need more," she begs after her second orgasm.

Not one to deny her what she needs, I make quick work of ridding us of our underwear before thrusting myself deep inside her glistening sex. Cassie spreads her legs wide, inviting me in further. It isn't long before I feel her muscles tense up again, making it harder to thrust.

"Oh god," Cassie pants franticly below me. Not letting up, I continue my pace.

"Fuck, Cass. You feel so fucking good," I grit between my teeth, my own release not far behind. But I want to push her over the edge first before following.

Reaching between us, I rub circles on her clit, giving her the nudge she needs. As Cassie cries out in ecstasy, I feel this flood of moisture. At first, I think it is me. But seconds later, as I feel my balls tighten before throbbing inside her and spilling my seed, my jaw drops as I realize the sensation was *her*.

As I slowly slip from her core, I watch as our combined fluids drip out. Looking up, I see the shocked expression on her face.

"Did I just—" Her embarrassed blush has me half hard again. *Fuck, this girl is going to be the death of me.*

"That was the fucking hottest thing I've ever seen." I quickly crash my mouth to hers, hoping to ease her panic.

"I've never had that happen before."

I give her one more kiss before sitting up and pulling her with me. "How about we go take a quick shower?"

· ♥ · ♥ · ♥ · ♥ · ♥ ·

Waking up in my old home, well, it's kind of weird. This is the first night I've slept here since the accident. Grabbing the bedding while Cassie works on blow-drying her hair, I sneak a glance at my parents' old room. As I suspected, Tilly and Jake have left it the same, not that I blame them. I admit it was strange sleeping in there. But seven months later, it feels like it is time to open this space back up, instead of keeping it as though it were a mausoleum in their memory.

I make my way to the kitchen after I get everything thrown into the washer. Jake sits at the counter eating grapefruit and oatmeal. Based on his shit-eating grin, I'm positive he was waiting for one or both of us to come down. No doubt, he heard us this morning; granted, neither of us were trying to be incredibly quiet. I made Cassie climax two more times while we showered. After what she did this morning, I was desperate to make it happen again—which I did, by the way.

"Not bad." Jake nods in greeting. "But I think you could have gotten at least one more."

Jake's never been shy discussing sex with any of us, and I usually never mind sharing a few details with him. But Cassie isn't just some random chick that I hooked up with; she is going to be the mother of my child—*my wife.* That thought is actually amusing. Not the idea of Cassie being my wife, but rather, the jealousy and not wanting to share any part of her. I never felt like this with Bianca. It's left me wondering... is this reaction because of what happened with my ex, or is it because of Cassie? Is it solely how I feel about *her* because she's... something more? Something different?

While I'm not interested in sharing details with Jake, I can at least play along a little. Leaning forward, I whisper to make sure that Cassie doesn't accidentally overhear. "Quality over quantity." I give him a big smile and pat him on the shoulder, before I make my way to the fridge to prepare us some breakfast.

"Quality, huh?" Jake ponders the meaning of my statement. There's no way I am elaborating for him—if Cassie ever found out, she would kill me.

"Quality of what?" Cassie asks as she enters the kitchen. Her long dark hair is down in soft waves that cascade over her shoulders. The yoga pants and tight t-shirt she's wearing show off the barely-there baby bump. It hits me... I can't wait for her to start showing. There is something so incredible about knowing that a part of me is growing inside her.

At first, I didn't believe Jax could really settle down here. He has had one foot out of this town since the kid learned to walk. I have been carefully watching him, waiting for any sign he might flee. I know he has loved Tilly for... well, forever. But that wasn't enough to make him stay before, or even come visit. I wasn't convinced her being pregnant would be reason enough either.

But I get it now.

"Orgasms," Jake says, unashamed as he takes a bite of oatmeal.

Cassie turns bright red. "Did you tell him I—"

I hold up my hand and shake my head, stopping her from accidentally spilling more details than I did.

"What did you do, Cassie?" I swat the back of Jake's head and growl at his prodding.

"You are not getting any details about what happens between me and my fiancée in the bedroom."

"Yeah, Jake, you might be my best friend and all. But there are certain things I will never share with you."

"Seriously, you too? It's just sex. I'm not sure what the big deal is?" Jake huffs. "Wait, did you just say I am your best friend?"

Cassie, now standing next to Jake, leans forward on her elbows talking in hushed tones I can just barely overhear. "Of course, you are, Jake. I said there are *certain* things I will never share—but that doesn't mean everything." Jake smiles at her. "Besides, it is kind of a big deal." She does a measurement with her hands and winks. I'm left stunned, uncertain what to say. Did she just do what I think she did?

"Yes!" Jake perks up. "You, me, root beer, pizza, and movies—Friday night. We'll have a besties night. I can give you a few pointers that will make certain he is wrapped around your pinky."

Jake has been the best roommate and friend to Cassie. I was surprised last night when I went to grab a beer and there wasn't a single drop of alcohol. He stocked the fridge up with healthy food—not that the kid eats junk. But he made certain not to buy any foods Cassie shouldn't be eating. He even tossed out the coffee and replaced it with some herbal teas.

"Sounds like a date." Cassie notices the time on the clock. "We better get dressed and go face the firing squad."

Placing my hands on Cassie's hips, I pull her close and place a soft kiss on her plump lips. "I thought getting married was going to fix things there?"

She rolls her eyes. "Kill seems to think so. But I'm not holding my breath. Fine, maybe they pull this stick out of their butts and realize how ridiculous they've been acting. That doesn't mean I'm ready to forgive and forget. I understand not jumping for joy at the situation. However, they shut me out. Their only daughter. It hurts."

I hold her close, kissing the top of her head. Jake takes this as his cue to exit the kitchen. However, as he leaves, he gives me a "told you so" glance, reminding me of the conversation we had weeks ago. There is a lot of pain Cassie's been holding on to. I think it is finally peeking its ugly head.

"We don't have to go, if you don't want to." I'm sure her brothers will come back to town and kill me for this, but all I care about is Cassie and the baby. I don't want her to go home if it is only going to hurt her more.

"No, it's okay." She wipes a tear from her eyes. "Let's just get this over with."

"All right, why don't we go get you dressed."

"I can get dressed on my own." She pushes my chest playfully.

Leaning down, I bite her earlobe before whispering, "Yes, but I have a feeling there are a few things I can help with beforehand."

Without another word, Cassie grabs my hand, leading me upstairs. Yeah, we have a lot of shit to figure out and deal with yet. But at least this is one area in which we are both on the same page.

30

Cassie

April 21st

"CASSANDRA," MA LEANS IN to give me a hug. Da eyes Robbie intently, but shakes his extended hand. So far, so good. It's not the warm greeting I'm used to. But at least it is not as hostile as the last time I was here. Da gives me a hug, but that sad look in his eye breaks my heart. I really hope we can get over this, move on, and be a happy family again.

It's strange... over the years, I've used this home as an escape, ran back here when things went bad. It was always my safe place. Now I feel as though I'm a stranger walking through these doors for the first time. Nothing about seeing my childhood home feels comforting or familiar anymore.

"Cassie," Moira yells, running at me with her arms open wide.

"Moira, what are you doing here? Not that I'm not glad to see you. I just had no idea."

"You can thank me for that," Kill says with a victorious smile.

"Yeah, doofus over there mentioned that you and Robbie were coming over today." Moira leans in so only I can hear her. "I wanted to be here in case shit goes down." She then goes to Robbie, who looks uncertain of the hug she is giving him. He awkwardly pats her back, as though he does not know what to do with his hands. "Come on, ya' big lug. You act like no one's ever hugged you before."

"Hi, Moira," Robbie states with a pleading glance.

"Come on, Moira, let the poor guy walk through the door."

"Shut up, Kill. I'm just letting him know he's welcome," she states pointedly.

Finally making our way to the backyard, I see Cian watching over the grill. I hesitate, not sure how to react after our last conversation. Studying me for a moment, he makes the first move by coming over and giving me a hug. "You look good, Cassie."

"You too." I squeeze him tightly. You'd think that Kill and I were closer, given the fact Cian is ten years older than me. But growing up, my eldest brother was my protector. Our parents had been gone a lot when we were young, working day and night to get the boutique off the ground. Initially, it had been a money pit and Da needed to work a second job to keep a roof over our heads. Cian was there to help me with my homework, make dinner, tuck me in, and check for monsters. By the time he was eighteen, my parents' boutiques were finally profitable enough that they were able to spend more time at home. I continued to go to Cian for everything until he enlisted. I cried for months. It took me a long while to get over the fact he left me.

"Are you sure about this?" Cian whispers as he practically holds onto me for dear life.

"I'm sure," I reassure him before breaking our embrace. As I glance up and see the concerned look on his face, I realize this has nothing to do with me, or my brother thinking I can't handle this on my own. As always, he is just looking out for me as best he can.

Quickly, everyone joins us at the table. Ma makes small talk, excited about the upcoming wedding expo in California next weekend. She and Da always make a mini vacation out of the event. Da remains quiet through the lunch, only making direct commentary with Ma's tales. Robbie and I even talk about the garage along with the expansion. Da perks up a bit more during that part of the conversation. Regardless of the situation, I know he respects the fact that Robbie built his own business. Thankfully though, everyone to this point has been polite. I pray it doesn't change once we break the news.

"We have an announcement," I snap. At this, Da sets down his fork and focuses all his attention on me. The rest of my family follows suit. Moira appears confused. Robbie gives my hand a reassuring squeeze under the table. We talked about this on the way, preparing for all the worst-case scenarios. Now it's time to see which action plan we need to follow next. Clearing my throat, I continue, "We're getting married."

No one speaks. The sounds of nature and the traffic from West 7th street are practically deafening. Da carefully studies Robbie and me, while everyone (except for Moira) has their eyes on Da. It seems whether this is good or bad news relies solely on his approval.

"Cian, *faigh an t-uisce beatha agus dha ghloine,*" he orders after what feels like hours of silence.

Wordlessly Cian leaves the table, following Da's directive. Robbie is looking to me, wondering which scenario this follows. Depending on what happens next, it could be Plan B exit strategy or plan F celebration strategy.

Returning, Cian passes the two glasses and a bottle of whiskey to Da, giving him a stern look. My brother isn't happy, and Da doesn't seem to care as he dismisses him. Filling both glasses, he takes one and passes the other to Robbie, who inspects it for a moment. I think he is actually contemplating whether it is poisoned or not. Robbie either decides it's safe, or doesn't care, as he follows my da's gesture and raises the glass.

"*Comhghairdeas,*" Da says, before nodding to me with a smile and tossing back his drink. As Robbie follows suit, Ma says a thank you to the heavens.

While Ma is talking excitedly, Robbie leans over and whispers, "To be clear, that was a celebratory drink, not a one last drink before I die type thing, right?" At first, I think Robbie is just being funny, but when I notice the worry in his pinched brows, I realize he took that drink knowing it might have been his last.

Placing a soft kiss against his lips, I respond, "Yes, you dork, he congratulated us."

"Thank fuck, I have a feeling I'm going to need to learn whatever languages you guy speak. Whenever you're around your family, I only understand what you say half the time."

With that, everyone laughs, even Da. Getting up, he pats Robbie on the back. "While the union might not stem from an ideal situation, you seem like a good, hardworking man. One, who recognizes his mistakes and owns up to them. Under better circumstances, I'd be proud of my daughter for bringing a man like you home. But we cannot change the past." Da looks pointedly at us, his words meant for both Robbie *and me*. "We can only look to the future, and strive to be better."

"Yes sir," Robbie agrees.

I nod, for fear that saying the words would cause me to vomit. I know I should be happy that Da is accepting of everything, now that Robbie and I are engaged. I guess I'm relieved. Unfortunately though, the current celebration doesn't repair the hurt he and Ma caused, nor relieve my worry that they won't forever think of my baby as an accident.

She might not be planned, but I will love her all the same.

Not feeling much like celebrating, I politely excuse myself and go to the bathroom. I take a few moments to splash water on my face.

"Okay, Cassie, it's time for you to put your game face on now." Exiting the bathroom, I bump into Moira. "Oh, sorry."

"Can we talk?" she asks, her tone serious.

"Sure." I motion to my left.

Entering my old bedroom, nostalgia washes over me as I think of the countless nights Moira and I had sleepovers in here. Heck, we had one just not too long ago on New Year's Eve. We celebrated a tad too much and stumbled home drunk. The hangover the next day was a little more brutal than we were used to. But I wouldn't change it for the world.

I'm sad to admit we will never sleep in this room again. In fact, I don't think *I* will ever sleep in this room again. This place no longer feels like home to me. My home is now in Tral Lake, with Robbie. The realization offers me some warmth, alleviating a bit of the chill this place causes now.

"What are you doing?" Moira asks in a hushed tone. "I thought you said you were taking things slow. Using your brain, not letting that glutton for punishment heart of yours take the lead."

I roll my eyes before sitting on my old bed. "My heart is not in the lead. This is all logical."

"No, Cassie. Marrying a man you've only known for a few months... A man who got you pregnant from a single night of irresponsible fun, who is also your boss and the older brother to your friend *is* not logical. This is fucking crazy, Cassie."

"Moira, I am going into this with my eyes wide open. I like Robbie. We are actually fantastic together. I love being in Tral Lake and my new job. Despite the current situation, I am actually happy."

"That's great. I'm glad. I'm not saying I don't want you and Robbie to be together. I just want to make sure you aren't rushing into things."

"The engagement was sort of a happy accident."

"What did he trip and slip a ring on your finger? Speaking of which, where *is* the ring?"

"No. My loving brothers paid me a surprise visit the other week. After Kill decked Robbie, in the face by the way, I took the numbskulls outside to give them a piece of my mind. Anyway, there was a slight misunderstanding when Robbie mentioned he asked me to marry him. Kill perked up, thinking we were engaged. Robbie didn't correct him. After seeing how this could fix everything, I went with it."

"Dammit, Cassie," Moira groans. "Why do you do this to yourself?"

"Do what?" I ask, crossing my arms.

"You never stop and think about what's best for you. You are constantly bending over backwards to please everyone around you. Even now, you are marrying a man to make your parents happy. I love them like they are my own. But did you hear your fucking dad down there? This is bullshit, Cassie."

"Whoa, calm down, Moira. This isn't as bad as you are making it out to be."

"Isn't it? This baby already ties you both together for the rest of your lives. Even so, you could find a man who loves *and* wants to be with you—the both of you could find someone. Instead, you are settling."

"Moira," I say sternly. "I love you. I know you are worried about me. But you don't know what my life is like down there. Yes, I won't deny this isn't exactly the fairytale I had imagined for myself. But that doesn't mean it is a death sentence. Like I said before, I like Robbie. Sometimes I feel like my head is spinning from the Tilt-A-Whirl we are on, trying to figure everything out. At the end of the day though, I feel like this is where we were meant to end up."

"Do you love him?"

"Yes," I admit for the first time out loud. "I've been ignoring it, Moira, I have. But every day, that pounding in my chest gets louder and louder."

"Have you told him?" She calmly sits next to me on the bed, taking my hand in hers.

"Not yet... I've been waiting for a sign that we are on the same page. I know he has feelings for me. I can't explain it. But the way he looks at me, I just feel it. We both have our own baggage, and I think something is still holding a part of him back."

She sighs. "Cassie, I appreciate that you are between a rock and a hard place right now. I hope everything works out—I do. But are you sure you can be happy marrying a man who might never fully open his heart to you? I'm sure Robbie is a great guy and will be an amazing father. I want you to have your happily ever after, not just a happy for now."

31

Cassie

April 27th

HAPPY FOR NOW. THE words keep running through my mind. The rest of the day, hell this week, I've felt like I'm on autopilot. Except for Moira, everyone seems happy about the engagement. *You knew she wouldn't be. It's why you didn't call and tell her,* I remind myself. Yeah, that was another crappy part of our conversation. To say she was hurt that her best friend didn't confide in her immediately, that she only found out as a happy accident because Kill invited her over, is an understatement. Thankfully though, we talked it through and all is forgiven.

Ma has been messaging me nonstop with suggestions and hounding me for a date. *Robbie and I should really start discussing that.* How is it that Chad acted like I twisted his arm until he agreed to marry me, and two seconds later, I was happily planning away? Is Moira right? Am I just going through the motions? No, I might not be shouting it from the rooftops, but I know I love Robbie. It's just the stress of the situation. If I think about it rationally, we have so many more important things to figure out then a single day—we have our entire lives to plan. Where to locate the new shop, where to live, getting a nursery set up, figuring out how to raise a baby. Yup, this is what maturity looks like. Tilly had the right idea. We should just go to the courthouse and call it a day. I contemplate how much simpler that'd be, but then dismiss the idea. Ma would be furious if we didn't have a wedding. She's already disappointed that I refused a traditional Catholic ceremony. While they might be beautiful, it's not for us. Not to mention, I didn't want to deal with Father Flanagan's requirements under these "special circumstances" as my ma so eloquently put it.

Making my way to the kitchen, I smile as I watch Robbie cook breakfast. Since the shop is closed on Sundays, I suggested we stay here. Not that there is anything wrong with the apartment, but it starts to feel a little cramped after a while. I enjoy having the big comfy couch downstairs to cuddle and watch TV on. Additionally, my bed is larger and easier on my back with the new mattress.

"Morning, Cass." Robbie places a kiss on my cheek as I walk past him, heading to the fridge to grab myself a glass of apple juice, courtesy of Rigiford Orchard right here in town. "Are you hungry?" I look at the pan of bacon and eggs, wrinkling my nose.

"No thanks. Food sounds like a bad idea this morning."

Robbie rushes over, inspecting me closely. "Are you sure you're okay? If you're not feeling well, maybe you should go back to bed. It's been a tough week. Scar and Letty would understand."

"Whoa, calm down there, big guy." I give Robbie a giant smile. "It's just some morning sickness, no need to call in the troops. It will pass. I'm just going to drink some of the mint herbal tea Jake got me and eat some toast. That always seems to do the trick."

"I will come and help set up. I have nothing going on today."

"Thank you, Robbie. The gesture is sweet." I kiss him on the cheek. "But I know you are supposed to meet the guys and do whatever it is boys do while the ladies are at the baby shower."

"It's really not that big of a deal. We are just going to grill and work on getting Jax's house ready for the babies. He'd understand if I were late."

"I'm good, seriously. Already feeling better. I should hurry and get dressed. I just want to get a glass of juice."

I kiss Robbie's frowny face once more before going upstairs to get ready.

"Wait," he calls out. "I have something for you."

I turn and look at him as he fidgets nervously. It's the cutest thing I've ever seen. He reaches into his pocket and pulls out a small black box. Opening the lid, he reveals a white gold band. Set in the middle is a center-cut pink diamond, with two small diamonds set on each side in what looks like little leaves. "It's supposed to look like a rose," he offers sheepishly.

"It's beautiful," I gasp as he slides the ring on my finger. I love it. It's simple yet elegant. I remember the ring Chad gave me. It was large and gaudy. Not that the ring didn't have its own charm, but it wasn't meant for the finger of a girl like me.

Robbie breathes a relieved breath. "I'm glad you like it. I was worried it was too corny. When I saw it though, I thought of your family's shop. Although I know you aren't a florist, it has always been a big part of your life."

"It's perfect, really. Thank you." I admire the ring on my hand.

"Great. I'm glad you like it and it fits. I felt terrible about sending my fiancée to a baby shower without a ring on her finger."

His words wash over me like a bucket of ice, watering that seed of doubt that eats at me. I begin to think things are going so well, that perhaps this isn't just all out of obligation. Then he says something like *that* and has me reevaluating every aspect of our relationship all over again.

• ❤ • ❤ • 💗 • ❤ • ❤ •

Despite the rocky start this morning, today ended up being the most perfect day to host a baby shower for Tilly. This time of year can be such a hit or miss. One year, you will still be trekking through two feet of snow, then the next, it is seventy degrees and sunny. Fortunately, this year, it is the latter.

Scarlett, Letty, and I decorated the courtyard of her Inn with balloons and streamers. The natural foliage made it so we didn't have to do too much. Patty was kind enough to make a variety of sweets. Then Scarlett's chef for the Inn prepared a bunch of finger foods. We kept it as a snacking menu. Everything is sublime.

"Hey, are you feeling all right?" Letty places a hand on my shoulder.

"Yeah, I'm feeling great." I give her my most convincing smile.

"Okay?" Letty studies me. "You just seem pale."

"Letty, I'm Irish—I'm always pale."

"Or sunburnt." We both laugh. I made the mistake of falling asleep at the beach during spring break. Napping with salt water on your fair skin is a recipe for disaster. I ended up getting a third-degree sunburn. "I'm going to go pick up Tilly. Would you mind helping with the sign in?"

"Sure thing."

Scarlett and I assist with greeting everyone and making sure they sign in and get a pin for one of the games we are playing. I guess no one can say the word "baby" for the duration of the party. If you hear someone say it, their pin is taken away. The one with the most left at the end of the day wins. I honestly have no idea how Letty and Scarlett came up with half of these games. The worst is the one where everyone has to smell baby diapers and guess what's in them. Yup, I'm good with helping host the party and being excluded from the activities. Given the fact I don't know too many people in town, this was a great way for me to introduce myself. It seems while I am not familiar with most of the guests, a majority somehow know who I am. Apparently word spreads like wildfire in a small town (or so they all keep telling me).

Everyone knew my name, that I worked at the garage, and the hot topic of conversation—that I'm Robbie's fiancée. While none of the other Moore boys have settled down, Robbie has been the most elusive. It seems after he and Bianca split, he had a line of ladies beating down his door that he wouldn't give the time of day. However, I know better than to believe all the gossip. Since Robbie hasn't had an actual girlfriend since his divorce and is now engaged to the new girl in town, the big question of the day has been: how was I able to reel him in? That sick feeling from earlier is nothing compared to the somersaults my stomach is doing now. I think we are in a good place, and each day we are growing closer. In the end though, no matter how we might feel about each other now, the truth is *we are only together because of the baby.*

We chose to keep the pregnancy under wraps for now. Most people don't make big announcements until after the first trimester. Our close friends and family know, and that's all that really matters. But I realize that when this town hears that tidbit of information, I'm certain the ohhs and ahhs of me marrying Robbie will turn into venomous tales about how I seduced my boss and trapped the up-and-coming business owner with a pregnancy. These warm smiles and kind words are conditional. I've seen how quickly everyone can turn on you. Just like my ex, this is Robbie's town and everyone here is loyal to him.

My heart beats rapidly as the warnings Moira has given me ring loud in my mind. Despite my best efforts, I am in the same situation all over again. Down here, I have no one.

Even my couple of friends are all loyal to him. When things go bad (which let's face it, given my track record, it isn't a matter of *if*—but *when*), I will be surrounded by people who side with him. No one will care about my version of things. He will be the victim and I will be the vapid snake looking to sink her fangs into him.

"Cassie, is everything all right?" Tilly startles me. In my downward spiral, I hadn't noticed her approach.

I nod, attempting to dismiss her, while my chest remains too tight to speak.

"You don't look fine. Sit," she demands, pulling out a chair.

I do as she says, trying and failing to take deep calming breaths—*why is it so hot?* I fan myself with a napkin. I squeeze my eyes shut as black spots appear.

"Letty, get a glass of ice water," Tilly calls out. "Cassie, I think you might be having a panic attack. Can you nod if you understand me?"

I nod.

"Good, I'm here for you. Are you able to take a deep breath for me?" Her words are calm and controlled, just like when Jake helped me last time. Unfortunately though, this time, they do not seem to do the trick.

I want to take a deep breath, but when I try, my chest squeezes tighter. The murmuring of people around us makes it worse. I can't hear what they are saying. But it isn't hard for me to imagine, since the situation doesn't feel all that different from my first panic attack after my breakup with Chad.

· ♥ · ♥ · ♥ · ♥ · ♥ ·

I can do this. I've been repeating this same mantra each day for the past few weeks. Cian is right. I worked my butt off to get where I am. I'm not going to let Chad ruin this for me, or allow him to push me out. I might be back to the drawing board when it comes to my relationship, but at least I still have my career.

I walk to his office, which is really the last place I want to be. But after he gave me my long weekend and time to think, I realized I can't just keep my head buried in the sand any longer. Obviously, the negative effects of our breakup have been rippling into our work. We are both adults. While hurt, I am not interested in getting him back. Katie can have him for all I care.

Taking a deep breath, I find the courage I was missing the last time I was in the office. I hold my head high and open the door. The sight of Chad with Katie on top of his desk, her legs spread wide and skirt pulled up high, halts my steps. Is he? Oh my god, he is.

Quickly, I turn and shut the door behind me. I don't think they even noticed my intrusion—much like they hadn't when I caught them together the first time. I inhale again, trying to swallow down the bile forming at the back of my throat. Why does this bother me so much? I literally caught them in the act just a few weeks ago. Maybe it's because merely a few days prior to that, Chad and I were doing the same thing. It was after hours and he got turned on talking about having babies (I had recently quit my birth control).

And just like that, it feels like the room is closing in around me and I can't breathe... I QUIT my birth control. We were having sex, with the full intention of getting pregnant. What day is it? I had my period, right? Oh god, please don't let me be pregnant. It's already embarrassing enough, having to work with him while he flaunts around his new girlfriend before the indent from my engagement ring is even gone.

Not caring about the presentation I've been preparing for, I rush back to my desk. I need to check my calendar. I stumble on my way back, holding on to whatever I *can to keep myself from falling. Everything is growing darker.*

"*Is she day drinking? I know she's Irish, but seriously, it is only nine in the morning. Can you say alcoholic? No wonder Chad left her.*"

I barely make it to my chair before I collapse, my heart thumping so loudly I can hardly make out the surrounding whispers. I can only catch bits and pieces.

"*What's wrong with her?*"

"*Should we call a doctor?*"

"*She's fine. She just wants attention.*"

"*This is just a pathetic attempt to get Chad back. What did he ever see in her?*"

·♥·♥·♥·♥·♥·

"Everyone, please give us some space." I faintly hear Tilly direct in the distance. "Cassie, I need you to focus on my words. What do you need?"

"I've got some Prozac if that will help?" someone offers.

"No, she's pre..." *Oh no, she is going to tell everyone* is the last thought I have as everything goes black, and the world falls away from around me.

32

Robbie

April 27th

"DO YOU THINK SHE will like this color?" Jax asks, looking at the section of wall he just painted a soft grey.

"I think it is a cool color. It will match whatever else you end up putting in here," Scott comments, his pose eerily similar to Jax's. Arms crossed, they both inspect the first coat as it begins to dry. Though Jake was being an asshole a while back (making Tilly think that by hooking up with Jax, she was subconsciously dating her brother because they look so much alike), now that Jax has been back in town for a while, just like when they were younger, they act exactly the same as well. It is sickening how they finish each other's sentences. I wonder if Tilly ever worries that Jax might leave her for Scott?

"This is why you should have found out what you are having, then you wouldn't need to worry about what color you decorate with," I point out.

"Seriously, you are still hung up on that? I told you it is going to be fun, just like in the old days. You guys will get to pace in the lobby, waiting for me to come out and say, 'It's a girl' or whatever they end up being," Jax attempts to justify.

"I think finding out you are having a baby is surprise enough. That is why we are going to find out right away, do that blood test or whatever."

"Did Cassie agree to that?" Scott muses.

"Yeah, last time I heard her and Tilly talking, she seemed to be on team Surprise." Jake chuckles.

"Fine, I will have them do the blood test and keep it a secret if she doesn't want to know. But I am not waiting nine months to find out we are having a boy. How are you supposed to buy them clothes and shit? No thank you."

Scott and Jax start laughing so hard, they practically fall over. "You know, I'm sure you'll end up having a girl."

"Not just a girl, but the daintiest girl ever. She'll probably hate cars, and only like flowers and lace," Scott adds to Jax's banter.

"Oh my god, don't Cassie's parents run a floral shop?" Jake points out, making the guys laugh harder.

"Even if the baby is a girl, she will have gasoline pumping in her veins just like her dad."

"Sure, keep telling yourself that." Scott wipes a tear from his eyes. "I can already see you with a tiara sitting and having a tea party."

"Yup, she is going to have daddy whipped," Jax says, adding a sound effect at the end.

"Shut up, dude, you are about to have two of them. With all the shit you are giving me, I'm sure you will be the one with twin daughters, stuck eating crumpets and wearing a princess dress."

"And I'll look damn good," Jax verifies, before reaching into his pocket to grab his ringing phone. Looking down, he frowns before he answers, "Hey, how's the party going?"

We all stop what we are doing, listening to Jax's one-sided conversation.

"Slow down, what happened?" Jax's eyes are dark as they look up at me. My heart plummets, knowing that something is wrong. Without waiting to hear the damage, I run around looking for my bike keys while he wraps up his call. "Okay, we're on our way." Jax hangs up. "Hold on, Robbie, let me drive."

"Where are they?" I ask, tossing around tarps and magazines.

"The ambulance is taking her to Fairview. Tilly is riding along," Jax says carefully, treating me like a rabid animal. "Let me drive—you are in no state right now."

"Robbie." Jake places a hand on my shoulder. "Please let one of us take you. The last thing we need is you wrecking your bike on the way to the hospital. I know you are worried, but she needs you in one piece, okay?"

I nod in agreement. "Let's go." I throw on my jacket, run down the stairs and hop into Jax's Jeep.

· ♥ · ♥ · ♥ · ♥ · ♥ ·

"Cassandra Murphy," I say impatiently for the second time to the receptionist.

"I'm sorry, sir. Unless you're a relative, I can't let you through," she replies again.

"She's my fucking fiancée and pregnant with my child. Isn't that good enough?"

"Again, I apologize, but no. The doctor can only speak with a relative. You will just need to wait in the lobby until she can have visitors."

Jake places a hand on my shoulder. "Robbie, go sit with Tilly. I know a couple of the nurses. I'll see if I can get any information."

"This is fucking ridiculous." I storm off and plop down next to Tilly, who takes my hand in hers.

"I'm sorry, Robbie. I tried to stay with her. But they wouldn't let me go back. I called Moira; she just texted me and told me the Murphys are on their way."

I run my hands over my face and rub my eyes. As much as I don't want to see them right now, I can't wait until they show up. Yeah, it seems they are all happy now that we are getting married. But it pisses me off they didn't even fucking apologize for being assholes. We fuck up in my family, but we have the decency to apologize when it's all said and done. I still can't believe her fucking dad, acting as though he was doing this grand gesture for her by welcoming me into their home. I wanted to shout at each and every single one of them. But I held my tongue, not wanting to make things worse for Cassie. Regardless of how sick they make me, I hope they get here fucking fast. Because I need answers. "What the hell happened? Everything was fine this morning. She said she had a little morning sickness, but otherwise she was good."

"I don't know." Tilly rubs my back. "I noticed she looked pale, and she was sweating. I can't be certain, but I think she might have had a panic attack."

"Did someone say something to her?" I growl.

"Not that I saw, Robbie," Tilly says softly. "She was smiling, talking to people. Sometimes these things just happen, or maybe she suffers from some sort of anxiety disorder."

"I should have never let her go. I thought she looked weak this morning. I offered to go help her set up so she could relax. This is my fault."

"No, it isn't. Like I said, she seemed fine until she *wasn't*. Even if she wouldn't have helped set up the party, she still could have had a panic attack. Usually, they are triggered by some sort of emotional stress."

"It's her asshole family," I growl again. Then it hits me. "The baby," I choke.

"I'm sure they are both fine." Tilly does her best to reassure me, but I see the uncertainty in her eyes. Tilly's never been known for her poker face.

"Here." Jake hands me a black coffee.

"What did you find out?"

He frowns. "Not much. A girl I know is on duty in the ER today, but she isn't assigned to Cassie's room. She took a quick peek for me, but all she could verify was that she was in a room and unconscious. She'll text me if anything changes."

Scarlett and Letty show up moments later, getting the same rundown I got. I tune out everyone around me, as I stare at the double doors, waiting for someone to come and get me. I'm not sure how much time passes before I hear a familiar voice asking about a Cassandra Murphy. I turn and see Cian at the receptionist's desk. I make my way to him in a few long strides.

"Robbie, what happened? How is she?" I can see the panic written all over his face. It is the same pained expression I had when I got a call late at night informing me that there had been an accident, and my parents and Tilly were being rushed to the hospital. I (along with my brothers) sped the whole way to the Cities, except it wasn't fast enough... Dad died on scene, and mom never made it out of surgery. I just fucking pray (to whomever may be listening) Cian is about to get better news than I did all those months ago. I wouldn't wish that experience on my worst enemy, and I don't think I am strong enough to handle if something's happened to Cassie and the baby.

"I don't know. The fucking staff here won't tell me shit." I glare at the receptionist, who doesn't cower.

"Sir," she says sternly. I doubt I'm the first person to get pissed at her for this. "As I stated before, without her consent, I can only update immediate family."

"I'm her brother, so how about you tell *me*," Cian orders.

"Yes sir, I've paged her doctor. If you take a seat in the lobby, he will be out shortly."

We walk back over to everyone else. Cian takes a seat, dropping his head in his hands. Rubbing his face, he looks up and asks, "What happened?"

"Tilly thinks she might have had a panic attack."

"A panic attack," he hisses under his breath. "What did you do?"

I growl as I grit out, "I didn't do anything. Things have been great between us. If anything, it's your fucking family's fault."

"What the fuck did you just say?" Cian and I stand chest to chest. I might have a few inches on him, but I don't doubt he could kill me before I got a swing in. Whatever, I'm sick and tired of his family's bullshit.

"You heard me," I egg him on, ready to burn off all the rage.

"Stop it." Jake gets between us, pushing us apart. "You're about to get everyone kicked out of the hospital. I'm not sure what's going on with Cassie. But this isn't her first panic attack."

"What," Cian and I yell in unison, quickly cornering Jake.

"When did she have a panic attack? Why didn't you tell me?" I'm pissed at Jake for keeping this from me. I can respect their friendship, and as much as it pains me, that she might even tell him things she doesn't tell me. But this isn't something you keep secret.

Jake holds his hands up in defense. "Calm down. It was a while ago. When she first moved here." Jake looks at Cian cautiously before continuing. "She was worried about you two hooking up. She was going on about everyone at work hating her. How she couldn't believe she had her first drunken one-night stand with her boss. Look, we've talked a little. But when it comes to some of the shit that happened with her ex, she has it locked up tight."

I take a step back. The realization that there is a ton of shit going on with Cassie, shit she isn't telling me... it hits me like a fucking freight train. I hate this feeling of doubt. I never thought I'd have a baby or hell, even get married again. Except, here we are about to merge our lives together. I've felt good about this, even given the unconventional situation, because she has been a partner to me, something I now realize my ex never was. But how can we truly be partners in all of this, if she is still keeping a big part of herself from me?

"Cian," Tilly approaches tentatively. "I'm not sure if you remember me."

"Tilly." He gives her a pained smile. "Congratulations, you look great." He motions to her belly.

"I'm so sorry. We were at my baby shower. Letty noticed she looked pale earlier, but Cassie assured her she was fine. I went to check in on her and she started hyperventilating. I do not know what happened. Maybe it's just the pregnancy." Tilly sniffles. "I feel awful. I wish I knew."

"Thank you, Tilly. I appreciate you being there for her." Cian calms down, taking a seat next to me.

"Family of Cassandra Murphy," a doctor calls out. I don't wait to be invited and follow behind Cian. "Are you both family?"

"I'm her brother," Cian confirms, before turning and giving me a once-over. "This is her fiancé and the father of her baby."

"Very well, follow me." We tread on the heels of the doctor, through the doors and down the hall, before stopping outside of her room. "Ms. Murphy is in stable condition. According to her labs, she was suffering from hypoglycemia—likely due to skipping meals—in conjunction with what appears to be an acute panic attack. The combination caused her to faint, which isn't that uncommon in pregnancies. We gave her a mild sedative, in order to help the symptoms, subside, along with some dextrose to raise her blood sugar levels."

"The baby—"

"Is fine. The medication we gave her is safe to take while pregnant. The baby's heart rate sounds strong and stable. I have a request in to an on-call OB to come down and do an ultrasound, just to verify that everything is okay. But at this time, there is no indication that the baby was in any sort of distress. I'd like to keep her overnight for observation.

Pregnancies can cause a lot of stress and anxiety, not to mention the increased hormones. This sort of episode isn't out of the ordinary, but you can never be too safe, which is why we will continue to monitor her glucose levels."

The doctor takes in both of our dumbstruck looks, before sighing.

"Look, I'm sure this has been a long day. Why don't you go in and see her, then we can talk about the next steps?"

"Thank you, doc." Cian pauses, turning to me before entering the room. "Look, I'd like to go in and talk to my sister first." He doesn't leave any time for me to argue as he shuts the door in my face. As much as I'd like to barge in there and tell him to fuck off, I know he is just doing what he needs to. So, I wait and pray that Cassie will let me in when he's finished. While I can't think of what I did that might have brought this on, I'm not stupid enough to think this attack has nothing to do with everything going on.

33

Cassie

April 27th

"Hey, sis," Cian says softly, waking me up as he brushes my hair back.

"When did you get here?"

"Moira called me. I came right away. How are you feeling?"

"Like an idiot," I admit, and Cian frowns.

"These things happen. You have no reason to feel like an idiot."

"I passed out in the middle of my friend's baby shower, in front of all of those people. This is a small town. I'm sure it will be headline news."

"Did someone say something to you? Is Robbie—"

"What?" I sit up quickly, which causes me to get dizzy. Cian helps me lie back down. "Robbie did nothing, okay? It must be hormones or something."

"I know you are lying," he says sternly.

"Drop it, Cian. Robbie has been nothing but amazing. We have been getting along really well."

He studies me for a moment. "Is it because of *us*?" he asks with a gulp.

"What?" I say, genuinely thrown off by his question.

"Out in the lobby, I might have lost my composure and insinuated to Robbie that I thought this was his fault. He was quick to counter that it's because of issues with our family. I was ready to put him in his place. Except when, I think Jake's his name, mentioned you had one of these attacks before, I started thinking about everything that's gone on recently, and well, Robbie might not be that far off. I need you to be honest with me here, Cassie, please."

Jake and his big, stupid mouth. *Oh no,* if Jake told Cian, I'm sure Robbie heard. *Darn it,* this is going to start a line of questioning I'm not sure I'm ready to answer. Not to mention, I'm stuck in the room with the one person in this world I can't lie to—and not for lack of trying.

"Cian, what do you want me to say?"

"The truth for starters."

"Please, I don't want to talk about this with you," I plead.

"Why not? Are you still mad—"

"What? No, look at me, Cian." I look him straight in the eyes. "I forgave you for going away a long time ago. I was nine—you had been like a father to me. But I grew up. I understand. This has nothing to do with *that.*"

"Then why won't you tell me what's been going on?"

"Because I'm embarrassed, okay. Are you happy now?" I cross my arms and turn my head, unable to handle the disappointed look I'm sure is on his face. I can't even imagine an eighth of the stuff my brother has seen during his years of service. Here I am, in a hospital bed having panic attacks because I'm worried about what some people are saying about me.

"I'm concerned." Cian takes my hand. "I hate that for the first time I don't know what to do. Or how to handle the situation. It kills me you are down here alone. I wish you'd take me up on my offer. We don't need to live near *them,*" he says the last word with disdain. "I'd even move down here if you wanted the baby to remain close to Robbie. But you don't have to marry him to make *them* happy. I promise I'm here. I'll help take care of both of you."

"Cian." I turn to look at him. "This isn't your problem to solve. I'm not a little girl you need to take care of anymore." He winces at my words. "I'm not alone. I'm about to have a whole new family, a life down here. I meant what I said before. I'm happy in Tral Lake. For the first time, I feel like I belong somewhere. I wish you could accept that. Especially since that is exactly what you told me when you joined the army."

We sit silently as Cian processes what I'm saying. It's the truth though. Despite everything, I *am* happy. I just need to figure out how to address the voice in my head that exploits my inner doubts.

"Okay, you're right. It's hard sometimes, you know, being back," Cian admits. "Before, my role was your guardian. Then I spent the last twenty years having a purpose. I've been trying so hard to slide back into my old life. But maybe that's the problem? My old life has grown up and moved on. Perhaps it's time I look for a new one? A fresh start maybe?" He gives me a rare smile that doesn't quite reach his eyes. I can tell he is trying though.

"Do you want to talk about it?" I ask carefully. Not once have I ever asked him about what he did in the military. I know some basic things, but I've never been brave enough to ask about the haunted expression he now carries.

He shakes his head. "I guess we both have things we aren't ready to share?"

I nod, accepting this as our compromise. Neither of us will force the other to reveal their deep, dark secrets. "Where's Ma?" I'm not sure what hurts more: being in the hospital and not having your mother there, or realizing that in a time of crisis, you don't yearn for her comfort. Placing my hand on my stomach, I make a small promise to this baby—she will never have to wonder if my love is conditioned by meeting certain expectations.

"They are at the annual bridal fair in San Diego. I haven't called them yet. I didn't want Ma blowing up my phone until I knew what was going on."

I breathe a sigh of relief. I'm not sure I could take the heartache of knowing she didn't come when she could have. "Cian..."

"No, Cassie, don't ask me to do this."

"Please don't tell. Things are finally getting better with them. If she hears about this, Ma is going to go back to nagging me about being down here. There is really no need to upset everyone all over again." At first, Ma suggested that Robbie and I move up there, saying that surely, he would have more success in the Cities. Fortunately, Da chimed in on that call and stopped her ridiculous request. But knowing her, she'd use this as ammunition to convince him otherwise.

"Okay," Cian states after considering my plea for a moment. "But I need you to promise me something."

"What?"

"If you will not talk to me about what's going on, talk to someone. My suggestion is that fiancé of yours out there, who is probably two seconds away from beating down this door."

I chuckle before wiping my nose. "Deal."

"Because if you don't, and this happens again, my offer will no longer be optional." I know Cian means it. He isn't one to just say things for the sake of saying them.

"Okay, I understand. I will talk to someone." We both sit silently for a moment. "Is Robbie...?"

"Yeah, yeah, your *fiancé* is right outside. He's been harassing the staff trying to get back here to talk to you. I'm going to get some coffee and snacks. I'll be back in a bit, okay?"

"Thank you, Cian."

He kisses the top of my head, then crosses the room to open the door for Robbie, who is by my side before the hinges are even able to swing back into place.

"Cass, what happened? Are you okay? Fuck, I was so fucking terrified," he says franticly, taking and kissing my hand.

"I'm fine, Robbie."

"I should have never let you go out. I could tell you weren't feeling well. This is all my fault."

"Really, Robbie, this isn't your fault. I think I just got overwhelmed." That voice from earlier is still nagging at me, subconsciously reminding me why I am here in the first place. It thinks I should take Cian up on his offer to whisk me away from here. Because there's no doubt I am the talk of the town. The nutjob who passed out from a panic attack at her soon-to-be sister-in-law's baby shower. It's incessant—the internal whisper that insinuates Robbie is only with me because of this baby—and it's getting harder and harder to ignore my fears.

That being said, I also hear another faint voice. One that is full of hope. While she isn't as loud as the other, I can hear her tell me to hold on. That Robbie isn't Chad. Even if all of this is stemming from the life growing inside me, that intense attraction was there the minute I laid eyes on him. *Yeah, you had that same feeling with all the others too.* I shake my head, willing that negative voice to quiet down. I'm praying if I focus on the hopeful one, the other will die out.

A knock at the door pulls both of our attentions. "I hope this is a good time. I'm Dr. Miller. They called me down to take an extra look at the baby and make sure everything is okay."

"Yes, please come in." Fortunately, the drugs they gave me are helping. But I've been struggling to keep calm, wanting to verify the baby is fine. While the ER doctor said the baby's heart rate was strong, I need to see that she's okay.

The doctor gets set up with her portable ultrasound machine. As she talks me through what to expect, she preps my belly with the warm jelly. Pressing around firmly, she talks us through what she is looking at, until she finally stops at what we have been impatiently waiting for.

"There you are." She studies the screen and takes a few measurements. "Everything looks great. The baby is measuring at around ten weeks, as expected. I see nothing that makes me believe the baby is at any sort of risk. That being said, I'd like it if you took it easy for the next couple of days. Avoid any strenuous activities or things that could cause high mental or physical stress. In addition, make sure you eat small meals throughout the day to stabilize your glucose level. If you are having problems keeping food down, we can look into some prescription anti-nausea medication. If you notice any spotting or bleeding, call your doctor immediately or come into the ER."

"Can you tell if it's a boy?" Robbie asks, making the doctor laugh.

"At this stage, no. I could make an educated guess based on some studies. But they aren't always accurate. We cannot positively determine the sex of the baby via ultrasound until closer to twenty weeks. If you can't wait that long, there is a blood test available that you can do as early as eleven weeks. I'd suggest checking with your primary OB."

"Thank you, Dr. Miller, but I'd prefer not to know."

Robbie grumbles something under his breath, but I ignore him. Tilly already warned me he would likely want to know the gender as soon as possible; he isn't too big on surprises. Honestly, I'd always planned on finding out. But messing with him is so much more fun.

"There is only one, right?" I ask nervously.

The doctor laughs again. "Yes, just one. For now."

"What," Robbie and I say in unison.

"Sometimes a twin likes to hide. But from what I can tell, there is only one."

The doctor runs through a few more things with us before taking off. Robbie and I study the images she left behind of the alien she claims is our baby.

217

"You see that there?" I point at the picture. "It looks like *she* has inherited her father's giant head."

"No way, *he* has a big brain just like his mom."

The smile Robbie gives me is enough to wipe away the last bit of anxiety floating around my imagination. He has been nothing but open and honest with me, willing to put himself all in to making this work. I need to stop letting the cruel whispers of my past mistakes get to me.

34

Robbie

April 29th

"Where's Cassie?" Chris asks, noticing it is ten in the morning and she isn't in yet.

"Upstairs. She isn't feeling well. I told her to take the day off." I continue pulling the carburetor from the old Mazda pickup that was dropped off over the weekend.

"I heard about the shower. Is everything okay?" Mack inquires.

I growl under my breath. I love Tral Lake. But there is no privacy here. I'm sure the entire town heard about her attack at the party before I even did.

"Everything is fine. The doctor said she needed to take a few days to rest." That was a fun argument this morning. Cassie fought me tooth and nail about staying home. She tried telling me she was only supposed to take it easy, not be put on bed rest. After much debate, I convinced her to relax until her checkup on Wednesday. If everything looks good, then she can come back to work on light duty.

The second battle was persuading her to stay with me upstairs. I like the idea of knowing I'm only a few feet away. I don't doubt the house is much more comfortable and open. But Jake is on shift for the next few days. I'd go nuts worrying about her home alone and across town. What if she had another attack, and no one was there? I suggested that if she really wanted to stay at the house, I could always call her family and see if one of them could keep an eye on her, so she's not alone. Needless to say, she packed her bags quickly.

"Why don't you take off? I imagine she must be bored sitting upstairs by herself in your apartment," Chris mentions.

"Thanks, but I'm sure she'd kick my ass if I spent all day monitoring her. No doubt, she's enjoying the break from me right now."

"How's the wedding planning going? I haven't received my save-the-date yet." Mack feigns insult.

"It's crazy to think that just a few months ago you were betting on her not lasting the week, now you're getting hitched. Don't get me wrong, Cassie is a sweetheart. But don't you think it's a little fast?"

Well, it seems the pregnancy is still under wraps. Even though Tilly assured Cassie she didn't let it slip at the shower, I could tell she was worried that the entire town knew by now. While Cassie hasn't come right out and said it, I know she wants to keep the pregnancy quiet until after the wedding. I think it is a wasted effort and only delaying the inevitable. Fuck, most people in this town couldn't care less about the timing of us having a baby and getting married. I'm not saying there won't be a few assholes, but fuck 'em. However, if this is going to keep Cassie calm and happy, then I'll play along. Unpleasant as it might be, eventually everyone is going to put two and two together.

"When you know, you know," I say with a shrug of my shoulders.

"I still think it's BS," Mack scoffs. I give him a pointed stare. "What? I saw her first," he says in a teasing manner.

"Yeah, there is no way she would have ever fallen for one of your cheesy moves. Cassie requires more than discount oil changes to get into her pants."

Mack opens his mouth, likely to toss another joke at my expense, but he is cut off by the snarl behind me. "Nope, apparently, she just needs a few shots of tequila." I clench my fists and turn to see Cian standing in the shop bay. *What the fuck? I thought he went home.*

"What are you doing here? I thought Cassie sent you on your merry way," I ask through my teeth.

"I need to talk to you," Cian states before turning on his heel and walking out front.

"Is everything okay?" Chris asks.

"Peachy." I sigh. "If you see Cassie, can you try to keep her away from the front?"

"Sure thing, boss," Chris says before resuming his work.

Walking outside, Cian is leaning against the building with a cigarette.

"Okay, what do you want?"

He lets out an exhale of smoke before flicking the butt. "I think we got off on the wrong foot."

"Which foot might that be? The one where you treated your sister like shit and ghosted her for a month when you found out she was pregnant? Or the one where you and dipshit came down here to kick my ass? I'm not a math guy or anything, but last time I checked, you only have two feet and both of them seem to be wrong."

"Point taken," Cian concedes. "That wasn't a proud moment for any of us."

"No shit. Did any of you even ask how she was doing or feeling? What if she would have been there telling you she was pregnant, and the guy was a deadbeat who told her to pound sand? I've got a little sister who dropped the same bomb. Believe me, I get being pissed at the asshole who knocked her up. Even knowing him since he was a kid, I wanted to beat his ass. But the first thing I did was ensure she was okay. Afterwards, if necessary, I'd hunt the fucker down and guarantee he'd never be guilty of the same mistake again. I'd never insinuate to Tilly that she did something wrong—because she didn't."

"I can't change the past, but I'm hoping to make it up to her."

"How's that?" My stomach twists in a knot. The fact that he is here talking to me, and not Cassie, tells me whatever he is about to say likely isn't good.

"What has Cassie told you about me?" He eyes me suspiciously.

"To be honest, not much. Only that you are in the army."

"*Was*," he corrects. "It's been difficult. I thought returning to civilian life would be easy, but I'm trying to fit into a world that doesn't exist anymore. Killian is happy and settled with his bar and fan club. My parents are... complicated." He looks off into the distance and shakes his head.

"What do you want, Cian?" I ask, exhausted.

"I need your help," he says with a smile that sends an icy shiver down my spine. "But first, let me tell you a little story."

Fuck, this guy is going to be the death of me.

35

Cassie

May 10th

"GET OUT OF HERE," I tell Robbie. Even though the doctor verified that the baby is looking healthy, he's refused to let me leave the apartment, insisting that I need to rest.

"This is my apartment." Robbie crosses his arms over his chest. I clench my legs tightly, willing my body to ignore the response his deep husky growl has on it.

"Okay," I say coolly before turning back to Jake. "Let's go back to *our* house and hang out."

"No," Robbie says quickly, losing a bit of his composure before shaking it off. "I don't get why I can't hang out with you guys?"

"Because it's girls' night. No boys allowed," I tease.

"Seriously," he scoffs, pointing to Jake, who gives him a giant, goofy grin in return.

"Yes, but not tonight. Tonight, he's my best gal pal, and we are going to hang out and plan the wedding while doing our nails."

"You've got to be kidding me." Robbie runs a hand over his face, scratching his couple of days' worth of stubble. "It's my wedding too. I'd maybe like a say in a thing or two."

"You will, sweety." I bat my eyelashes at him. "Don't worry, you're going to get to help with plenty. We are just going through the girly stuff. Like what flowers, dress ideas..."

"Lingerie," Jake adds unhelpfully, eliciting another growl from Robbie.

"I only have four short weeks to plan this wedding. We got lucky that Eli had an opening. I know Scarlett would have been fine with us having everything at the Inn—which is definitely beautiful. When Jax showed me the images for the barn though, I'm sorry but I couldn't resist. It was like everything just made sense. I could see the wedding, the reception, maroon and gold... It's going to be perfect."

Since the panic attack, I've been listening to the optimistic voice in the back of my mind. The one that whispers words of encouragement, reminding me that this is the right thing to do. My stomach still twists in knots at the fear of people in the town thinking that I trapped Robbie into marriage. But this voice reassures me that even though that four-letter word hasn't been shared between us, it's there. Well, certainly on my end anyway. I have to believe he feels it too. Because I refuse to believe that the universe is so cruel she'd make my heart skip a beat each time Robbie smiles at me, if he didn't feel the same way.

"I've come prepared." Jake unzips his hoodie, to reveal a hot pink t-shirt underneath that says: *Maid of Honor*. Then he leans down to his bag, pulling out nail polish and face masks.

"See?" I defend. "Not to mention, we already ordered pizza I know you'll hate and have lined up gory 80s slasher flicks I know you don't like." Seeing that Robbie still isn't convinced, I follow up with a low blow. "You're the one who has kept me locked up here for weeks, refusing to let me go back to my place. The least you can do is allow me to have some fun with my friend since we can't go anywhere."

Jake and Robbie share a suspicious look before he huffs out, "Fine. Please tell me he isn't actually your maid of honor?"

"Hey!" Jake says, offended.

"No, I'm sorry, Jake. We've discussed this. Moira is my maid of honor, but you'll still be a groomsman."

"Fine." He rolls his eyes. "I'd look fabulous in maroon, by the way."

"Whatever." Robbie shakes his head. "I'm just going to be at the bowling alley with Chris and Mack, so if you need me, call."

"Yeah, yeah." Jake waves Robbie out the door. "We will be just fine. You seem to forget I'm a first responder with actual medical training. *If* something happened, I'm better equipped to handle it than you are. Now go."

Shortly after Robbie leaves, our food is delivered. I waste no time digging into our pepperoni, green olive, and pineapple pizza. I wanted jalapenos also, but I've been getting bad heartburn recently. So, I went with a sweet and salty combo instead.

Settling in, we queue up our movies and scarf down dinner while going through some bridal magazines. This barn is gorgeous and it's already well decorated with rustic charm. I only really need to worry about floral arrangements and centerpieces. Eli's setup is impressive, and a dream for a bride who doesn't want to spend thousands on a wedding planner. He has several package deals to choose from, including menu ideas. Everything is sourced from local businesses. Given how little time I have to plan, this has been a lifesaver. With the exception of the flowers, everything will be from a homegrown vendor. All I have to do is make my selections in his packet, give it back to him, and voilà—I'm done. His staff takes care of all the event organizing based on my selections. I only have to meet with Patty about the cake and Carla about the dress.

So far, the only problem is the dress. "What about this one?" Jake asks again.

"No, it's too puffy."

"You said the last one was too tight," he grumbles.

"With the baby, I don't want to be strapped into a tight dress where I can't breathe. But that is too much. Ugh, this is a disaster." I throw the magazine to the floor.

"What are you looking for?"

"I want something simple, country. I know the trend is to make the wedding look simple and elegant, but still have it be expensive. Except, that isn't what I want. I want it to be genuine. I love that Tral Lake is down to earth. I don't want to change it."

"Well then, none of these New York hoity-toity magazines are going to help you." Jake throws his magazine next to mine, then checks his phone. "We've got time. They don't close for a couple of hours."

"What?"

"I'm sure Carla has a ton of dresses or could make you a beautiful one that looks like something from these magazines. But since these aren't what you're looking for, I think I have an idea. I was at Tral Treasures the other day and if it's still there, I think it's exactly what you have in mind."

"Jake, I'm not buying my wedding dress from a sex shop."

"It's a secondhand store, you pervert. You're thinking of Fantasy Gifts. Come on, grab your purse and keys."

"What about Robbie? He'll kill you if he catches us out."

"Well then, we better hurry."

Laughing, I grab my stuff, and we quickly walk down Main Street to the shop. I'm sorry, but any store with the word "treasures" in the title and dark drapes on the windows screams 'sex shop'. But I'm proven wrong when we walk inside, and the store is a variety of secondhand items. They have a little of everything.

"Hi, Maud." Jake waves to the elderly lady at the counter.

"Oh, Jake, hello. Do you have more donations?" she asks, her voice as shaky as her wrinkled hands.

"Nah, I'm actually here helping my soon-to-be sister-in-law find a wedding dress. I saw something last week. I hope it hasn't sold."

"Let me know. I recently had a donation of nice dresses that I haven't had a chance to put out yet."

"Thanks." Jake leads me to the back of the store. I make a mental note to come here later and do some shopping. Tonight, we are on a mission.

"Donations?" I ask.

He shrugs his shoulders. "I thought it was about time to start cleaning out my parents' stuff. They'd hate knowing it's been sitting around taking up space when it could go to good use somewhere else."

"Are you doing this all on your own?" I place my hand on Jake's arm, stopping and turning him to face me.

"Not completely. It's okay, Cassie. It's been therapeutic." He gives me a reassuring smile.

"If you need help, tell me."

He nods before his eyes light up. "It's here." He rushes to the rack and pulls out a dress. I can't believe it... he is right. Jake holds up a creamy white, lace, short-sleeved, A-line dress. The cut just below the bust makes the midsection forgiving—not that I expect to be huge, but I won't need to worry about sucking anything in. The torso and groin area are solid enough to be decent, but the rest of the dress has layers of sheer lace that offers a nice silhouette in the sunlight. It is the absolute perfect dress for a summer barn wedding. It's beautiful and elegant without outshining the allure of the venue. Even better, it is only fifty dollars and right next to it, I see a fabulous pair of dress boots to go with it.

I wrap my arms around Jake. "Thank you. This is exactly what I was looking for."

"See? I told you I'd make an outstanding maid of honor."

"Yes, you would. Hey, since we snuck out anyway, how about we live dangerously and stop to get some ice cream at the diner on the way back?"

36

Cassie

May 22nd

"WHAT ARE YOU UP to?" Robbie says, wrapping his arms around me from behind.

"Just going over a few proposals for the expansion," I respond, flipping through the reports I printed out.

"You're sexy when you are working." He places a kiss on my neck.

Leaning my head back, I grant him access to my throat. "*Numbers*," I whisper. Robbie growls and bites my neck. "*Projections*." I moan, as he squeezes my exceedingly sensitive breasts.

"Fuck, Cass," he grumbles. "I was going to ask if you'd like to go to the café with me to pick up our lunch orders. But now I'm thinking I need to carry you upstairs and have something else to eat."

I glance at the clock and see that it's only eleven. "We could be quick."

"Are you serious?"

"Does this feel serious to you?" I slide his hand under my dress to feel my drenched underwear.

Going to the door, he glances down the hall, making sure no one is there, before he closes and locks the office. Turning around, he is already stripping out of his blue jumpsuit, revealing his tight grey t-shirt and briefs. "You're going to need to be quiet," is all the warning I get before Robbie bends me forward over the desk.

His fingertips tickle my thighs as they travel higher, bringing up the hem of my dress. Kneeling behind me, he trails soft kisses up the inside of my leg before licking me through my underwear, his tongue tickling my lips and teasing me. I'm grateful when I feel his fingers hook into my waistband to pull it down, spreading me wide open, wet and fully exposed. Using the flat of his tongue, Robbie exacts long, slow licks from my clit to my bottom—each stroke agonizing. It's just enough pressure to tease me, but not enough to give me the release my body is shaking for.

I gasp when he sucks my clit between his teeth. "Shh, you need to be quiet." Leaning further forward, I stifle my moans with my forearm, biting down when I feel his rough finger enter me and apply pressure to my G-spot. One more hard suck, and I fall apart around him.

"Oh my god," I breathe into my arm.

I'm hardly finished with my orgasm when I feel the head of his erection push past my folds and enter me in one swift thrust. The intrusion catches me off guard and I fail to cover my cry. He pulls me up, causing my back to arch. Robbie turns my head to face him. Capturing my mouth with his, he plunges his tongue, allowing me to taste my juices. Suddenly, he picks up his pace, thrusting his hard shaft deep inside and hitting a nerve I didn't even know I had until him. As his swollen head keeps pressing on my new spot, a warm sensation starts in my toes and travels up to my core. Like a switch, he presses his thumb against my clit and I'm set off like fireworks. He's doing his best to swallow my cries. But as he finds his own release, he moans into my mouth. If anyone was walking by the office, it would be clear what we were doing. Surprisingly, I don't care.

Spent, I lean forward on the desk, resting on my arms. Robbie's body covers mine as he presses a soft kiss to the back of my neck. "I think this should be our normal lunch date."

I laugh before he gives me one more kiss. We both get cleaned up and ready to walk to the café.

I soak up the sun as soon as we step outside. Right now, it is perfect. The sun is bright and warm with highs in the mid-seventies. There is no humidity with a light crisp breeze. I pray the weather will stay this nice for the wedding. *I can't believe I'm getting married in a couple of weeks.*

Walking to Moore Books and Coffee, I smile like the cat who got the cream, basking in a post-orgasmic glow as Robbie holds my hand. It's the small moments like these that I've grown to cherish. These are the things I choose to hold on to. When Robbie touches me, that's when I know what we have is more than just out of obligation. It's his words that sometimes make me doubt the deafening thump in my chest that is screaming to let her out. *Soon,* I remind her. I'm just waiting for a sign. *Chicken. O*kay, fine. I'm terrified that as soon as I open that door, I won't be able to close it. If for some reason I'm wrong, I don't think I'll be able to recover from that earth-shattering revelation. I'd much rather live in blissful ignorance and hold on to these moments, than find out I've been making mountains out of molehills again.

Entering the shop, I notice Scott's frustrated and on the phone. When we get up to the counter, he is hanging up his cell, murmuring some insults under his breath.

"What's up?" Robbie asks.

"This stupid oven," Scott huffs out. "When we did the inspection, they said it was good—just needed to replace the hood. Now the health inspector is saying I need to replace the whole fucking rig."

"Seriously? That sucks."

"Yeah, not to mention, there is a brand-new leak that is dripping right into the cooler. I'm waiting for the maintenance guy to show up, but I'm suspecting I'll need a new walk-in. Fucking McCalesters, I knew we shouldn't have trusted them."

I look at Robbie confused, but he just shakes his head. "Long story. Do you want me to take a quick look at the cooler?"

Scott looks relieved. "Yeah, would you mind just giving me your opinion? I'd like to make sure I'm not getting ripped off."

"Sure, let's go look at it real fast. Cass, I'll be back in a minute." He leans down and presses a kiss to my cheek.

I grab our food from the counter and find an empty table to sit at, while I wait for Robbie and play on my phone. I decide to take a selfie of me drinking my tea and send it to Moira.

Moira: Did he give it to you good?

Me: Yes, it made for a nice late-morning snack. With this new diet and exercise regimen, I will fit my dress for sure.
Moira: I could use some good D. Ugh, B.O.B. just isn't hitting the spot these days... or helping me burn as many calories.
Me: At the wedding, I'm sure there will be one groomsman willing to help you with some housekeeping.
Moira: Don't tempt me.

"*Did you hear she's pregnant?*" I pick up on a girl whispering behind me. I close my eyes and take deep breaths. *They might not be talking about you, and even if they are, it doesn't matter.* I remind myself, hoping to prevent another attack.

232

"*I know. I wouldn't be surprised if she did it on purpose—only way she could get him to commit,*" another female replies.

"*Do you think they're going to get married?*"

"*Didn't you hear? They're engaged.*"

"*Lucky girl. He's definitely a prime cut of meat.*"

"*They all are.*"

"*I tried asking him out one time and he acted like I didn't even exist.*"

As I look at the girls, my heart plummets. Before, I could have assumed that *maybe* they were talking about someone else. But I recognize them almost immediately. They were at the baby shower. While Tilly assures me she kept my secret, it seems it has somehow leaked out. I thought I was strong enough to handle people like them. That if I focused on the fact that this has grown to be more than a relationship of convenience, it would make jerks like them meaningless. Instead, their whispers and overt laughter (as I catch them sneak side glances at me) stoke the flames of the venomous voice of self-doubt. It takes all my strength to not burst into tears. The last thing I want to do is make more of a fool of myself.

"Hi, Robbie," one girl says in a singsong voice, giving him a small finger wave. She pays me absolutely no attention—as though I don't even exist.

"Madison," Robbie says, disinterested.

"Oh, hi, Cassie. How are you? You look great. *Glowing.*" Madison gives me a big smile. *I'm sure it's fake.*

"Did you have something you wanted to say about me or my fiancée?"

"What? No." The girls both hold up their hands and shake their heads.

"Okay, so you just prefer talking about someone behind their back? Or at least loud enough that they can overhear you. But if they confront you, they'd look like the asshole because they were eavesdropping. Can I share a secret with you ladies?" Robbie leans forward, and the sneer he gives them raises the hair on the back of my neck. I've never seen him act like this before. "I don't give two shits about looking like an asshole. Next time you have an opinion about Cassie, my engagement, anything, don't. Because I don't give a flying fuck what you think. Cass, are you ready?"

I nod my head. Too stunned for words, I grab the bags. Pulling me into his side, Robbie drapes his arm over my shoulder. We walk out the door, and I've never been so turned on and angry at the same time. Once we are far enough away from the café, I stop and turn to Robbie. "Why did you do that?"

"Do what?"

"Make a scene?"

"Are you mad at me?" He studies me carefully.

"Yes." I shake my head. "No... I'm just... Everyone overheard that. It's going to add to the rumor mill that is already going on. Aren't we just making more problems for ourselves?"

"Maybe." He shrugs. "But I don't care. And clearly, neither did she. If she had any self-preservation, she wouldn't have talked shit, one table over from where you were sitting, in an establishment owned by my family. I promise you if any of my siblings overheard her, even an extremely pregnant Tilly, they all would have done the exact same thing."

Robbie wipes a tear from my face I hadn't even realized I shed. I have so many conflicting emotions right now. I feel like my head is spinning.

"Cass, don't cry. They aren't worth it. Come here." He tucks me under his arm. "Look, most people in this town aren't going to think one way or the other about the baby, and how we ended up together. I can promise you folks in Tral Lake have enough of their own skeletons to deal with. Don't even get me started on the McCalester scandal. What I'm trying to say is... *fuck 'em.*"

"I just don't enjoy being the focus of everyone's attention. It was bad enough, knowing people were probably going to talk about us. But now, what are they going to say?"

"Cass, I need you to listen to me real good." Robbie turns to face me, lifting my chin to look me in the eye. "I will do just about anything to make this work. To make sure you and the baby have a good life. But I will never allow someone to disrespect you or my child. I don't care who they are. Do you understand that?"

I wrap my arms around his neck. Standing on my tippytoes, I kiss him deeply, the restraints holding my heart back now threatening to snap with that four-letter word on the tip of my tongue. Even though I get the sneaking suspicion that Robbie is holding a part of himself back from me. *Aren't you still holding a piece of yourself back?* I've learned that when it comes to him, actions speak louder than words. The fierce determination he has to make sure I know he will protect us, even if I'm not strong enough to defend myself, is better than any speech proclaiming his love in flowery words. I've received enough of those in my time to learn that they are all just filler and no substance. For the first time, I honestly feel loved and cherished by someone who isn't my family. Crazy as it seems, I am now thankful to Chad, my co-workers, my other exes. Because if it wasn't for them, I wouldn't be here right now.

"I'm ready." Robbie raises an eyebrow, confused by my statement.

37

Robbie

May 22nd

Walking upstairs, I'm blown away. My place had never been unkept. I keep things clean and put my shit where it belongs. Just like the shop, I don't want to waste time searching for something. I don't have to think about it; I can work on instinct. But since I moved into this apartment, even after all the remodeling and despite when Bianca cluttered it with her girly shit, this is the first time it has ever felt like a home.

When Cassie told me she was ready, I didn't know what she was *ready* for. Once we got back to the shop, she asked for the rest of the day off, urging me not to come upstairs until six and not a moment sooner. I've been standing outside my door for the past forty-five minutes, waiting patiently. Usually, I'd have no problem keeping myself busy, especially since the Mustang is just about finished. However, I haven't been able to think about anything all day other than that kiss and the determined look in her eye.

"I hope you're hungry?" Cassie says with a bright smile. It doesn't hide the fact that she's nervous. She's hardly able to make eye contact, and she keeps biting her bottom lip while she twirls her ring around her finger.

"I'm starving. It smells great. I don't think it's ever smelled this good in here before." I'm not the best cook. I can keep myself alive and that's about it. If I ever wanted a home-cooked meal, I had to go, well, *home*. I eat probably one too many meals at Harper's and the diner.

"Thanks. I've always loved cooking—especially baking. I'm not nearly as good as Scott, or even Jax. But I make a mean steak and salad."

"You'll get no complaints from me. Jax is a good cook, but he gets a little out there for me. Not that I don't enjoy trying new things. That meal Jax made last week with the meat and eggplant that looked like a lasagna was pretty good. But I prefer mom's tater tot hotdish or Scott's meatloaf any day of the week."

"Moussaka." Cassie smiles before chuckling. "My ma makes it every now and then." A sad expression washes over her face. "Sorry, I've never actually met anyone from my ma's side of the family. I guess there had been some falling out before I was born. Whenever she misses them, she likes to cook some of her yaya's recipes she learned while visiting her in Greece." She shakes her head. "No matter, we aren't here to talk about that."

I swallow the bitter taste of keeping my conversation with Cian a secret. I've wanted to tell her since the moment he blindsided me out front. But he made me promise on a threat of death and dismemberment to keep my mouth shut, saying that it'd only hurt her more than anything.

"Okay, what would you like to talk about?" I ask hesitantly. Based on her continued fidgeting, I can tell whatever conversation we are about to have will not be an easy one. With the exception of Madison's bullshit earlier, things have been going smoothly—*too smoothly*. Now I get the feeling that was all just the calm before the storm.

Cassie gestures for me to sit at the small two-person table I have as my official eating area. She went all out, decorating the spot with a little table cloth and a vase with flowers. My gut sinks. *These are from the house*—when was she there? I have to hope (from the lack of yelling and the fact that Cian isn't blowing up my phone) that she didn't catch him there.

Yeah, Jake wasn't too happy about keeping the little detail of her brother staying there a secret. It's been hard as hell coming up with excuses for Cassie not to stop by home. Jake or I have been grabbing whatever she needs and bringing it here. Cian assured me it would only be for a week, but he's had a few bumps in his plan—probably why he wants to keep it from Cassie. In the event things don't work out, he doesn't want to disappoint her.

Cassie takes a deep breath. "I want to talk about something that happened. Specifically, about what happened with my ex."

I swallow. I wasn't prepared for that. I'd assumed this conversation was about her getting cold feet or worse, wanting to move back home because of assholes like Madison. I didn't expect this.

"Cass, we don't have to open old wounds if you don't want to."

She nods in appreciation. "I know. But that's the thing about wounds. If they weren't properly cleaned and irrigated, they can fester. Eventually you need to go back in and poke around so they can finally heal and scar over." Cassie chuckles. "Sorry, probably not a thing you want to talk about with dinner. It's just with Kill, I became pretty good at wound care. Let's just say in the beginning, his fights weren't all in a regulated ring and he needed a medic. Anyway, what I'm trying to say is... I never actually talked about what happened with Chad or work. I mentioned a few things to Moira, and gave an even more abbreviated version to my family. I'd been too embarrassed. But after the panic attack and what happened today, I realize maybe it's time to open up. We're about to be married, and have a baby after that. For better or worse, we are planning a life together and I don't want this always holding us back. As I've recently realized, keeping all this bottled up is doing more harm than good."

I swallow, preparing myself. I have a feeling I'm going to have to rein it in, if I don't want to scare her off. "Okay."

"All right, well, it might help if I start at the beginning. The problems were established long before Chad. My brothers did a good job at scaring the bejesus out of all the boys at school from ever wanting to date me. They were all too terrified that Kill might beat them up, or that Cian would murder them and their bodies would never be found. College was my first chance at freedom. While most people knew who my brother was, it was the height of his fighting career and that fact made me popular by proxy. Of course, I had a type. I had been helplessly drawn to the bad boys. Leather jackets, tattoos, motorcycles—I was in love instantaneously. I was drawn to their whole aesthetic and romanticized the idea of being loved by the reformed rebel. I know this sounds bad, but it's the truth."

"I don't think anyone makes the wisest romantic choices when they are young."

"No, especially not a girl who had been ready to fall in love since she was six. With my religious conservative parents and overprotective brothers, I was smothered. I got drunk on the freedom and didn't make the best choices. I thought Mark had been the worst one yet. I'd met him shortly after graduating college. Moira had left for some fellowship, Tilly returned home, Cian was god knows where, Kill was in Vegas training, and my parents were busy at the shop. For the first time in my life, I was alone. I hated it. Enter Mark. He checked all the boxes and then some. I wanted a bad boy, and I finally found one. It just turns out I got more than I bargained for. I ignored the warning signs at first: excessive drinking, dabbling in drugs, questionable late-night calls. It wasn't until he became aggressive with me that I knew something was wrong."

My nails cut into my palm as I squeeze tightly. I already know where this story is going, and it is taking all my willpower not to find this asshole and kill him. Fuck, when this is over, I'm telling Cian he has one more mission, to gather as much fucking intel as he can on this asshole and make sure he is never found.

"The relationship was over almost as quickly as it began. We were out at some bar—he was plastered. Some guy slapped my butt. Mark flipped out and ended up getting us kicked out. Once we left the bar, all that anger was turned towards me. It was all my fault. I was dressed like a slut and asking for every guy to stare at my ass. I was nothing more than a cock-tease. His words, not mine. He didn't stop at words though. It wasn't over until I had a busted lip and a broken rib. Before you freak out, just let me finish. That night was awful, but it opened my eyes. I never saw him from that day on. I didn't even bother to go back and retrieve my laptop from his apartment. It just wasn't worth the risk of him hurting me again.

"After that, I was done. I got the job I'd dreamed of at the firm. I'd sworn off bad boys. Wild, crazy Cassie ceased to exist. Well, mostly. At least *that* part of her did. Then I met Chad; he was the exact opposite of every guy I had ever dated. No tattoos, no leather jacket, no motorcycle. At first, I had no interest in dating him, especially since his family owned the firm. But he was persistent, charming. He wooed me with flowers and chocolate. I'd never experienced any of that before. I thought, '*This is how it's supposed to be.*' This was romance. And for the longest time, it was. He was the first boyfriend I'd ever brought home to meet my family. When they told me they didn't like him, I thought that was just them being overbearing and overprotective. Or that it was because they were judging him. That since he was from money, they just didn't know how to act around him.

"It took me four and a half years to learn he was nothing more than a wolf in sheep's clothing. He might have worn an

Armani suit and driven a Porsche, but at the heart of it, he was no better than Mark. Except I never saw *him* coming. There was no anger or aggression; it was all manipulation. And that's the kicker... Looking back, the busted lip wasn't so bad. Those physical wounds heal, but the emotional ones... they stay with you. They follow you long after the scrapes and bruises scab over and fade away with time. So, while Mark was an uncomfortable bump in the road, Chad was the real villain in this story.

"The mind games started so subtly I never even noticed. He fooled me, lied to me, broke down my barriers and exploited me. Prior to Katie, I had a suspicion he was cheating on me. Extra late nights, sudden business trips, the hint of perfume on his collar, hushed phone calls—all the signs were there. But when I confronted him about it, the confidence he exuded when he looked me in the eye and told me it was all in my head... well, it was disarming. He had a logical explanation for each one of my accusations and so much conviction with his denial that he had me doubting myself. I actually thought I was going insane. I remember finding lace panties under the bed when I was cleaning one day. I knew for a fact they weren't mine. I've never owned crotchless anything. He had an entire story about how and when he bought them for me and the amazing night we had together afterwards. I knew he was lying—I didn't remember a single thing he was telling me. He turned it completely on me, mentioning how I had one too many that night and didn't remember, and how I'd been drinking too much lately. Somehow, the conversation went from me pointing out women's underwear that didn't belong in our bedroom, to me having a drinking problem. That was the next thing, manipulating me into thinking I was some sort of alcoholic. I won't lie. I enjoyed having a beer or a glass of wine with dinner. Or going to the pub with Moira. But I've never been blackout drunk, or done something I regret because I was drinking—even us and our situation," Cassie makes her point clear.

"That night together, I knew exactly what I was doing. I wanted it as much when I was sober as I did after six shots of tequila. I regret nothing. Not what happened, how it happened, or the baby. No matter what happens with us, I will regret no part of it. Sorry." She shakes her head. "I'm getting off track. I haven't even got to the worst of it yet."

How much worse can this get?

"After I caught Chad and Katie together, physically in the act... Well, the next day when I went back for my stuff, he actually tried convincing me I was making it all up. But I knew he was lying. It was like the pain from my heart shattering somehow knocked me out of whatever daze he had me in. The worst of it though, was afterwards. Because not only had he fooled me, lied to me—for years. He had the whole firm aligned with him. Or if not completely in his corner, not coming to my defense either, out of fear of losing their own jobs. The manipulation didn't end with the status of our engagement. If anything, it got worse. Because instead of lying to keep me with him, it was to push me away. Telling me how my coworkers were making complaints. The partners unimpressed with my work. Giving my projects to others. The rumors about me were vicious. It only helped strengthen his story. I was the cheater, the liar, taking advantage of him to advance my career. It broke me. One day, the whispers got so loud I couldn't breathe. After the holidays, everything seemed to get worse, like he amped up his tactics. That was the first panic attack, and what lost me my job."

"Wait..." I feel like a dick. I don't want to interrupt, but I'm holding on by a thread. "They fired you for the panic attack?"

Cassie gives a small nod. "I had been the talk of the company, not in a good way. So, when I collapsed, causing yet another scene, Chad's father more or less gave me a choice:

accept his settlement offer and be laid off with a letter of recommendation, or continue working there and eventually get fired then blacklisted. I didn't even need the settlement. I was done. I wanted to be strong like Cian told me to be. But I couldn't handle it. I was broken. Taking the settlement didn't matter anyway, and the letter of recommendation did nothing. No one would hire me. The rumors spread far past just inside that office. Three of the smaller agencies in the Cities are even under their umbrella, so applying wasn't even an option.

"At first, I was sad. I worked my butt off to get where I was. That was all me—it had nothing to do with Chad. When I came here though, and sat in your small office looking at your archaic filing system, I realized it was all wrong for me. I've always loved numbers; something about them centers me. But I chose to study business and accounting because of my love for small family-owned operations. My parents struggled so much to get their boutique off the ground; there was little to no help for them, no resources. They had to learn everything on their own, from trial and error. Even if I think the name is ridiculous, bet or not, I love working at Moore Body and Lube. The guys are great. The owner happens to actually care about his business and works to serve his community, not to become a millionaire. Don't play it down. I do your books and see the customers. Conveniently, it seems that all the single parents, elderly and less fortunate get a special discount and free services. You're a good man, Robert Moore Jr.

"That's why I'm risking telling you all of this. Because I want you to understand how difficult this next thing is for me to say." I actually can't breathe. I knew a storm was coming. I just never expected her to unload everything, and then leave me. I'm still caught somewhere between wanting a list of her exes and going on a murdering spree, and holding her tight and never letting her go. "I love you."

I hesitate, completely surprised. I wasn't prepared for her confession. *Do I love Cassie?* I'm planning on spending the rest of my life with her. We're about to have a baby together. We make awesome partners. The thought of a bitch like Madison saying anything derogatory about her flips a switch inside me, needing to protect Cassie, to defend her. So why can't I say the words that she is eagerly waiting to hear? I said them to Bianca—*daily for years*.

"You don't need to say anything," Cassie chokes out. The pain in her watery eyes is like a knife twisting in my gut. Casually wiping her face, she sits up straight. With her shoulders held back and chest thrust out, she continues, "Actually, I don't want you to. I just laid a lot on you. Whatever you say right now is going to be motivated by this conversation. So, unless after hearing all of this, you don't want to get married... I guess I would want to know that much now. Otherwise, please drop it." The twist of her ring is the only sign she gives me that if I were to call off the wedding, it would devastate her. The last thing I ever want to do is hurt Cassie. *Except that is exactly what you are doing right now, asshole.*

38

Cassie

June 7th

"LIKE THIS?" MOIRA HOLDS up the mason jar filled with LED string lights.

"Yes, perfect," I say, finishing one of my own. Fortunately, the wedding and reception are small, so we don't have many to make. I would have finished them myself, but last weekend, I went home to talk about the floral arrangements with Ma. We probably could have discussed them over the phone, but it was a nice excuse to get away.

It's been difficult to pretend that Robbie's hesitation when I said that stupid four-letter word wasn't a big deal. I chastised myself repeatedly for taking what felt like a rejection at the time to heart. I was prepared for that scenario—*it's what I expected*. Actually, his hesitance was a better reaction than the disgust I was ready for (at the very notion I would feel so strongly so soon). I was putting everything out there, laying all my cards on the table prior to the wedding. I'm not sure why, but the idea of carrying that baggage into this new phase of my life made me feel sick to my stomach. Like if I didn't dump it now, it would always be a part of me. The entire experience was terrifying, but cathartic. I never told anyone about Mark. I told my parents someone mugged me to explain the injuries.

Even though it felt good to get everything off my chest, a small part of me really, truly believed that if I stopped holding my heart back, Robbie would do the same. I convinced myself that he loved me, but because I was hiding so much, he wasn't going to reveal himself to me. I hoped this would bring us closer together. Instead, it has pushed us further apart. I've tried to not read into things, telling myself I'm acting crazy. But that voice of self-doubt has gotten stronger as the wedding day approaches.

First, he practically kicked me out of his place. Okay, I might be exaggerating a bit. But for weeks, he's had every excuse in the book as to why I should stay with him in the cramped apartment. Even when I mentioned something as simple as wanting to just grab more clothes from the house, he would insist on taking care of it. Though sometimes it got a little annoying, I thought it was sweet. Like he didn't want to be without me—practice for when we are married and living together, which by the way, we still haven't discussed that whole arrangement. I'm sixteen weeks pregnant and don't know where I should set up for the baby. Then, after I opened up to him, he suggested I head back to the house. He had some major work to do on the Mustang and wouldn't be around, stressing that there was no need for me to be alone and bored upstairs, when Jake was home. Admittedly, none of this is too concerning, *on its own*. Except, after Memorial Day weekend was over and Jake was going back to the station, I suggested maybe I would crash at his place again so we could finalize wedding details. He insisted he was very busy with a few projects he needed to wrap up before the wedding and I'd be stuck all by myself. The house is more comfortable and blah, blah, blah.

Second, the hushed phone calls. This is what truly made the hair on the back of my neck stand up. All of a sudden, secrecy. Robbie, whether it be a personal or business matter, has never stepped out of the room for a conversation before.

Third, I asked him about the expansion. A few weeks ago, I had provided him several different projections on his time and financial commitment. Unfortunately, no matter what, most of his time would need to be spent at the new shop, especially because all the locations he has been looking at are almost an hour away from here. I started calling them "Automotive Repair Deserts". Like Moore Body and Lube, each of these areas has little to no resources for major repairs or fabrications. The few that did, offer little within the range of affordability. The perfect location, which was about an hour and a half west of here, only had one tow in the area. He had already reached out to the company; it's a private operator. There had been discussions about contracting with him if he opened a shop in the area. I really liked the location; it didn't have as much charm as Tral Lake, and the economy wasn't nearly as stable. But it has potential. A bit of a gamble, but no matter what, Robbie would be taking on a risk. There is no guarantee that any of the new locations will be profitable. Most projections ran a forty-five percent failure rate, and best-case scenario, he wouldn't be in the black again for five years. We went from talking about this daily to nothing.

I was prepared to marry Robbie, well aware this was no more than him fulfilling some sense of familial responsibility. Despite it not being the magical fairytale I'd dreamed of growing up, I could accept a loveless marriage, because all of the other elements that made a robust relationship were there. We work well together, like the perfect duo. We have similar values and work ethic. We have fun and laugh with each other. The sex—off the charts. It seemed like I was going to marry a friend with benefits, and then we'd raise a baby. Basically, it'd be me marrying Jake—not that I've ever done anything like *that* with him. You get the idea. But, since I opened my big mouth and dumped all my crap on Robbie,

I feel like we are barely even acquaintances. Except for the occasional kiss, we haven't been intimate since that day in his office.

"Pre-wedding jitters?" Tilly asks.

"Yeah," I admit.

"I was so nervous before the wedding with Jax. Even without having an actual ceremony, I had been terrified of all the ways the day would go wrong. Would he not show up? Would I be sick and throw up on him during the kiss? Would there be a blizzard? Would the courthouse shut down? Every possible worst-case scenario, I thought of it. But don't worry, everything will be great tomorrow." Tilly winces and holds the side of her belly.

"Are you feeling okay? You look a little pale?"

Tilly waves me off. "Yes, *Jax*," she says sarcastically. "I'm fine. At your stage, the kicking is cute, and *this amazing experience*. At mine, it feels like a scene from *Alien* and I'm waiting for a hand to burst out."

"I still don't know how you manage to stand?" Letty jokes.

"Sheer willpower," Tilly retorts. "Have you felt any kicking yet?"

"Yeah, it just started the other day." I cried for hours afterwards. It happened while I was lying in bed watching *Supernatural*—alone. Robbie and I had been bingeing it together before bed. I was going to hold back, but after a week of not spending a night with him, I decided to keep watching. I still haven't seen the final few seasons, and I'm too impatient to wait for him. When the baby kicked, I got super excited, yelling out for him to hurry and come feel. Then I remembered he wasn't there. I thought about calling him, then changed my mind. That's when the tears started—the realization that no matter what some piece of paper said, I was going to be by myself. The only thing keeping me going is knowing I need to be strong for the baby.

"I remember freaking out the first time they kicked. Jax and I were, well, you know, and they kicked the hand that was on my stomach. He went..." Tilly makes a flopping motion and snaps her fingers. "Like that."

We all burst out laughing. Even though I might have gotten my hopes up, believing Robbie felt the same way about me, at least I have everyone else. Tilly and I picked up right where we left off in college. Having our babies grow up together will be amazing. I love Jake; he is my best friend—best *male* friend. Scar is hilarious; she is constantly sending me taboo romances to read. Letty and I have been getting together in the mornings to discuss some business plans. I've offered to review a few things for her and give her a couple of projections.

Maybe we don't need to get married? That thought has been rattling around in my head nonstop, as the big day approaches. Given his distance, I'd honestly hoped Robbie would be the one to call things off. The only reason I haven't is out of fear of being labeled the bad guy, and having all my newfound friends thinking I am standing Robbie up. I'm not sure any of them would understand that I'd probably be saving us from a divorce. Also, I'm not sure I want to deal with my family and their complaints again. So, if Robbie is still willing to go through with this sham of a marriage, so am I. Then, at least when this doesn't work out and we separate, I can say I tried. It's probably not a great idea to be planning your divorce the night before your wedding, but this is all just for show. I figured I'd give it one year, two max. Ideally, I'd like to be divorced before the baby is old enough to realize mommy and daddy don't actually love each other.

"Okay, that's it," Moira says, tugging my arm. "We are going out."

I roll my eyes. "Where do you plan on going in a small town, with two pregnant women, one of whom is ready to pop at the seams?"

"Anywhere that's not sitting here watching you fret over the wedding tomorrow. While you've been planning your big day all these years, I've been concocting your bachelorette party, which I'm being denied. So, as your best friend and maid of honor, it's my duty to ensure you have one more fun night, before you tie the knot and become a boring old married person with children and responsibilities."

"You know, Moira, when you get married, I'm going to make certain to include this tidbit of information in my speech."

"One, I'm never getting married. There is no man capable of tying me down. I'd need at least three of them."

"You should read some of the books Scar sends me. Having three or even four guys tie you down isn't that uncommon anymore."

"Okay, well, when I find three guys to tie me down, and it's legal for all of us to get married, you can make sure to include this in your speech. In the meantime, we are going out. I don't care where. But we are not sitting around here all night while you stress about tomorrow."

"Nails," Letty yells excitedly. "It's still early enough. I'm sure we could all go get our nails done."

Tilly grabs her phone and starts frantically texting. "Yes, Amanda says she'll stay open later, and ask Lauren to stick around to do a special last-minute bridal party spa day. I don't know about you, but the idea of letting my feet soak while getting a rubdown sounds amazing."

I go through the checklist of the few things I still need to do, which really isn't much. Eli and his crew are handling almost everything. Ma will be here with the flowers in the morning. "Okay, a little pampering sounds nice."

"Yes." Tilly reaches her hands out for Letty to help her stand. "Jax is nowhere as good at rubbing my feet as Lauren. He tries, but she has the special touch. Oh, then we could stop by the diner for burgers and milkshakes. I've been craving one all day."

Everyone excitedly slips on their flip-flops and heads out the door. It's a beautiful evening, and I'd love to walk. I'm not sure Tilly would make it that far though. We are barely three steps out the door before Tilly says, "Oh shit." We all look back at her panicked expression. "I think I peed myself."

39

Robbie

June 8th

"How long does this normally take?" Jake asks, pacing the hall with his hair pulled in all directions.

"Calm down, dude," Scott complains.

"I can't calm down. Tilly is in there right now being torn apart and there is nothing I can do about it," Jake cries, collapsing in the chair next to Cassie. He puts his head in his hands and rests his elbows on his knees. Cassie leans over, rubbing circles on his back and whispering that everything will be fine. So far, she's been the only one to get any semblance of composure from Jake. It's taken all my willpower to bite my lip and ignore my jealous rage, which wants nothing more than to remove her hand from him. *They are just friends. Jake needs her right now.*

This is not exactly how I planned my night ending up. We had a pretty typical stag night going: cigars, poker, talking cars and business. I was up a grand on Jake, which never happens. Part of me still thinks he somehow twin-linked with Tilly to have her go into labor, so he could get out of losing. As ridiculous as that sounds, I guarantee he at least attempted it.

"How are you feeling?" I ask Cassie. She looks up at me before glancing back at Cian. She was a little surprised when he showed up at the hospital with us. Apparently, her brother being down here (and at my little party) before the rest of the family was too suspicious for her, especially since everyone else isn't arriving until tomorrow. Saying that we had become friends over the past month was laughable. Granted, she isn't completely off on her suspicions.

"Good. I just hope that Tilly and the babies are doing okay." She turns her attention back to Jake.

I glance at the time on my phone; it is almost two in the morning. We are supposed to be getting married in eleven hours and most of the wedding party is here at the hospital. "Let me bring you home. You look exhausted."

"I'm fine," she yawns.

"Cass," I say sternly. "You're about to topple over any moment. You need your rest."

"Come on, Cassie," Jake prompts, sitting up and motioning for her to snuggle in next to him. *Just friends, just friends, just friends.* I remind myself as my nails dig into my palms.

"Fine," she huffs, before scooting closer to Jake and resting her head on his shoulder.

I hate that since our talk, things have been strained. There is so much I've wanted to tell her, but when she looks at me, I cease up. That's when I remembered I suck at words. I always say the wrong words. So, I've been working on a few surprises for her—ones that I'm hoping will convey the things I can't seem to verbalize. We just have to make it through tomorrow. We'll be down two members of the bridal party, but it won't be the end of the world.

After a couple more hours, Letty walks down the hall, a big smile on her face. Yeah, that was another reason for Jake's meltdown. Tilly was allowed only two people in the room once the labor started, and much to his dismay, she wanted Letty. Jake goes to stand, then remembers Cassie is leaning against his shoulder and, from the looks of it, she is already passed out. I knew she was exhausted. Cian gets up from his chair, gently lifts Cassie's head and motions for Jake to stand.

"You guys go ahead. I'll stay with her." Cian slides into Jake's spot and lays her head back down. I hate leaving her here like this. I know she'd want to see the babies. But she needs her rest. Jake's told me about the late nights she's had, watching TV in bed. I can only assume the pressure of the wedding is making it hard for her to turn off that brain of hers.

Placing a soft kiss on Cassie's head, I leave her with Cian and Moira before following Jake, Letty, and Scott to Tilly's room. Once we enter the suite, we are greeted by the new parents, both clearly exhausted. But the smile on their faces says it all. This is likely the best moment of either of their lives.

"Who do we have here?" Jake asks softly, before extending his hands to Jax, who then reluctantly places the baby in his arms.

"That's Alexander, and this one here is Gavin," Tilly says, motioning to the twin in her arms.

"Two boys." Jake smiles large, knowing he just won the pot.

Jax shakes his head before laughing. "Yes, Jake. Both are boys."

"You named him after Pops?" I comment.

Tilly smiles. "Yeah, we had a few name combinations picked out. I wanted to name one after dad, but I thought that was your honor, to pass it down if you wanted. Alexander was perfect, given it was Pops' first name as well as dad's, and I guess *your*, middle name. It seemed fitting."

"I couldn't decide between my dad's or my grandfather's name. It was a tough choice. I used both. His full name is Gavin Dean."

"What's *his* middle name?" Jake motions to Alexander, who's still in his arms.

Tilly has a goofy grin. "Jacob."

"Alexander Jacob," he repeats in awe, staring down at the baby he's cradling. "It's perfect."

Tilly rolls her eyes. "Would you like to hold him?" Tilly asks me.

I raise my hands, suddenly very nervous. I haven't held a baby since Tilly and Jake were this size. "Scott can go ahead."

"You're a good man." Scott pats me on the shoulder. "You need the practice anyway. This will be you soon."

Jax gently takes the baby from Tilly before he thrusts him in my arms, not giving me a choice. I'm speechless, looking at little Dean's face. Yes, I'm going to call him Dean. First off, come on, James Dean. Secondly, I've been watching *Supernatural* with Cassie, and Dean is my favorite character. She likes to joke that I am Sam's build (well, a little bulkier) with Dean's personality and love for cars.

"I think he's got baby fever," Jax teases.

"Good, because he's about to have his own soon," Tilly adds.

I'm about to have a baby... with Cassie. Cassie, who I'm supposed to marry today. But as I look up at Jax, who is brushing back Tilly's hair as she tries her hardest not to fall asleep, it is obvious to even a complete stranger that, despite all the heartache those two have experienced, they are without a doubt madly in love and meant to be together. Then the realization hits me... *I can't marry Cassie.*

40

Cassie

June 8th

"Cassie." I FAINTLY HEAR Robbie's voice. Cracking open my eyes, I see him squatting before me in the hospital lobby. *The babies.*

I sit up quickly. "Is Tilly...?"

Robbie smiles. "Tilly and the babies are great. They are all sleeping right now, but I'm sure they'd love to meet you when they wake up."

I search around for my purse. "What time is it?"

"It's eight in the morning."

"Oh no, the wedding! I still have so much to do." Rubbing the soreness from my neck, I get up, looking for my coat and purse before realizing Robbie has them both. I take my belongings from his extended arms. "I better get going."

"Cassie, wait." Robbie's words cut through me. Something about his tone sounds ominous.

"Robbie, we're supposed to get married in five hours. Unless..."

His sudden wince tells me everything I need to know. "Cass, can we talk outside?"

I wrap my arms around my midsection, protecting myself from what I know is about to come. This is what I wanted.

His decision to back out now means I can still be friends with everyone, without being the villain. Not that anyone really is the bad guy in this scenario. But no one could hate me for cancelling the wedding. All of this would be his own choosing. "It sounds like there is nothing left to discuss."

Robbie runs a hand over his face, the bags under his eyes and disheveled hair, evidence he hasn't slept. "Please, can you give me a second to explain?" His sad amber eyes tug at the strings still attached to the heart he's just obliterated. Clearly, there are a few functioning pieces left, as I nod in agreement and follow him outside to the courtyard.

The sun is shining brightly. It is still a little chilly and dewy this morning. But it's obvious that today was going to be a beautiful day for a wedding. I better call Eli and warn him not to set up; hopefully he hasn't done too much already. I should also tell Ma to take the flowers home. Maybe she can use them for someone else or donate them before they wilt. *Crap,* my parents are going to flip. I quickly pull out my phone, hoping I can catch them before they make it too far down here.

Robbie gently grabs my wrist. "Cassie, hold on."

"No, Robbie," I cry. *Stupid hormones.* As much as I want to be strong, I can't stop the tears from falling. "Just so you know, I'm not crying over you. I'm pregnant and this is an involuntary reaction. I can't help it. Now let me call Ma before my parents waste their time."

"Cian already took care of it. He's got everything handled."

"Of course, he does," I sneer. "Then what do you want to talk about? Clearly, you've already made up your mind without talking to me. It's fine. None of this was real anyway. You were only doing what you thought was right. It was stupid to think we could go through with this."

"I never loved Bianca," Robbie yells as I walk away. I stop with my back towards him as he continues, "She was the first girl I ever thought was pretty, so I thought that meant we were in love. Growing up, that's how Pops explained it to me. He told me how he thought grandma was the most beautiful thing he'd ever seen. He asked her out, and before they knew it, they were married with a baby on the way. He ran the junkyard while she managed the house. My parents were the same way—high school sweethearts, who got married, opened a shop together, and had a baby. I idolized them. I wanted to be a good man, just like the long line of men in my family. So, I followed suit, because that's what I thought I was supposed to do. There were so many signs that she never loved me. That she had just hoped I'd be her ticket out of this town. I told her I loved her every day, because that's what Pops raised me to do. Do you want to know the saddest part? If she hadn't left me, I'd probably still be married to her. Because I didn't realize I never actually loved her, until I met you."

I turn to look at Robbie, who is staring down at the ground. When he glances up and meets my eyes, I notice the slight quiver in his lip. He takes a tentative step towards me, close enough that he can take my hand in his.

"I've never experienced this rumbling like a V8 in my stomach, or my pulse racing at 526 horsepower, getting me from zero to sixty in 4.2 seconds, until I saw you—even before we spoke a word. I never would have believed it possible to feel such an intense bolt of electricity by accidentally brushing someone's arm, like one of those incredibly lame romance movies Jax and Scott would force us to watch. Except, that next morning at breakfast, I thought someone hooked jumper cables to me. Fuck, the night of our first actual date, you literally, not figuratively, made me weak in the knees at just the sight of you. What I'm really trying to say here, Cass, is I love you. Not because I feel obligated to. Not because we are going to have a baby. I love you, just because you are the most amazing person I've ever met. I know without a doubt I will never meet anyone like you again in this lifetime, or the next...

"And that's why I can't marry you."

"What?" I pull my hand from his, and just as quickly, he takes it back.

"I can't marry you, because I never properly asked." Robbie gets down on one knee. "I'm definitely no Prince Charming. I don't know any poems, and I have no intention of learning any. I doubt this is the fairytale you envisioned all those years ago. While I'm not exactly a bad boy, I do have tattoos, a leather jacket, and a motorcycle. I'm definitely reformed from whatever shell of a life I had before the day I saw you sitting doe-eyed in my office—if you can even call what I was doing living. I love you, Cassandra Grace Murphy, and I'd be honored if you'd choose to spend the rest of your life with me."

I lean down, take Robbie's face in my hands and press a firm kiss to his lips. Standing tall, he lifts me up and I wrap my legs around him. "Wait." I break the kiss. "Are we still getting married today?"

Robbie rests his forehead against mine and chuckles. "If you want. Cian has been coordinating the final details. All you need to do is get dressed and say yes. But we don't have to *today*. We can get married next week, next year, in a decade. I know you've been planning your dream wedding since you were young, and this isn't exactly what you had envisioned."

"That's the thing about being young, you don't always make the best choices. I might have made the plans quickly. But whether we get married today, next week, next year, or in a decade, I wouldn't change a thing. Because the only detail that matters is knowing when I get to the end of the aisle, you are the one standing there, the one I'm saying yes to."

"So, we're going to do this?" he asks with the brightest smile I've ever seen, even brighter than Jake's.

"Yes." And with that, Robbie devours me with an all-consuming kiss.

"Aye, save some for the actual wedding, why don't ya?" I turn to see Killian standing there with an amused grin. "Cian sent me to collect you. He said to tell you he's got everything ready, minus the bride and groom. He might be talented, but he isn't a magician. So, unless you want him acting out your parts with sock puppets, we better get going."

41

Cassie

June 8th

"You look stunning," Moira says, while adding one last layer of hairspray to my long curls. In theme with keeping everything simple, I decided against some crazy updo with too many bobby pins. Moira pulled my bangs back with a twist, securing them in place. To the rest of my hair, she added large curls that fall like a black curtain down my back. It is a dramatic contrast to my cream-colored dress. As a final touch, she pinned in a mix of maroon flowers and gold leaves, as I decided against a veil.

"Move over, Moira." Ma nudges her out of the way. "Hold on, I need to adjust the flowers."

"Ma, they are perfect," I object.

"No, a few of the petals are bruised," she says, removing and then adding a couple more flowers. Stepping back, she further inspects. "I really wish you had worn a veil, Cassandra. It's bad enough you are not being married in the eyes of God. The veil is a symbol of protection, to ward off evil."

"More like a symbol of modesty or obedience," Moira grumbles under her breath.

My mother turns, giving Moira her signature disappointed glare. "Moira Ann O'Connor, watch your tongue."

"What? Most of the classic wedding traditions stem from archaic practices such as arranged marriages, where women were handed off by their fathers in exchange for goods. The veil was to hide the bride's face until she was given to her husband."

"That is ridiculous," Ma scoffs. "My grandmother used to tell me tales of how the veil was used to protect the bride's identity, not from her future husband, but to ward off spirits which mean to do her harm and cause misfortune—such as the groom seeing the bride before the wedding."

"Well, we're a little late on that one, considering the groom not only saw the bride this morning but proposed to her." Killian laughs. Moira and Letty join him.

I look over to Cian, who is sitting there silent with his arms crossed. His gaze hasn't left our mother or father since they arrived. While he has been nothing but warm towards me, I can't help but wonder why he is being so cold with them. As it stands, everyone is getting what they want, well, mostly (Ma isn't the happiest on some of the wedding details). I'm marrying the father of my baby, which should make my parents happy. I'm marrying someone I love and who loves me in return; to say I'm elated is an understatement. So why does Cian look as though Killian peed in his Corn Flakes? Maybe he's just exhausted from helping coordinate all the last-minute wedding details this morning? But when I glance over at Da, who is also glaring at Ma, I know something is up.

"Okay, spill it," I say, placing a hand on my cocked hip, as everyone turns to look at me with matching confused expressions on their faces.

"What are you talking about?" Ma is the first to brush off my question. At this, I notice Cian glare at her with distaste as Da appears almost guilty.

"*That*, that right there," I say, pointing to Da and Cian. "Something is up, and I want to know what. I'm about to get married, and it seems only half the people in the room are happy about it."

"Cassie, you know I had my concerns, but I'm happy for you. After this morning, I have no doubt about you and Robbie," Moira cries, wrapping her arms around me—careful not to mess up my hair.

"I know, Moira. I wasn't talking about you. I was talking about *them.*" I gesture to my parents and Cian. Killian is looking around, obviously clueless, but as he starts to notice the odd tension, he crosses his arms over his chest.

"Cian?" he asks, knowing that if he wants answers, he will not get them from our parents.

"Moira, Letty, would you mind excusing us for a moment?" Cian requests, his tone polite.

Moira looks to me, double-checking that I'm okay with her leaving. I nod in agreement. Quickly, she and Letty flee the awkward situation.

"Cian, this is completely inappropriate," Ma states, fidgeting. Clearly there is something more going on. But seeing as she's already on the defense, I know I will get nowhere with her.

"Da?" My voice feels small as I say his name in the form of a question.

Cian glares at our father. "Tell her, or *I* will."

Da rubs an exhausted hand over his face. It's only then I realize it looks as though he's aged dramatically over these past few months.

"We will discuss this later—"

"Stop, Sophia," Da cuts off my mother. "That's enough."

"Fergus, we agreed. This has nothing to do with Cassie."

"Like hell it doesn't," Cian interjects.

"Cian," Da scolds, "watch your tone. You may be a grown man, but I'm still your father and you will show us respect."

"Respect?" Cian laughs. "Like the respect you showed Cassie?"

263

At this, Killian stands next to Cian; his stance indicates he's ready for a fight. I've seen this sort of posturing from my brothers before. It is nothing new. What's different is I've never seen them act like this towards our parents. Realizing this is a lot more than I thought, I step in to deescalate.

"Cian," I say carefully, "if this is about how everyone acted when I announced the pregnancy, that's over with. I think we all said or did things we aren't proud of, you and Killian included. Let's just drop it. I'm marrying Robbie, who I'm head-over-heels in love with. That's all that matters."

Cian's features soften as he looks at me. "I agree, but this isn't about you marrying Robbie. It's about *them*." He turns back and looks at our parents, his expression morphing to one of disgust. "They don't deserve your forgiveness, Cassie, not when you don't comprehend all they did wrong."

I find myself at a loss for words, when I look to my parents and see the guilt etched on Da's face while Ma is flushed and clenching her jaw.

"Last chance," Cian challenges.

"I'm sorry," Da says, barely above a whisper. "This has gotten so out of hand. Please sit, *mo stoirín*." I do as he says. His pained expression already has my heart breaking. Ma is about to object but Da raises a hand, silencing her. "When you announced your condition..."

"Pregnancy," I clarify defensively.

"Yes, pregnancy." He swallows as though the words are difficult to say. "It caught me off guard. Not just because my precious daughter announced she was unwed and with child. But because it felt as though everything was coming full circle, and fate had thrown us a challenge we were not prepared to handle. Do you recall the story I told you of how I met your mother?"

"Yes. You met while she was visiting Ireland with her cousin. It was love at first sight. You couldn't live without her, and against your parents' wishes, you fled to the US to marry her. Ma's parents weren't thrilled with the match either, and you both went off alone, starting your own lives together." As you can see, my desire for my one great true love stemmed from more than just fairytales and movies. My parents were a genuine "rise above all odds" romance of their own, turning their backs on their families for the sake of genuine love.

"Aye, well, there is a bit more to the story than that." Da looks down, ashamed.

"You lied?"

"Not exactly. There are just certain pieces we left out, as they are not things you tell your children. I met your ma in Ireland while she was visiting. The part I left out of our whirlwind romance was the reason I followed her to America—she was with child." He glances over to Cian. "Her parents were going to send her to a convent to have the baby, and then place it in a god-fearing home. The thought of never seeing my child, I couldn't do it. I took your mother from the convent, married her, and we never spoke to her family again."

I feel the tears pooling in my eyes. "Why were you so hard on me? *You*, more than anyone, should have understood how things just happen sometimes."

"Because we raised you better than this, Cassandra." Ma finally speaks up.

"Like your parents raised *you*?" I guffaw, surprised that for the first time, my mother's look of disappointment has no effect on me.

"Watch your tone," she orders, but I just let out a hollow laugh.

Da attempts to take my hand, but I pull it back as though his touch burns me. I step in line with a glaring Cian and Killian. "I cannot believe you both." I pause for a moment, shaking my head. It's as though whatever filter I had on has vanished. Instead, I can hear Robbie standing up for me in the back of my mind, except I don't need him to. I'm strong enough to defend myself. "Scratch that. It doesn't surprise me that Ma would lie and manipulate me like this. I've always

265

just been one enormous disappointment to her. But you, Da. You broke my heart. You were prepared to have your only daughter, your *mo stoirín,* potentially enter a loveless marriage out of obligation, all because of an archaic opinion that suggests I am somehow less of a person if I have a child outside of the matrimonial bed."

I feel the sting before I register what happens. Reaching up, I caress my burning cheek as I look at my mother, who is being held back by my father.

"How dare you speak to your parents in such a disrespectful tone!"

That's when *the lie* reveals *the truth.* My parents were not some tale of young love. It's just like with Chad. Now that they have broken my heart, the rose-colored lenses have been shattered and I can finally see them for who they are. For what they represent. They are nothing more than the epitome of a loveless marriage, forged by obligation. Killian is about ready to step in, but I stop him.

"Leave," I say sternly.

"You can't be serious," Ma starts, but as Da squeezes her shoulder, she quiets.

"I am serious. You've already tainted enough. I don't want to look back on this day and be reminded of your hypocrisy. I'm about to walk out those doors and start a relationship based on love and mutual respect. I have no intention of carrying this baggage into that."

"Sophia, stop." Da stops her from speaking again. "Go wait outside." Ma looks between the two of us before she stomps out the door in a huff, yelling Greek profanities along the way. I allow Da to approach me and caress the spot my mother struck. While I am angry and hurt, I also know that if I search through my childhood memories, the only genuine love we had in our home was my father's love for us. Eventually I will get over the pain he's caused, but not today, not anytime soon. "I'm grateful that you are marrying a good man who loves you. I will never be able to express how deeply sorry I am over my role in all of this. I intended to come to you after your announcement. I admit... it was a shock, and it took me a moment to process. Instead, I sent Cian to keep an eye on you." I look back at Cian, who shrugs. Funny enough, I am not all that surprised. "When he reported you were happy down here, that the relationship between you and Robbie was blossoming, I didn't see the need to interject. I just hope you can believe that if, for even a moment, I thought you were marrying a man who did not love you as you deserve, I would have never let you go through with such a thing. It is not a life I would wish for any of my children."

I wipe away my tears. "I know, Da. It's just, right now, I'm so hurt. You have no idea how much pain you've both caused me. How terrified and ashamed I've felt. I'm not ready to forgive you just yet."

Da places a kiss to the top of my head. "I would not expect you to. This will always be my greatest regret." Stepping back, he wipes away a tear of his own. "I will be heading back to Ireland for a while. I feel it is time I start to repair the damage my actions have caused, before it is too late, and I cannot make amends. Perhaps this time apart will be good for the both of us—give us a chance to heal. I will be back before my grandchild is born. It will be painful enough missing my daughter's wedding, but I'd never forgive myself if I missed the birth of my grandchild."

I give him one last big hug. I wanted to ask more questions about his return to his homeland, and why he specifically said "I" not "we" when referencing his plans. But as I glance at the clock and myself in the mirror, I know I'm running out of time to clean up before starting my new life. "I love you, Da."

He breathes a sigh of relief before squeezing me tighter. "*Is breá liom tú, mo stoirín.*" With that, he walks out the door. It takes all my energy to not collapse into a puddle of tears.

"Go get Moira. We need to get freshened up," Cian orders Killian, as he leads me to my cushioned stool. "I'm sorry, Cassie. I should have said something sooner or, *fuck*, after... Please don't let this ruin your wedding day."

I give him a big smile. "It's okay, Cian. It hurts. But I'm glad it's out in the open. As I said, I don't want to look back on this day and cringe whenever I see them in my wedding photos. Did you know about Ireland?"

He nods. "Yeah. Our grandparents are too sick to care for their farm. Da's initial concern was leaving his daughter after finding out she was pregnant. It's why he had me look into Robbie, not that I wouldn't have done it in the first place." Cian smiles. "Granted, I was not aware of the potential change in plans. But, let's not worry about that now, all right?" He grabs a tissue and wipes away my remaining tears, careful to not further smear my makeup.

Moira rushes into the room, taking in the scene. Immediately, she panics as she grabs her makeup bag and pushes Cian off to the side. It only takes her a few minutes to have me back to perfection. As we line up outside the door, Kayla (the wedding organizer) asks for my father. It's then that I realize I sent away the person who was supposed to walk me down the aisle.

"Kayla—" I start to say, but I'm soon cut off.

"Sorry, there has been a slight change in plans," Cian states as he and Killian approach.

"Aye, we'll be walking her down the aisle." If I wasn't smiling so hard, and trying to prevent tears of joy, I'd roll my eyes at the ridiculous accent Kayla instantly swoons over.

As she regains her composure, she continues to direct everyone, getting us all in position.

"You ready?" Cian leans in and whispers.

I squeeze both of their arms tightly. "I've never been more ready in all my life."

42

Cassie

June 8th

I KISS MY HUSBAND, yes, *my husband*. Today Cassandra Murphy walked down the aisle and said "I do" to a man she loves. Even better? He loves her in return. It's the best feeling in the world—like winning the lottery, but better, since (unlike money) you never run out of love. It just keeps growing. It makes all the previous heartaches worth it. If I had to do it all over again? Knowing that the prize at the end of it all was Robbie, waiting for me in his leather jacket and that silly grin, one which he only ever has for me, then *yes, a thousand times yes*. Do you know why? Because when she returned from that journey down the aisle, she wasn't alone. Now she is Cassandra Moore. Wife. And soon-to-be mother.

Swaying to the music, I trace my fingers lightly on the back of Robbie's neck. I couldn't even tell you what song was playing. I don't think I've heard a single thing since we said our vows. It has been a blur of hugs, congratulations, and clinking of silverware indicating it's time to kiss again. Not that either of us needs to be told to do so—I think we are good in that department. Robbie didn't seem all too surprised when I walked down the aisle without my father, replacing him with both of my brothers. Although Jax and

Tilly weren't able to join us, Eli made sure to have one of his staff livestream it to them. Scar had no problem stepping in as the unofficial photographer for the event. Jake was a little bummed at the change in bridesmaid (Letty stepped in for Tilly). Fortunately, they were able to put aside their bickering for twenty minutes, just long enough to get down the aisle and through the ceremony.

"Wait." I stop swaying. Robbie looks down at me, confused. "What was your deal the past couple of weeks?"

"What was my deal the past couple of weeks?" He repeats, rubbing his chin.

"Yeah. At first, you refused to let me out of your sight. Then I told you all that stuff. After that, you did a complete one-eighty. I thought..." I take a deep breath. "I thought you didn't want me."

"Shit," Robbie grumbles, giving Cian the side-eye. "He's going to kill me."

"Cian?" I hate I didn't ask about this earlier. I was so surprised by the proposal, my parents, and the wedding, I'd forgotten about his suspicious behavior.

"Cass," Robbie pleads. "Look, I can't tell you everything. Some of it's not my place—also, it's not exactly what I want to discuss on our wedding day."

"You mean the fact that my parents are the world's biggest hypocrites?"

His wince says it all.

"Why didn't you tell me? If you knew all this time..."

"I'm sorry." He places a kiss on the top of my head. "Cian told me. I'm not sure why, because it didn't make me feel any better about what you went through. He made me promise not to say anything, that it was a family matter and needed to be handled between you all."

"Okay. I can understand that. Also, keeping a secret is a great way to win his favor. But no more secrets," I say pointedly.

"No more secrets." Robbie kisses me.

"Why were you keeping me from the house?"

"I didn't want you to go to the house because Cian had been staying there, and he didn't want you to know."

"He was staying there. Why? Why wouldn't he want me to know that?" That makes no sense.

"At first, he didn't want to get your hopes up, then he didn't want to distract you from the wedding. Your brother is moving to Tral Lake."

"He's what?" Why would Cian move down here?

"Yup, he is officially Tral Lake's newest deputy. He starts on Monday. Only *he* can tell you why. He came and talked to me the day after we got you back from the hospital. You were already staying with me, so I didn't see the harm in letting him crash at the house. It was only supposed to be for a week—until he found a place. There were a few complications, but he got everything situated a couple of weeks ago."

"Cian has been here for a month and didn't want me to know it?" I ask, hurt that my brother wouldn't want to see or spend time with me.

"I don't know his reasoning. He only told me that he didn't want you to be disappointed, if things didn't work out. Please don't be mad."

"I'm not mad, just confused." I think for a moment. "Okay, that explains why you wouldn't let me go to the house. But why didn't you want me around the shop? And what about all the hushed conversations?"

"I might have been working on a few surprises for you," Robbie says sheepishly, rubbing the back of his neck and smiling.

"Surprises?"

"Yeah. It wouldn't have been so bad if you could have gone back to the house sooner. But since Cian was there, I had to hurry to get everything finished. I couldn't have you around."

"When do I get these surprises?" I ask, my tone sultry.

"Hmm." He pulls me closer and I can feel him growing harder between us. "Tonight."

"I like the sound of these surprises."

"Hey, Cassie," Jake says, patting my shoulder and ruining the moment. We both turn towards him, growling. "Sorry, do you know where Moira is?"

"No, why?" I reply.

"Shit." Jake looks around, panicked. "Time's running out. I've got a bet going with Killian on who can get the most numbers by the end of the night. We're tied, and I only have five minutes left. I figured with Moira being the maid of honor and all, her number has to be worth double points."

"It's not," Killian yells from across the room. He's looking around, trying to find his next target.

"Seriously, you two?"

"What?" Jake shrugs. "We wanted to prove what was hotter: a charming, well-endowed firefighter, or a washed-up fighter with a fake Irish accent?"

"I think I saw Moira take off with Derek. Sorry, dude." Robbie laughs.

"Fuck, thanks. I better hurry. There's no way I'm losing to your brother. His bets are a bit too steep for my liking. Congratulations, *sis*." Jake presses a quick kiss to my cheek before running off.

"Do I even want to know?"

Robbie shakes his head at me. "No, probably not."

As the song finishes, I decide I need a break. I've been on my feet all day. I take a seat next to Letty at the bar. Her arms are crossed and if looks could kill, Jake would be a dead man.

I lean in and whisper so that no one else can hear me. "You should tell him."

"What?" Letty's face reddens.

"That you like him," I say matter-of-factly.

"I feel a lot of things when it comes to Jake. *Like* isn't one of them." Letty finishes her drink before slamming it down on the counter. She walks over to the man in question, who's arguing with Killian over the terms of their tie-breaker. The next number wins. Approaching the pair, Letty puts extra sway in her step. "Hey, Kill." Her voice is like honey as she traces a finger down his arm and grabs his hand. Pulling a pen from between her breasts, she removes the cap with her teeth before quickly writing something on Kilian's palm. She replaces the cap once she's finished, leans up, pressing herself against Killian, and kisses him while sliding the pen in his breast pocket. With her back turned to the boys, their mouths visibly agape, Letty throws a wave in the air before tossing a seductive, "Call me," over her shoulder.

Killian comes out of his daze first. "Jesus, Mary, and Joseph," he utters with that god-awful accent. "I guess that makes me the winner. Catch ya later, lad." He pats Jake on the back before following Letty. "*Oi*, Letty, hold up." Draping his arm over her shoulder, he leans in and whispers something in her ear. She laughs loudly before they walk out of the reception area.

I turn back to see Jake's face red, his nostrils flared. *He is furious.* I don't think I've ever seen him actually upset before. Stomping over to the bar, he grabs a couple of shots from the tray, tossing them back in rapid succession. He wipes his mouth before he storms off.

"What was that all about?" Robbie asks, returning from the bathroom and somehow missing the entire exchange.

I just laugh and shake my head. "Nothing. Your brother just lost a bet."

"Wow, he almost never loses. Are you ready to get out of here?"

The suggestiveness in his tone reminds me of what Jake interrupted earlier. I nod. We quickly make our rounds, saying goodbye to the remaining guests. I give Cian a big hug, thanking him and reminding him we need to have a serious conversation later.

As we get to the door, Robbie covers my eyes with a silk scarf.

"I'm all for a little tie play, but don't you think we should start that in the bedroom." I press my butt against his growing erection.

"I have more than a silk blindfold planned for the bedroom tonight, Cass. This is so you don't see your surprise," he whispers before biting my earlobe.

Walking outside, I'm vibrating with excitement. I never get surprises. *Okay*, not ones like this.

"Are you ready?"

"Yes."

Robbie removes my blindfold and I'm stunned. "Is that what I think it is?"

"Yes." He wraps his arms around me, placing his hands on my belly. "Do you like it?"

"Like it?" I exclaim. "I love it!"

I give him a quick kiss before inspecting the black, four-door, '67 Chevy Impala before me. It has "Just Married" written on the back and a string with cans attached to the bumper.

"This is one of those surprises I had going that I needed you gone for. It took me a while to find one in decent condition. I've been working on it the past couple of weeks after closing."

"I seriously can't believe that you got me the same car from *Supernatural*. You have no idea how much I'm fangirling right now."

"Are you ready for your next surprise?"

"There is more?" I bounce with excitement.

Robbie nods and smiles, before he guides me into the front seat. Once he starts the car and the stereo turns on, blasting "Carry on Wayward Son" by Kansas, I burst out laughing.

"You went all out. Didn't you?"

"For you, anything." He kisses my hand before we take off.

I'm so caught up appreciating the car, I didn't even realize we were driving the opposite direction from town. We pull up and stop in the driveway of an old farmhouse—it looks familiar, but I can't put my finger on it.

"Where are we?"

Robbie exits, comes around to my side of the car, and helps me out.

"Okay, don't get mad..."

"Usually when someone starts a statement with *don't get mad*, it means there is something to get mad about," I retort.

"True, but just hear me out, okay?"

I turn, crossing my arms, before giving Robbie my full attention.

"The other reason I didn't want you at my place was because it isn't *my place* anymore."

"What?" I yell.

"Let me finish." He looks at me sternly. "I rented it out to Cian. I've been staying here. This is our new house."

"You bought a new house? Without talking to me?" I think for a moment. "Wait, what about the expansion? We discussed looking at real estate between Tral Lake and the new location, making the commute easier on both of us."

"I'm not expanding." He places a finger to my mouth, silencing me before I start. "Hear me out. I don't want to expand. It had been a thought of mine for a while because I had nothing else going on. Besides the financial risk a new location would cause, it would also mean missing out on time I'd much rather spend with the both of you. I'm tired of missing things." Robbie has a mournful expression as he places his hand on my belly. "I remembered, after that first barbeque at Jax's, you pointed out this house. You mentioned how cool it would be to live on the adjoining property. That way the kids could always play. I stopped by a few weeks ago. And to my surprise, the house had been vacant for some time. I called the city and found out they assumed possession a while back and hadn't put it on the market yet. I took the money I was planning on using for the expansion and offered them cash. When my dad left us the inheritance, he asked us to do something for ourselves with it—not reinvest it in our businesses... *like we all have basically been doing*. I know I should have talked to you. I just got so excited when I found out it was available. It was like fate; everything just lined up perfectly. Cian needed a new place. For the first time, I felt like I was *actually* doing the right thing. Not because it was logically correct. But because deep down, it felt right." Robbie pauses, realizing he's now rambling. "Are you mad?"

I couldn't see it at first—the only illumination coming from the night sky and the porch lamp—but as my eyes adjust to the dark, I recognize the home. Out of all the parceled lots near Jax and Tilly's, this one is the closest and has no fence separating the properties, with the backyards connecting. It would be perfect to let the kids play between the two houses, each of us being able to keep an eye on them.

"This is what you want? You had mentioned talking to Jake about your parents' house and us taking it over."

"Yes, this is what I want. I only ever said that as a suggestion, because it seemed practical at the time. Truthfully, I never wanted to move back into my old house. It hasn't felt like *home* for a while now. I want to start something new, fresh, with you. This house has good bones but will need a lot of TLC. I would have shown you sooner, but Cian was helping me ensure it was livable."

"So, this place is a clean slate. One that we can make our own?"

"Exactly. Your brother just helped me get the basic necessities up and running, then we moved my stuff from the apartment over here. I even had him pack up a few of your things and drop them off."

I look from Robbie to the house, then back to him again and smile. "In that case, I love it."

Robbie lets out a relieved sigh, before scooping me up bridal-style. "Well, *in that case*, Mrs. Moore, welcome home."

Epilogue

Robbie

USING A RAG, I wipe the sweat from my brow. It's hot out tonight. That ridiculous humid heat, where (short of hugging your AC) you get no relief, not even at night. I'd much rather be sitting inside with Cassie, watching a movie in the luxury of the central air we recently had installed after moving in. Instead, I'm out here finishing up the last few touches on the Impala. I rushed to get her ready for our wedding, mostly focusing on the fact that she ran, and the bodywork was done. It still needed a few final touches. As I wrench down the last bolt, I think I can say she is as good as new. I glance over to the Mustang. "Don't worry, sweety, you're next."

"Whatcha doing, big guy?" I look up to see Cassie as she steps into the garage, wearing a thin white night gown. Her growing baby bump pulls the garment up high enough that I can see the flash of her white underwear.

"Cass," I scold. "What did I tell you about coming to the garage barefoot."

She pouts but doesn't stop her descent towards me. "I know, but it's too hot for shoes. Not to mention, the cement is cool on my feet."

I look around and make sure there is nothing she might cut herself on. Just like at the shop, I try to keep the garage at home clean. But there is always the possibility of small slivers of wood or steel lying around.

"Are you still pouting?" Her smirk tells me she has something up her sleeve. Her finger lightly traces the fresh tattoo I got on my chest: a rose with her name. It remains the only pop of color amongst the black ink. I surprised her with it shortly after the wedding. I still thank god for giving me enough common sense to never have engraved Bianca's name on my body. With Cassie though, I had zero reservations. Subconsciously, I had left this spot blank over my heart, open for her.

"I'm not pouting," I say, pulling her closer to me.

"No, you seem to have a stick up your butt since the ultrasound yesterday." Much against my protest, Cassie refused to find out if we were having a boy or a girl. Just like Tilly, she wants to be *surprised.* I even tried a few tricks Jake assured me would persuade her. But *mind*-blowing orgasms did nothing to change her mind.

"I don't have a stick up my butt," I growl. "But if you'd like me to stick my—"

"Robbie!" Cassie squeals as I pinch her ass. "*That* is never going in *there.*"

"Really?" I challenge as I lean down and bite her bottom lip. "You didn't seem to object too much with my thumb the other night. I think you said, and I quote: *best orgasm of my life.*"

"There is an enormous difference between your thumb and your cock." As if on cue, he grows at the word. Cassie almost never uses dirty words, but when she does, it is like an immediate on-switch. I feel her clench when she notices how hard I am. Without hesitation, and in one quick sweep of my arm, I clean off my workbench before picking Cassie up and placing her on top of it. Glancing down, I notice that my greasy fingerprints not only stained her gown but also left smudges on her creamy thighs. I warned her it was a terrible idea to ever wear white around me. Now I'm glad she did, because it is such a turn-on, seeing her dirty like this. *Just like the day she was changing her oil.*

Leaning forward and pressing myself between her legs, I devour her mouth. "That's fine." Kiss. "This is." Kiss. "Enough for—" I stall as my hand goes to enter her waistband and I feel a piece of paper. Carefully, I remove the document and glance down to see it is an ultrasound photo from yesterday. "Cass, why do you have a picture of our baby in your underwear?"

"Well..." she drags out.

"Cass," I say sternly. "As much as I love looking at ultrasound images with you, this isn't exactly the place you should be keeping them. Not to mention, it's a bit of a boner killer."

Cassie frowns, and I hold my hands up defensively.

"That's not what I mean. Your baby bump is sexy as fuck. I'm just referring to looking at the picture of our baby." As my palms are up, I notice that something is written on the back of the image. "What's this?"

I freeze as I read the words.

"Is this—" I try to ask, but my mouth suddenly feels dry.

"I had always planned on finding out. I just thought it was funny getting you riled up. I called ahead and asked the doctor to write down the sex on one of the images and give it to me in my paperwork. I thought us finding out alone together would be more fun."

I stay silent, repeatedly reading the words scribbled across the paper in front of me.

"Are you okay?" Cassie asks, her brows pulled together in concern.

"Yeah. I just—"

"It's crazy, right? It somehow makes it feel more real."

"We're having a—"

"We are." She smiles. "Are you okay?"

I carefully place the picture on the shelf, so I don't ruin it more than I already have with my filthy hands. I kiss

Cassie, who moans and is nothing more than a puddle of want and lust. "I couldn't be happier," I admit. "I love you, Mrs. Moore," I say as I pick up where we left off, sneaking my hand behind her waistband.

"I love you!" Cassie cries out in ecstasy, as I plunge my digits into her core. I don't know shit about fairytales. But watching Cassie fall apart around me as she finds her release, well, it makes me pretty fucking happy, and I could do it forever and after.

The End

Want moore Robbie & Cassie? Sign up for my newsletter to get access to bonus content.
Visit: https://bit.ly/ExpectingMooreBonus
or scan

The Moore Family Series:

Forever Moore (Tilly and Jax)

Expecting Moore (Robbie and Cassie)

Want You Moore (Jake and Letty)
Fighting for Love:

Flirty at Murphy's: A Murphy's Bar Novella

Last Round
Rose's Inferno Trilogy:

Retribution (Book 1)

Desolation (Book 2

Pandemonium (Book 3)
Standalone Novella:

Learning to Love Again

New books are always coming visit

WWW.FRANKIEPAGEBOOKS.COM
to see the current list of titles available

Milton Keynes UK
Ingram Content Group UK Ltd.
UKHW040734030823
426269UK00004B/218

9 781088 138250